Zingerman's® BAKEHOUSE

Amy Emberling & Frank Carollo

Photographs by Antonis Achilleos

CHRONICLE BOOKS
SAN FRANCISCO

Library of Congress Cataloging-in-Publication Data

Names: Emberling, Amy, author. | Carollo, Frank, author.
Title: Zingerman's Bakehouse / by Amy Emberling and Frank Carollo ;
  photographs by Antonis Achilleos.
Description: San Francisco : Chronicle Books, [2017] | Includes index.
Identifiers: LCCN 2016057669 | ISBN 9781452156583 (hc : alk. paper)
Subjects: LCSH: Bread. | Zingerman's Bakehouse. | LCGFT: Cookbooks.
Classification: LCC TX769 .E54 2017 | DDC 641.81/5—dc23 LC record available
  at https://lccn.loc.gov/2016057669

Manufactured in China

Designed by Alice Chau & Anna Carollo.
Illustrations by Ian Nagy & Ryan Stiner, Zingerman's Service Network

10 9 8 7 6 5 4 3 2 1

Chronicle books and gifts are available at special quantity
discounts to corporations, professional associations, literacy
programs, and other organizations. For details and discount
information, please contact our premiums department at
corporatesales@chroniclebooks.com or at 1-800-759-0190.

Chronicle Books LLC
680 Second Street
San Francisco, California 94107
www.chroniclebooks.com

APPRECIATIONS

Most books have an acknowledgments page, but we've decided to make this a page of appreciations. In Zingerman's Community of Businesses, we end our meetings with appreciations. The completion of this book seems like the end of a long meeting. Here are our heartfelt appreciations:

Thank you, Bakehouse staff past and present, for your contributions in creating the bakery. Without you there wouldn't have been a book to write.

Many appreciations to the current and former members of our BAKE! staff for your early work on recipe documentation, help with recipe testing, and baking for photos.

Jake Emberling and Emily Ramsey, thank you for so diligently testing many of the recipes. The book wouldn't have happened without your help.

Anna Carollo and Margaret Carollo, it was fun to work together in this different way, and we loved your enthusiastic, detailed feedback and color commentary about the recipes you tested.

Ruby Emberling, thank you for your super-helpful feedback about our essays. Your thoughtfulness and encouragement made a difference.

Kathy Shipan, thanks for being such a joyful and energetic recipe tester and for working on the "project" recipes.

Geoff Emberling, we can't thank you enough for your conversations, which helped us form our thoughts; your editing suggestions, which improved our writing; and your formatting skills. Also thank you for your patience and support during this year of unprecedented work.

Thank you, Judith and Bernard Leviten and the entire Carollo clan, for your constant love and encouragement for all our work at the Bakehouse.

Thank you, Ari Weinzweig and Paul Saginaw, for setting out on this adventure, for being strong role models, and for our conversations about the book and your emotional support throughout the process.

Thank you to our Zingerman's partners. Without your support, cooperation, and counsel, we'd have a very different bakery, and one not nearly as good.

Thank you, Michael London, for being our first and most influential baking teacher.

Thank you, Lisa Ekus. Your support, guidance, counsel, and advocacy on our behalf were fantastic.

Thank you to the team at Chronicle, especially Sarah Billingsley and Alice Chau, for your professional expertise in editing and design.

Antonis Achilleos, we love the photos you took of our food. We will think of you every time we look at our book.

CONTENTS

FOREWORD

"The search for great bread," my friend the food writer Paula Wolfert once wrote, ". . . has been my passion. Whenever I travel I constantly ask people: 'Where can I find the best bread around here?' 'Who is the best baker?' And nearly always, as soon as I ask, the eyes of my respondent will light up. He or she will utter a name and an address. And then I am off upon the hunt."

I'm not much different. My own search started 35 years ago when Paul Saginaw and I opened Zingerman's Delicatessen in a slightly out of the way, oddly angled, two-story, turn-of-the-19th-century orange-brick building at the corner of Detroit and Kingsley Streets in Ann Arbor's Kerrytown neighborhood. My hunt took a great leap forward when, in the fall of 1992, we joined with our friend Frank Carollo to open our own bakery. Today, if Paula Wolfert were to come to town, inquiring about the best bakers, I'm pretty sure that almost every local food lover would send her to 3711 Plaza Drive, to Zingerman's Bakehouse.

It's hard to imagine eating well in Ann Arbor without the breads, brownies, pies, and pastries from the Bakehouse. While it's certainly not perfect (what is?), I can say with great certainty that Zingerman's Bakehouse is very much what we hoped for—and much more—back in 1992 when we first sat down to talk: a special place that would produce traditional, full-flavored, artisan baked goods; a business in which the staff would feel a part of something special; a place that was rooted in its community, one that the community cared for with equal reverence and respect. The Bakehouse succeeded on all counts!

To be clear, I'm a cook, not a baker. Perhaps because I don't do it myself, I hold everyone who bakes well in high esteem. The best home bakers, I believe, deserve a lot of credit. Special occasions at their houses are always marked by marvelous-looking and great-tasting baked goods. They wow their family and friends on holidays, weekends, birthdays, anniversaries. They make everything from scratch, by hand, with great love—each item is baked with the care that you would put into making something for someone that you care deeply about.

I think what impresses me most about what Frank, Amy, and the Bakehouse crew do is that all of those same things are totally true of what goes on at Zingerman's Bakehouse. But instead of one baker working solely when inspired to feed his or her loved ones on special occasions, what happens at the Bakehouse is anything but occasional. It happens literally every day, all day, all year. Over a hundred caring people on staff relentlessly working their collective butts off 363 days a year to craft a million and a half loaves of artisanal bread and more than a million pieces of pastry, plus a whole array of soups and savories to serve in our shop for over two and a half decades!!! And yet, as big as those numbers may sound, they do it with the same care, the same love, the same commitment to making people's days better as does the best skilled home baker. Businesses that can bake this well for so many years, stay healthy, take care of their crew, create financial stability, contribute to the community and continually improve every year are very few and pretty far between.

One of Paul Saginaw's great sayings is "Professionalism is sticking with something long after the initial glamor wears off." Knowing Frank's ability to remember minutiae (and his deadpan humor) he could probably rattle off the exact hour that the glamor of being an artisan baker wore off. And yet he and Amy and everyone else at the Bakehouse continue to craft amazing food every single day. I would know. Being on a high-gluten diet, I eat something from the Bakehouse pretty much every day of the year. I even take Bakehouse bread in my bag when I travel. My current favorites? The Roadhouse bread. The Jewish rye with caraway. On the sweet side: the Obama buns, Rigó Jancsi torte, ginger cookies, and the Big O's. But really, I will testify from personal experience and nearly 40 years as a food professional, it's all very, very good!

On the surface at least, it would seem that really anyone could do what we do at the Bakehouse. There are thousands of books on baking, schools that teach it, training programs to participate in. The food business is hard, but it's not nuclear physics. While there are clearly many more good bakeries in the United States than when we opened ours in September of 1992, they're hardly common. Those that are out there, sprinkled around the country, stand as relatively rare beacons of great artisan baking in a commercial world that has taken on the form of the traditional but—as it almost always does—has taken a pass on the substance. Fast food chains now feature croissants and every supermarket has some kind of "artisan" bread section, but the quality of what you'll get when you buy it is not what an old-school artisan would aspire to make.

While many people have contributed to Zingerman's Bakehouse, this book is a testament to the creativity, caring, unique blend of skills and studies, and relentless pursuit of excellence of Amy and Frank. Both Frank and Amy have a deep love of food, a passion for baking, a strong drive to learn and improve, and a commitment to doing meaningful work and to making work more meaningful for those around them. Without Frank, the Bakehouse would never have successfully gotten off the ground. Without Amy, it would not be the extensive, eclectic, and excellent business it is today. Without the Bakehouse, Zingerman's would be a very different organization. Without Zingerman's, Ann Arbor would be a pretty different town. Frank and Amy's willingness to work long and hard, to work together, to work productively over the last 25 years has created an exceptional bakery, one from which so many—both in Ann Arbor and around the country—have benefitted big time.

One very cold winter's morning I walked into the Bakeshop to get a baguette. Jamie Sharkey and Cathy Zemina were working. Their energy, the way they treated me and every other customer in the shop, the passion with which they were talking about every product on the shelves, the enthusiasm with which they handed me the baguette (just a few hours out of the oven) would have made you think it was a special occasion. But it wasn't. It just a cold Wednesday morning, just shy of 25 years after Frank and I sat down on another cold Wednesday morning to have our first discussions about the bakery. Their energy—and by the way,

the excellence of that just-baked baguette—is a testament to the special place that Frank and Amy and everyone else at the Bakehouse and in the Zingerman's Community of Businesses helped to create.

The book you're holding in your hands, like everything from the Bakehouse, is the product of a great deal of care, good intention, long hours of conversation, and a whole lot of hard work. Like most of our breads, it's leavened naturally. It's been proofed, punched down a few times, proofed again, and after a few years in the "intellectual" oven, it's ready to read. Take a deep breath. Sip some good coffee or tea. Settle in. Read. Bake. Eat. Enjoy. The world can use some positive perspective, a sense of collaborative achievement, respect for diverse traditions, the drive to make a positive difference. I hope that what follows in this book will have as much positive impact on your life as Zingerman's Bakehouse has on mine, on our organization, and on our community. Good bakeries really do make a difference.

ari weinzweig

Co-founding partner, Zingerman's Community of Businesses, and author of *Zingerman's Guide to Good Eating* and *Zingerman's Guide to Good Eating, Part 4: A Lapsed Anarchist's Approach to the Power of Beliefs in Business*

INTRODUCTION

zingerman's bakehouse is 25 years old and we're celebrating!

In 1992, when the bakery opened, we were eight people with a lot of enthusiasm, just six bread recipes, and one now seemingly tiny hearth oven in a shiny, new space. We had one customer, Zingerman's Delicatessen. Frank Carollo, the founder of the Bakehouse, brought unmatchable energy, charisma, and determination. He hoped to create a successful artisan bread bakery with a small team of happy people. I was one of the original bakers, just looking for good work in the food business with good people. At a time when real artisan bread wasn't readily available in Michigan, we were excited to be rediscovering traditional baking methods like naturally leavened starters and hearth baking. Together we believed we were making a difference to the daily eating pleasure of our community. It was an exciting, challenging, and fully engaging time.

The Bakehouse soon became more than an artisan bread bakery. We started making pastries in 1994, opened a retail shop in 1996, started making wedding cakes in 2000, and added a baking school (called BAKE!) in 2006. We've spent time researching food traditions that were new to us (particularly Hungarian food). We now make hundreds of recipes, from cake to soup to many more breads, with 150 people working around the clock in a much larger space than we started with, and serving a broader community reached through our 100 wholesale customers. And our once-shiny bakery is now well broken in and in the process of facelifts and remodeling.

Fundamentally, though, we have not changed. For 25 years, the bakery has been shaped by the interests and passions that attracted Frank and me to the work in the first place—our love of traditional food, our respect and concern for people, and our belief that business can be good both for individuals and for communities.

As food, people, and business are intertwined in our work, they are intertwined in this book. There are three primary narratives running through the book that mirror our experience in the bakery.

NO. 1: A COOKBOOK

At its core this is a cookbook, just as the Bakehouse at its core is an artisan bakery. In all of our recipes we use traditional methods, which require attention to detail, dedication to process, and full-flavored ingredients. We selected only recipes that are particular favorites of ours or of our customers, and ones we think are interesting either in method, ingredient choice, or historical background.

The recipes have a range of difficulty, from easy to medium to day-long projects. We are sharing with you the exact recipes we use or teach at our school, scaled for home bakers. We include our secrets, which are really just knowledge gained after years of thoughtful work (and correcting mistakes). Don't be alarmed by the length of some of the recipes. "Don't freak out!" as we say at the bakery on unusually hectic days. You can do them!

NO. 2: HOW WE WORK

The way we do our work, our underlying values and beliefs, and our daily practices are critical to us at the Bakehouse. We aim to create an environment that enriches all of us and teaches behaviors and values that support positive personal development. Part of the book is about these values, beliefs, and practices, and part is lighter anecdotes about our baking life.

NO. 3: OUR BUSINESS STORY

We have many visitors at the bakery and at our partner businesses. Visitors often want to know how we develop a Zingerman's business. By telling the bakery's story, we hope to show some of what is involved in building a locally rooted artisanal business.

We also wrote this book to honor Bakehouse staff and customers. We hope that the team, past and present, takes some pride in this book. More than 1,000 of us and millions of our actions have created the bakery. And our customers might be surprised at how much they inspire us during our daily work. Their enthusiasm for our food has sustained us. We are well aware of the responsibility placed on us when we are preparing food. Frank often says as we roll loaves of bread, "This is someone's special loaf. Remember that."

HERE'S WHO WE ARE.

ZINGERMAN'S COMMUNITY OF BUSINESSES

We are 10 businesses and 700 people strong in the Ann Arbor area, all providing the Zingerman's Experience of great food and great service.

It all started with Zingerman's Delicatessen, which was opened in 1982 by Paul Saginaw and Ari Weinzweig in a historic district of Ann Arbor. Many people told them a deli wouldn't last in Ann Arbor. Almost four decades later, the Delicatessen is one of the country's leading specialty food stores, with an emphasis on education, flavor, tradition, and integrity of ingredients.

In 1992, after 10 years and some success, Ari and Paul wanted to do more. Over the next 25 years they and their partners created many other businesses in what we call the Zingerman's Community of Businesses (ZCoB). Each business has a managing partner or partners who bring a particular passion for their craft to the day-to-day leading of their business. We make fresh cheese and gelato, roast coffee, cook candy, serve classic American and now Korean dishes, cater events, teach our management practices, and ship our food all over America. There are nine other businesses that customers can visit in Zingerman's Community of Businesses: the Delicatessen, ZingTrain, Mail Order, Creamery, Coffee, Roadhouse, Events at Cornman Farms, the Candy Manufactory, and now Miss Kim, a Korean restaurant.

The primary focus of our work in the ZCoB is full-flavored traditional food, making it and selling it, but we are equally engaged with the process of our work. We are a highly open and participative business community, which believes in continuous learning, the lavish sharing of information (open-book management), group decision making, and the power of visioning. We aim to make great food and a great workplace and to be a significant positive contributor to our community.

Zingerman's Bakehouse was the second Zingerman's business created, in 1992, and this book's authors, Amy Emberling and Frank Carollo, are the managing partners.

FRANK

I grew up in the suburbs of Detroit, the middle child and only boy in what felt like an immigrant family. My dad's parents came from Sicily to Detroit in the early 1900s, and while he was born and raised in Detroit, we definitely identified as being Italian. My mother was from Austria, a World War II bride, so I was a product of two cultures in which food played a significant role. My childhood was rich with food. There were our daily meals, with Central European standards such as *schinkenfleckerl* (ham and noodle casserole) and *pasta al sugo* (pasta with sauce), and holidays, with items like *mon strudel* (poppy seed strudel), still a personal favorite, and *arancini* (Italian rice balls). My most prominent memories are of being in our basement, or at my grandma's or an aunt's house, sitting at a long table with dozens of relatives preparing to celebrate a holiday or birthday. And that celebration was always centered on food.

As a child of the '60s I grew up with Wonder Bread—or Silvercup Bread, to be precise—my family's weekday bread. But on weekends, I would ride with my father to a small Italian bakery and we'd buy flour-covered bread with a crispy crust that came in a paper bag rather than a plastic one. I was told that my grandfather always favored the crusty heel of the loaf because it had the most flavor. Even as a child, I sensed that this weekend bread was treated with more respect than the Silvercup.

As a kid I often felt uncomfortable about being different—my mom wanted us to behave like Europeans (we brought our own bags to the grocery store, a source of incredible embarrassment for me, long before American culture got with the program), while I longed to be just like everyone else in my neighborhood. This sense of not really fitting in followed me throughout my childhood and adolescence, and into my college years.

I moved from St. Clair Shores to Ann Arbor in 1972, and that 58-mile ride was like beaming into a different galaxy. Ann Arbor in 1972 was a world unlike any I had ever seen—diverse, socially progressive, and the epitome of a countercultural liberal college town. I further continued not fitting in by studying engineering in a place and time where that field of study wasn't popular or the norm.

After an eye-opening and disheartening summer working for one of the car companies, I began to realize that being an engineer at a corporation was not going to be a satisfying life for me. Shaped by the liberal social mores of the '70s, I grew my hair, did a few other things common among young people at the time, and started to search for another way to live. Ever cautious, I hedged my bets and applied to graduate school in engineering just to keep my options open.

That's when something really special happened for me. On a whim I applied for work at Bicycle Jim's, a restaurant in Ann Arbor where all the employees had just revolted and quit. I viewed that as an "opportunity" to convince the owner that I would be a good choice to work in the kitchen, although I had zero experience. I managed to persuade him to give me a chance, and a week later I started my journey in the world of professional food.

When I began to work as a cook, my life was transformed. I was doing work that I loved and felt a little guilty that I was getting paid to do it (all of $2.45 an hour). I didn't feel qualified or confident to be an engineer, but the engineer qualities hard-wired into me—being organized and creating systems—were very valuable skills to have in the food business. My coworkers liked to work with me because things went smoothly during my shifts, and that made work more enjoyable for me. I also noticed immediately that my coworkers preferred certain jobs and stations over others, though all were critical to having a successful night. So I began to try to work the least desirable station—the fryer—to avoid conflict and to actually make people glad to be working a shift with me. We were a team making good food joyfully, and that made me really want to keep doing this work.

During the last four months until graduation I was feeling more and more like cooking and less and less like getting a master's in bioengineering. My acceptance into the graduate program was good for a year, so I decided to defer enrollment and to keep working and save some money.

One year later, in October 1977, I was working at a brand-new restaurant in Ann Arbor called Maude's. That's where I met Ari Weinzweig and Paul Saginaw, who were working there as well. It was the beginning of a long friendship and business partnership. Ari and Paul went on to found Zingerman's Community of Businesses.

I decided to forego graduate school as long as I was enjoying cooking, which, as it turns out, meant that I never went. I spent a total of seven years working at different restaurants—as a cook, assistant kitchen manager, and assistant dining room manager, learning to tend bar, and finally coming back to Maude's as general manager. It was all good experience, but I was ready to try something different.

I spent a year as a stay-at-home dad caring for my two-year-old daughter, Anna. After a few months, feeling rejuvenated and desiring some adult contact, I began to work weekends at Zingerman's Delicatessen. At the time the delicatessen was a bit more than two years old. I had never worked in a retail setting and really loved learning about cheese (goat cheese seemed so exotic in 1984!), charcuterie, and tea. It also led me into a partnership with Paul in Monahan's Seafood Market.

I spent seven years as a fishmonger, learning the retail seafood business from one of the most knowledgeable seafood men in the country, Michael Monahan (also one of the most personable and friendliest people I've ever met). Shopping at Monahan's is still one of my favorite things to do.

But I had an itch to try something different. On March 12, 1992, with one day left as a partner at Monahan's, I walked across the street to Zingerman's Delicatessen and had a cup of coffee with Ari to see what ideas he might have. He mentioned that he was thinking of starting a bread bakery. Six months later to the day, I was feeding our sourdough starter for the first time. The rest is (our) history.

food experiences that inspired me

- *Going to the International Baking Industry Exposition show with Paul Saginaw in 1994 and meeting many bakers just like us. This was before much written information was available about naturally leavened bread. I distinctly remember a successful baker from Minneapolis telling me that you couldn't bake yeasted breads in the same bakery with naturally leavened bread. Although I didn't tell him this, we had already been doing that for a couple of years.*

- *Attending a Bread Bakers Guild event at the Culinary Institute of America in New York in 1999, where I took classes with Didier Rosada and Jeffrey Hamelman. They both made a big impression on me, inspiring me with their experience, teaching style, and cumulative knowledge.*

- *Visiting Acme Bread in Berkeley, California, the bakery that I measured our own bread baking against for the first two decades of our existence.*

- *Visiting Tartine Bakery in San Francisco and being inspired by their bread and the bakery experience they provide to their customers.*

- *Attending the Slow Food Salone del Gusto in Turin in 2002.*

People's favorite frank jokes

AMY: *Humor can go a long way toward making a work day more pleasant, especially one that is full of routine. Frank is our primary jokester. He does funny things, he says funny things, and he has a repertoire of specific jokes and one-liners. Many of them are silly and sort of stupid or annoying, but he says them so consistently that they become funny (to me at least), almost because of their predictability. They're so predictable, actually, that we often find ourselves saying them at the appropriate time even when Frank isn't there. Along with great bread and leadership, jokes might be an important part of Frank's legacy. I asked the staff which jokes were their favorites, and I was deluged with responses. Clearly they make an impact. Here are some of the responses, plus a few of mine peppered in:*

- *Comedically he is a quadruple threat, and it is almost all situational. The constant punning, like when he insists that Jason Whipple's favorite band (in his role as bakery receiver) is "Haulin' Oats." He's also a very talented mimic, both physical and verbal, and it is always funny to see him transform himself into someone we all know.*
  —Josh

- *When he says a phone number out loud not following normal rhythm, like "734-761-722 long pause 5," and when you ask him, "Did you get a haircut?" and he answers "Actually, I'm going to this new place where they cut them all at once."*
  —Jessica F.

- *Frank is quite good at altering song lyrics. His favorite for Savory (kitchen staff) is when we play Sade's "Smooth Operator." He'll change the chorus to "smooth sandwich maker."*
  —Thomas

- *(Frank's favorite for this team is his version of an AC/DC song: "She's a prep machine, she kept her French knife clean.")*

- *Tried-and-true sight gags, like pretending to be hit in the face by an opening door. He gets a hurt look on his face suggesting pain and emotional anguish. He does this one so often that it worked against him one day. He was leaving his office and a trophy fell off the top of a bookshelf and hit him in the face. He made the same gestures he does for his gag. Fiona, our accountant, saw it all happen and just ignored him. He implored her to pay attention. She continued to ignore him, certain that he was joking.*

It turned out that the trophy had cut him above his upper lip and he needed stitches.

- *When he sneak-calls the (service) office from his cell phone, picks up the office phone, and pretends to give terrible service to a customer. He loves to do this in front of new employees, who are shocked by his rudeness.*

- *Of course, the hardest thing is that he is often so deadpan that sometimes he is serious when you think he is joking, or joking when he is serious, which can make for some interesting moments.*

- *Buckteeth—he puts sliced almonds over his front teeth and walks around the bakery pretending that nothing is different.*
  —Patti

- *When discussing cold-brew coffee, he always says, "You know what's great about cold-brew coffee? When you heat it up it tastes just like coffee."*

- *Dancing like Stevie Nicks when a Fleetwood Mac song comes on. Swirling his apron like she'd swirl her flowing skirts. Picture a full-figured guy, dancing like Stevie Nicks in the middle of a bread bakery. It's enough to get you through several hundred more loaves of bread rolling.*

- *Frank doesn't understand what all the fuss is about gluten free. He says the gluten has always been free at the Bakehouse.*

- *Frank's annual questions: What day is Thanksgiving this year, and when is Christmas? Or he announces that Thanksgiving's on a Thursday this year and that Christmas is December 25th, as if it's big news. He does this every year, multiple times, throughout the fall.*

AMY

I spent the first 18 years of my life on Cape Breton Island in Nova Scotia, Canada. Food of all sorts was a primary interest for me from the time I was a very young child, and even in far eastern Canada, on a relatively sparsely populated island, I was introduced to a variety of cuisines and eating experiences.

I grew up in a Jewish family and enjoyed standard Jewish fare like brisket, rye bread, pickled herring, and matzoh ball soup. I loved my Nanny's gefilte fish and chopped liver—begged for it, even! For more typical local flavor I'd visit my neighbors the Malloys, a family with eight children. Their kitchen was always full of what seemed like exotic foods, Scottish and Irish, so different from the food of my family. I particularly enjoyed their Christmas treat of plum pudding and hard sauce.

Every year at Christmas, our beloved Italian housekeeper, Elva, made deep-fried, honey-coated cookies that she called fry cookies. She also made pizza for lunch on many Fridays. She'd fry any extra pizza dough in a pan (my first version of focaccia), and my three siblings and I would devour it before returning to school. Summertime brought visits to my New York grandparents and bakery delights like charlotte russe and checkerboard cakes. It was all so tasty and different. I was intrigued by the mystery of how simple ingredients could be put together to make this world of food.

To satisfy my interest in understanding how food was actually made, I watched the classic Canadian cooking show *Galloping Gourmet* and, as an elementary student, read cookbooks after school. Every month we'd get *McCall's* magazine, which featured a cooking class in each edition. I couldn't wait for it to come to see what I was going to learn about next. I still have three photocopied recipes from the magazine, and we use a version of one of them at the bakery. I particularly loved baking—my eldest brother used to call me "Bakerwoman."

I liked to make food, and I also loved to go to restaurants. Fortunately, my mother supported my interest by making many varied dishes at home and letting me help cook, and my parents took us to wonderful restaurants. My first choice in celebrating was always related to food—at 16 I wanted lobster for my birthday and a bouquet of yellow roses. Luckily, my birthday landed during lobster season! Graduation from college was marked by several special

dinners in famous Boston restaurants, and my wedding ceremony and reception were held at a traditional French restaurant in Boston, Maison Robert (which has since closed). Where else would you get married but a French restaurant, a temple to cuisine? Food captured my attention in a way nothing else did.

Besides being interested in food, I grew up in a family that owned a small business. My grandfather came to Canada at age 20 from Poland and established a wholesale grocery business in my hometown that my father eventually bought, ran, and expanded. Our family owned this business for 75 years before we sold it. Business talk was common in our house—profit, employees, bank loans—and my parents worked constantly to keep it thriving.

What I didn't realize until I had my own business was what helpful preparation this was. I had learned early on that owning a business took an incredible amount of energy and emotional resiliency. I saw firsthand that there were good years and bad years but you have to persevere regardless. I learned that you have to innovate and use technology—all valuable lessons that still help me today at the Bakehouse.

Although I loved food and actively cooked and baked when I was younger, becoming a professional chef wasn't a real possibility in my mind. College was my certain future, and then perhaps a law degree or a Ph.D. in a social science. I attended Harvard College, where I studied social movements in American history. I was interested in how people organize to make a better life for themselves and others. This was definitely one of the foundations of my desire to create a workplace that values people and their full participation.

After college, I decided to take some time off to have fun (before more studying) and to follow my still-great passion for food. I worked in several restaurant kitchens in Michigan (having moved to Ann Arbor with the man who would become my husband) and soon realized how much I love to make food in a professional setting. The energy, the rush, the wild mix of people, the smells and tastes were all compelling. After several years of hands-on experience, I was fortunate to receive a scholarship from Les Dames d'Escoffier to study cooking and baking at the cooking school of the Ritz Hotel in Paris.

When I came back to Ann Arbor, I approached Ari Weinzweig, one of the two founders of Zingerman's, and asked him for a recommendation of where to work, if not at his Deli. I loved the feel of the Deli. It was dynamic and fun, smart and rich with food and information, yet still friendly. Probably most appealing was its sense of irreverence. It was fancy food, but not sold by or only for fancy people. It was like no other place I had ever been. I wasn't sure that I wanted to make Deli food, though. I was still under the spell of French cuisine and baking.

That conversation was a life changer. Ari suggested I try to get a job with his friend Frank, who was opening a bakery. (He failed to mention that it was going to be his bakery too!) Baking! I hadn't really considered doing only baking, but why not? It was still my first passion.

I went for an interview at the not-yet-open bakery. Frank was sitting at a folding card table in the middle of the shiny floor. I don't remember anything about the interview, other than thinking, "I really want this job." I was hopeful that it might come to be. Several days later, however, I hadn't heard from Frank. Overcoming some shyness, I gave him a call. Frank let me know that he hadn't called because he was concerned about how I would support myself, my graduate-school husband, and our young son on the modest starting wage he was going to pay everyone. I responded pretty rapidly and maybe inappropriately (holding my tongue has always been a problem for me), blurting out, "Isn't it my decision about whether the pay is enough?" That was the beginning of a wonderfully argumentative and productive relationship that is now more than a quarter of a century old. I don't even remember the rest of the conversation. I did get the job though!

I stayed for four years, was the first manager, quit twice (I wasn't an obedient worker and narrowly escaped being fired), and then left Ann Arbor with my children and husband when he completed his Ph.D. program. I was certain that I'd never return. We landed in New York City with two children. I weighed my options for the rest of my life and decided it was time to make rational decisions rather than passionate ones. I got an MBA from Columbia University to prepare myself for a "real" job (leading to an internal question: banking . . . or baking?).

That real job in a consulting firm lasted for about 10 months. In 2000, Frank and Ari and Paul said, "C'mon back and partner up in the bakery." I realized that although I knew objectively that life as a business consultant might be lucrative and more comfortable, I could not resist a life in food. As corny as it sounds, I realized that making, sharing, and learning about food was my personal calling. Some people get hedge fund and some get baker! I went back to following my heart. Two years of measured rationality was all I could manage.

The negotiations for returning to the Bakehouse were quintessential Paul and Ari and Amy. Frank was too busy baking to talk much, and he's the quietest of the bunch. Paul and Ari were all about the vision and the rightness of the fit and assumed that all the details would work out if it was the right thing to do. I was much more focused on the practicalities and the details of our financial arrangement. I vividly remember asking Paul, "Well, how much will it cost for me to buy in, and what kind of salary can I expect to draw at the beginning?" I was concerned about my family income and paying off the enormous debt I had amassed by going to business school. His response was, "Amy, if it's the right thing to do, the money will work out. Just come and we'll work it out." My family and I returned joyfully and it has all worked out—more than worked out, really. It's been great. The rest of my professional story is in the following pages.

food experiences that inspired me

- *My mother's perfectionism in the kitchen. I tease my mother that she cooks with a measuring tape. I often wish I could have the patience to be as precise as she is. I'm still trying.*

- *Madhur Jaffrey's books on Indian cuisine, which some graduate-student tutors introduced to me while I was in college. Following her well-written recipes was the first non-Western cooking I did in the late 1980s. I still use her books.*

- *Greens Restaurant in San Francisco. In 1987, at the age of 21, I had a magical meal of fresh flavors there, perfectly combined to my novice palate. The setting and view were beautiful. It felt like a place with a purpose. It was inspiring, and I've returned many times since.*

- *Eating dates that were mashed together in a block and drinking cardamom-flavored coffee on the dry, rocky ridges of Oman while on an archaeological expedition with my husband in 1989. We sat in a circle and the Omani we were working with supplied the refreshments. He had one cup and we all took turns having some coffee and pulling off a mass of dates from the block. Experiencing simple traditional foods in authentic settings inspired me to keep these traditions alive and known.*

- *The chefs who taught me at the Ritz Hotel in Paris. They were uncompromising about quality and would go to extreme lengths to make the best possible food they could imagine. They were incredibly joyful about it, so excited when something tasted great.*

FRANKENAMY: BEING PARTNERS

Our paths to the bakery were quite different. What has it been like to be partners?

When members of the staff speak about us, they often list both of our names and run them together so closely that it sounds like one name—Frankenamy. What we take from that is that we represent a unified experience or perspective. We're a consistent and single voice . . . much of the time. That seems good.

Our partnership works well and is a source of inspiration, energy, and comfort. We've started to consider having other partners, and through that process we've begun to reflect on what makes this partnership effective. Other partnerships will be different, of course, but there are some areas that we think are musts for a successful partnership with one of us.

Although we have different natures and social personas, we have many similar behaviors and beliefs that give our relationship a strong foundation and help us avoid sources of disagreement that can hamper a business partnership.

- We both love food. We love making it. We love eating it.
- We both like to work a lot, can work a lot, and do work whenever it's necessary, no matter how inconvenient.
- We have a very similar approach to managing money. We are both relatively deliberate and cautious in spending, but when we decide to do something, we spend what we need to do it right.
- We both prioritize people and value people.
- We are both generous, in different ways, but we each have our way and respect the other's.
- We're rule followers.
- We keep our word. Maintaining personal and business integrity is important to both of us.
- There's no blaming. We make decisions together and both own the consequences.
- We both enjoy learning and are dedicated to always getting better.
- We are appreciative of each other's strengths and are able to learn from each other.

Sounds pretty aligned, doesn't it? Well, we are, but we still disagree about many things and debate regularly and with high energy. This is also part of the charm of the relationship. There is enough trust and alignment that we can disagree with vigor and not find it disconcerting.

Probably the most surprising thing that we've learned is that our differences have actually been the most productive part of our relationship. We have different skills and approaches—Frank is more of a details guy and Amy tends to be big picture. We characterize each other as the Optimizer (Frank) and the Innovator (Amy). Of course, the reality is not so black and white. Our different perspectives on topics lead to productive conversations and better decisions.

Our partnership is very interactive and collegial. We see each other daily and rarely make a decision of any significance without consulting the other. We have a division of labor, each being the primary person responsible for a particular area of the bakery, but we still consult each other on the larger decisions.

Of course, we've had less joyful moments working together, when we felt out of alignment, but we've soldiered through them.

From this strong relationship we have been able to lead and manage the bakery and, more importantly, have been able to engage the staff to lead and manage the bakery with us.

our top 5 temptations at the bakery

AMY:

1. Our French Baguette
2. Pecan Pie
3. Boston Cream Pie
4. Onion Rye
5. Cabbage Strudel

Many of my favorites are parts of recipes or stages of recipes: chicken fat from the roast chickens used for chicken salad (it's really good on the ends of French baguettes), freshly made chocolate buttercream, also good on the ends of French baguettes, Sour Cream Coffee Cake batter, and trimmings from the roast beef we use for our sandwiches.

FRANK:

1. The ends of Sicilian Sesame Semolina Bread with a bit of butter
2. The pecan praline for the blondies before it's busted up and put into the blondies
3. Walnut and Currant Rugelach—they don't look special, but they pack a really wonderful experience for my palate
4. A very dark loaf of Farm Bread
5. A Big O Cookie

chapter 1:

Setting the Stage for
SUCCESSFUL
BAKING

A PROCESS OF BAKING THAT LEADS TO SUCCESS

If you're going to read anything before diving into the recipes, read these simple steps.

- Read the recipe all the way through before you start to do anything else.

- Look for ingredients you need. Do you have them? Do you have enough of them?

- Notice steps you need to take before starting, like toasting and grinding nuts or melting and cooling chocolate.

- Gather the equipment you need. Make sure that it's clean and that it works.

- Look up directions you aren't sure about. Look for an explanation in this chapter, or research it.

- Know when to preheat your oven.

- Measure your ingredients. We have two strong opinions about this step. Here they are—tips from the professionals!

- Weigh rather than measure. Weighing is much more accurate than using measuring cups. We always weigh at the bakery. When we started to write the book, we wanted to include volume measurements because we knew most home bakers used them. As we created the conversions and tested the recipes, the inconsistency of volume amounts became strikingly obvious. Not all measuring cups are actually the same size! Flours can be compact or loose. And then there's brown sugar. Do you measure it loosely or do you pack it into the cup? If you weigh ingredients, you don't have to think about these factors. As you'll see, we generally use volume measures for smaller quantities, because home scales are not always accurate in very small quantities.

- Measure all the ingredients you need into separate containers. Yes! We mean it. This helps to make sure that you measure items correctly and don't leave anything out of the recipe or put anything in twice. It also allows you to get all of your ingredients out at once with your scale, do the weighing, and then put all the containers away, allowing for a neat and organized workspace.

- Clear your work area of anything unnecessary for the project. A neat space makes it much easier to bake.

- Read the recipe again—what did you miss?

- Bake away!

For those of you who think this is a creativity-stifling OCD process, follow your own way. It might work out, and what you get at the end could be an exciting surprise!

FIRST RULE:
DON'T FREAK OUT! READ, PLAN, AND ENJOY.

Some of the recipes in this book look short and straightforward. You'll think, "No problem; I can do this." Other recipes will look long. We mean looooooong, with many steps. When you see lengthy instructions, you might be tempted to skip the recipe, but don't be discouraged! When the recipes are long it's because we want to tell you everything you will need to know. We want you to make beautiful and delicious breads and pastries, and that sometimes requires a detailed explanation.

There's a full range of recipes in this book, in terms of difficulty and time requirements. Some are familiar and easy, and some are moderately difficult, mainly because they require scheduling for fermentation times. A few recipes are real projects—they could take a full day of active work and involve a range of techniques. Some could take many hours of elapsed time but not a huge amount of active work. Some have multiple components that can be made over many weeks and refrigerated or frozen and then assembled on the day you want to serve them.

So how can you know what you are getting into? Read the recipe. Read it all the way through, and you'll get a good sense of the kind of work and time the recipe will take. Please also remember that the first time you make anything new it takes longer than subsequent times. This happens to us in the bakery, too. During the first week of making a new item every day, we learn a lot, and by the end of the week, we're making the recipe with greater ease and speed. It will happen for you too. But we also think you can be successful the first time through on all of these recipes (our detailed explanations will help!).

This chapter includes basic information, which will help you successfully execute our recipes. Let's get to it!

SERVING AND STORING THESE BAKED GOODS

There is a fair amount of uncertainty and confusion in our world about how best to serve and store baked goods. Perhaps the confusion comes from years of eating highly processed foods with lots of preservatives, as well as the food safety information and misinformation floating around. Here's how we suggest serving and storing our baked goods to enjoy the best flavor, texture, and shelf life.

Bread: Store in paper bags at room temperature. There is no need to refrigerate our bread. There are no pathogens in the bread that we are trying to stop from developing, so there is no reason to keep it cold. Additionally, the humidity of the fridge will destroy the crust. The breads in this book that don't contain butter or eggs take a very long time to stale and weeks to mold, so keeping them on the counter in a bag does not decrease the length of time you can enjoy them. After three days or so, they do lose moisture and become hard. But they are not "bad"! They can still be great to eat. Take a slice and warm it or toast it, or put the whole loaf in a 350°F [180°C] oven for 10 minutes and you can fully revive it. While warm, it will seem as though it was freshly baked. This cannot be done twice.

Enriched breads: For those with fat in them, like Challah and *Somodi Kalács*, storage and handling can be exactly the same as above. However, because of the enriched dough, these can mold, so they need to be eaten within several days.

All of these breads can be frozen and then reheated as just described for great results. If you are going to freeze them, we recommend wrapping them in paper first and then in plastic.

Sweet recipes: These are best served at or near room temperature, 72°F [22°C] or warm if that's your personal preference. Since so many of them contain butter, they taste best and have the best mouthfeel when the butter is at least at room temperature. If the butter is cold, it feels dry in the mouth initially. The cream fillings and buttercreams in these recipes will be smooth and tasty at room temperature.

Pastries or cakes: Those that have some sort of cream filling should be stored in the refrigerator. Otherwise they will spoil. To bring them to room temperature before eating, take them out of the fridge for two to three hours. We suggest handling anything with buttercream the same way.

The remaining sweet recipes can be stored, preferably covered in paper or in a plastic container, for three to five days. Hopefully, they'll be eaten long before that!

All of the sweet items in this book can be frozen. Wrap them well!

MOST COMMON BAKING MISTAKES

Not enough color. Many of us are afraid to let our breads and pastries get some deep color. We're worried that they will taste burnt. There are actually many shades between flavorful color and burnt, and we often don't take advantage of them. Embrace color! It almost always enhances flavor.

Changing the recipe the first time through. We recommend not changing a recipe until you really know and understand it. Changing the proportions of ingredients, even a little, and adjusting the actual ingredients can negatively affect the recipe in ways that you may not anticipate. We recommend trying the recipe as written first and then considering modifications.

Changing more than one variable at a time. Making improvements is great. However, we suggest adjusting one variable at a time.

Not measuring properly. Home bakers sometimes tell us that they made something twice and it was wonderful the first time and off the second time. We think this is often a result of mismeasuring. We think we're paying attention, but we make mistakes. Using a scale and measuring everything separately first will help prevent this.

Not having the right ingredients and substituting. Ingredients are chosen for a reason, and when we make substitutions we cannot be sure of getting the results intended in the recipe.

Using a different pan size and not adjusting the baking time. The dimensions of a baked good have a major impact on the baking time required. When you choose to use a different-sized pan, rely on the visual clues stated in the recipe to determine when it is fully baked.

Incorrect oven temperature. Home ovens don't always work well, and this causes real problems. If you are having difficulty with baking times, try putting a thermometer in your oven to see if it's calibrated properly.

CHOOSING INGREDIENTS

One of the key factors in making flavorful baked goods is using the most flavorful ingredients you can find. Perfect execution with flavorless ingredients will create a nice-looking bread or pastry that will be disappointing once you taste it. As we say at Zingerman's, "You really can taste the difference." The following are our recommendations for the most common ingredients in our recipes.

Our basic advice is to use the most flavorful ingredients you can find to make these recipes as special as they can be. Don't skimp on flavor! Yes, it may cost more, but eaters will appreciate the difference.

Butter! And What About Lard?

Butter is our fat of preference. Here's why:

Butter is more flavorful than shortening and margarine. It also browns more during the baking process, which makes many baked items more visually attractive. Start using butter in your baking and you'll never go back to another fat.

We use unsalted butter in all of our recipes. The amount of salt in salted butter is inconsistent, depending on the brand. It's easiest to control the salt in a recipe by using unsalted butter and adding the amount of salt that is optimal for the recipe.

Many of the recipes call for room-temperature butter. Two to three hours will do, and overnight is great. Don't worry about spoilage. Butter can sit at room temperature for several days without any problems. Some of the recipes call for cold butter. Having it chilled will help you achieve the desired end texture, so it's important to follow this direction.

Brands of butter we particularly like are Plugra, Lurpak, and Kerrygold. If you can purchase any of these, choose the one with the flavor you like best. If you can't get any of them, taste the unsalted butters that are available to you and choose the one you prefer.

Lard can be great too, and you will see that we recommend it for a variety of recipes. Lard was the fat most commonly used in American baking for a large part of our history. It fell out of favor and was supplanted by margarine and butter, and now most of us are not used to its flavor in sweet baked goods. To accommodate current tastes, vegetarians, and the dietary practices of some Jews and Muslims we use it sparingly. Feel free to substitute it for butter in equal proportions in any of the recipes. Technically, it will work just fine.

All-Purpose Flour

We always use unbleached and unbromated flour. Bleaching is an unnecessary step that is taken purely for cosmetic reasons. Bromation is a controversial process to age flour more quickly, saving companies time to market. It's illegal in some countries and in California, and it's totally unnecessary for baking. Any brand of all-purpose flour should work in our recipes, even the bread recipes. The term "all-purpose" refers to the protein content in the flour—all-purpose flour is in the 10 to 12 percent range.

Sea Salt

In the bakery, we use finely ground Sicilian sea salt. It allows us to avoid the off flavors of iodized salt and to benefit from the more complex flavors of sea salt. If you don't have sea salt and you are ready to bake in every other way, though, go right ahead. It's critical that you use finely ground salt so that the amount is correct in the recipe and the salt dissolves properly.

Vanilla Extract and Vanilla Beans

Use the real stuff. It is exponentially more flavorful than the artificial version and will make a significant flavor difference in the recipes. There are many good brands on the market. Just make sure that the label says it is 100 percent real. If the label says how many "folds" it is, more is better. Vanilla with 1.5 to 2 folds is the most common strength used by professional bakers. Vanilla extract made from beans from different parts of the world will taste different. If you have the choice of Tahitian, Madagascar, or Mexican vanilla, taste them and choose the one you prefer. The differences are quite remarkable and you may care, especially if vanilla is going to be the shining star in the recipe you're making.

Plump beans are most desirable, a sign of their freshness and good handling. If you have some dry vanilla beans in your spice cupboard, don't throw them out. You can salvage them by hydrating them in vanilla extract. Once they're supple again, go ahead and use them.

Never used a vanilla bean before? Take the pod and slice it horizontally down the middle. Scrape the seeds out of the pod with the back of your knife. Now you're ready to add them to the recipe.

You can still get more use out of the pod, so don't throw it away. You can put it in your sugar bowl and flavor your sugar or just leave it exposed to the air. Either way, let it dry out until it's brittle and then grind it in a spice grinder. Now you have vanilla powder. This is great to add to things like cookie doughs, scones, or muffins.

Granulated White Sugar

There's a debate in the baking world about which is better, granulated white cane sugar or granulated white beet sugar. Sugar beets and sugar cane are very different plants, so it would not be surprising that a sweetener refined from each of them might have different properties and therefore a different effect in baking. Since beet sugar and cane sugar look the same, we may not always consider that possibility. I've heard bakers say that beet sugar can't be used in baking. That is categorically not true. Many European countries use primarily beet sugar. Our recipes were created with cane sugar, but for many years we used Michigan beet sugar in our school with the same recipes, and they were delicious! Feel free to use either interchangeably.

Brown Sugar

We are fans of muscovado brown sugar. Muscovado is cane sugar that is refined less than white sugar, leaving much of the molasses in the end product and a great deal more flavor. Organic brown sugar is not the same as muscovado. Typical American brown sugar is actually cane syrup refined to white sugar, with molasses removed as a byproduct of the process and then some molasses added back. This explains the availability of light brown sugar and dark brown sugar. If you can't get muscovado brown sugar, use dark brown sugar.

Since muscovado has a strong and distinctive flavor, at times we choose not to use it because it can overpower the other flavors in the recipe. We make it clear in the recipe what kind of sugar we recommend.

Chocolate

Chocolate is basically made of cacao, cocoa butter, vanilla, sugar, and occasionally milk. The percentages of each of these elements in the chocolate are one of the primary differentiators of one chocolate from another. On chocolate packages these days, producers note the percentage of cacao on the

label. The rest of the ingredients in the chocolate make up the remaining percentage.

Chocolates also have particular flavors, depending on the bean and region of origin. The flavors can range from fruity to earthy to coffee or nutty. Chocolates made of a single variety of beans from a particular region emphasize the difference in these flavors. Other chocolates are blends of beans chosen by the chocolatier to achieve a particular flavor profile.

We've noted the minimum percentage of chocolate necessary for many of the recipes. If you prefer more intense chocolate, feel free to substitute a higher percentage, up to about 70 percent. We don't recommend using chocolate with a lower percentage than what the recipe calls for, because that usually means it will have more sugar and may make the recipe too sweet. We like sweetness to be one of the flavors in our desserts and pastries, but never the predominant one.

If you're choosing to use a varietal chocolate, we recommend that you sample it first and make sure you enjoy the flavor profile.

Cocoa Powder

We recommend using nonalkalized cocoa powder with a high butterfat content. The process of alkalizing cocoa prepares it to be combined with a liquid more easily, as in hot cocoa. It is not at all necessary for the cocoa we use in our baking, and the process actually decreases the flavor of the cocoa. Note that nonalkalized cocoa is lighter in color than the alkalized version most of us are used to. The final baked good will be less deep in color as a result. If darker color matters to you more than the flavor, use alkalized cocoa.

Nuts

Nuts are used in many of our recipes. It is important to buy nuts that have been handled properly and taste fresh. Since they have lots of oil in them, nuts can go rancid relatively quickly. For the best chance of finding good nuts, go to a market  that does a brisk business. The best way to store nuts for any length of time is in an airtight container in your freezer. Remember that nuts are a seasonal item. They are harvested annually, and one year's crop can taste slightly different from another year's. Depending on the yield of the crop, the prices may also change dramatically.

Spices

Spices, like practically all foods, come in a full range of quality. For the best spices, your best bet might be finding a specialty grocer in your area. Not all of us have specialty spice grocers, however. An alternative is purchasing from an online store, like Zingerman's Mail Order, www.zingermans.com. If you don't want to use either of these options, the next best choice, which can be a very good one, is to use newly bought spices. Spices lose their aroma and flavor over time, so new ones from the store will be much better than the year-old jar in your cupboard. If you can buy them in bulk, buy just what you need, so that you can get fresh ones again for the next recipe. We also recommend buying whole spices and grinding them yourself. Using a mortar and pestle will give the best results, but a spice grinder is a great second choice.

Eggs

We use large eggs in our recipes and, unless otherwise stated, suggest that they be at room temperature. If your eggs are cold, a quick way to warm them up is to submerge them in a bowl of warm water for five minutes. For the best results, use the freshest eggs you can find. Eggs contain protein, which often plays a part in the structure of baked goods. As they age, the protein breaks down and won't be able to do its job as effectively.

Dairy

We use full-fat dairy products in all of our baking, and we look for the most flavorful option available to us. The fat in milk, cream, and sour cream has an impact on the flavor, structure, and color of the baked items. Many of the sweets in this book are treats, made for special occasions and not eaten every day. We recommend using full-fat dairy so that they'll have the best texture, flavor, and color possible.

In terms of brands, we choose local brands that process their dairy products minimally. For example, our cream is pasteurized but not ultrapasteurized. The difference is the temperature of the pasteurization and the length of the heating. We find that ultrapasteurization destroys some safe and flavorful bacteria that we prefer to taste. For the dairy producer, it gives the cream a longer shelf life. We prefer to prioritize flavor over shelf life.

When choosing between local brands, we also choose based on flavor. Sample what's available to you and use your favorite.

Yeast

There are three forms of yeast available in the United States: instant, active dry, and fresh (cake) yeast. Our recipes are written for instant dry yeast. This yeast is created using a process that allows the yeast to be mixed with cool or room-temperature water and does not need to be proofed first. It is very convenient.

If you prefer to use fresh yeast, we recommend multiplying the weight of dry yeast in the recipe by 3 to get an equivalent amount. If you are using active dry yeast, the conversion is 1 teaspoon of instant yeast to 1½ teaspoons of active dry. Regardless of the kind of yeast you're using, check the date for freshness. Once the package is open, store it in your refrigerator.

EQUIPMENT

We want baking to be as approachable as possible. To achieve this, we try to choose the simplest equipment for home bakers to use that will allow for success. We even encourage you to use your hands! They're great tools. If you come to our baking school, you'll see that it's relatively humble. We often use just a metal bowl, a fork, a wooden spoon, and a plastic scraper. Stand mixers are a rarity and are never a part of bread-making classes.

Some of us like our equipment, though. And some of us need it for a variety of reasons, so we also tell you how to make these recipes with tools like stand mixers, pastry bags, portioners, and more. For this book, we've written many of the sweet recipes assuming that you will want to use a mixer. It is easy to use a bowl and a wooden spoon instead, if you prefer. The bread recipes are mainly written to use a bowl, a spoon, and your hands. A few of the more enriched bread recipes call for a mixer.

Below is a list of the most common tools the recipes require.

Oven

The temperatures for these recipes are intended for conventional home ovens. If you have a convection oven, it will work perfectly well for pastries and cakes—just decrease the baking temperature by 25°F [14°C]. Bake the items for the same amount of time stated in the recipe. For bread recipes, we highly discourage the use of convection ovens. The blowing air often dries the surface of the bread before it is able to reach its maximum volume.

Teaspoons and Soup Spoons

Spoons of different sizes work very well to fill things, and they can substitute for a portioner if you don't have one.

Knife or Food Processor

Many recipes in this book require chopped or ground nuts. A sharp chef's knife or a food processor will do this best.

Digital Scale

Look for a simple digital scale in your price range. They are available at many cooking equipment stores and online. Make sure they weigh in a variety of measures, including grams.

Wide Mixing Bowl

We like to make many recipes without a mixer. Why? Because a mixer isn't 100 percent necessary if you're up for a little physical labor. If you're going to mix up a recipe the old-fashioned way, we highly recommend a wide metal bowl (but any material will do just fine). This shape makes it much easier to stir effectively and to scrape down the sides while mixing to ensure a homogeneous batter.

Stand Mixer

All of these recipes can be made with a basic home stand mixer. We indicate the appropriate attachment and speed in each recipe. A mixer with a 5-quart bowl is adequate.

Wooden Spoon

We love wooden spoons for mixing. They're strong enough that they help us bakers put the force we need into activities like creaming. They stand up forever, they are readily available, and they're cheap. Amy still has a spoon she bought when she moved into her first apartment in 1988!

Silicone Spatula or Plastic Scraper

The mixing directions in these recipes will often instruct you to scrape down the sides of the mixing bowl to make sure that all of the precious ingredients are incorporated into the dough or batter. Typical silicone kitchen spatulas will do the trick. However, professional bakers also like something we call plastic scrapers or plastic cards. They have a rounded side that makes it easy to scrape a bowl. We also find them handy for lots of other baking needs, like scraping flour off work areas. If you like equipment, you might look for one. They're inexpensive.

Rolling Pin

Our favorite rolling pin for the recipes in this book is a traditional French pin with tapered ends. They are light relative to the larger pins with separate handles, and a little easier to control. They're readily available in stores that sell baking equipment.

Dough Knife or Bench Scraper

This is a very helpful and inexpensive tool used by professional bakers. It's a rectangular implement with a metal blade and a wooden or plastic handle. It cuts dough easily and is also handy for cleaning work surfaces.

Proofing Baskets and Linen Couches

Our French Baguettes, Chestnut Baguettes, and True North Bread all call for linen couches. They are available in our shop or online (search for "couches for bread baking"). They are made of heavy flax linen, and either an 18-by-36-in [46-by-91-cm] or 26-by-36-in [66-by-91-cm] piece would work well for home baking.

The Farm Bread is formed into loaves and then placed in proofing baskets for its final period of fermentation. The baskets hold the shape of the loaves during their relatively long fermentation time. They also leave decorative flour markings on the exterior of the loaves. We use traditional baskets made from willow. Some bakeries now use plastic ones because they clean more easily and cause less anxiety with health inspectors.

Portioners

Using portioners is one of those little baker's tricks. They allow us to have all our cookies, or whatever we're making, be exactly the same size, which makes it easier to bake each one of them accurately and have them look more perfect when they are displayed. We suggest a portioner size for each recipe where appropriate. They are available online and in some cookware stores. Portioners aren't 100 percent necessary, though. You can use your hands and eyes and a spoon and get cookies or scones pretty close to the same size.

Pastry Bag and Tips

Sometimes using a pastry bag allows for neater portioning and for making particular shapes. We suggest buying disposable ones. Both tips and bags are available in most cookware stores and online. We state the size of the tip needed in the recipe instructions.

It takes some practice to become proficient at using a pastry bag. First you cut enough off the tip of the bag to allow one-third of the chosen tip to poke through. Make sure it fits snugly in there. Now hold the bag in your non-dominant hand and fold about one-third of the bag down over the hand. Still holding the bag, fill it with your dominant hand. Avoid overfilling it. The more batter there is in the bag, the more force will be required to push the batter out. Better to put too little in than too much. Now, twisting the top of the bag closed to create pressure, push all of the batter to the tip and squeeze out any extra air in the bag. Place your dominant hand at the top of the bag to create pressure and use your nondominant hand to guide the tip. In general, keep the bag perpendicular to the surface you're piping onto. We suggest looking online for a short educational video. Having the visual will really help.

Sheet Tray

A basic rimmed baking tray, or sheet, that fits into your oven is necessary for many of our recipes. Most home trays are quarter sheets (9 by 13 in [23 by 33 cm]). We recommend also investing in half sheets (13 by 18 in [33 by 46 cm]). Having a few of these handy will make it easier to make large quantities so that you can bake two trays at a time and have two more ready to go into the oven. Nonstick is not a bad idea if you want to skip the parchment paper.

Parchment Paper

Parchment paper is possibly one of the most convenient items professional bakers use. It saves on cleaning, makes transferring items easier, and reduces the time needed to prepare (and clean) pans and trays.

Baking Stone

A rectangular baking stone replicates the effect of baking on a stone hearth. It can be put in a home oven and heated prior to baking bread or pizza. Bread baked on a baking stone gets the direct heat necessary for a good oven jump, and a stone also aids in creating a crusty, well-colored exterior. Baking stones are readily available in houseware stores and online.

Baking Peel

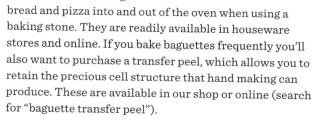

A peel is a convenient tool that aids in sliding bread and pizza into and out of the oven when using a baking stone. They are readily available in houseware stores and online. If you bake baguettes frequently you'll also want to purchase a transfer peel, which allows you to retain the precious cell structure that hand making can produce. These are available in our shop or online (search for "baguette transfer peel").

Cake Boards

It's often nice to build a cake on a cardboard cake board that can be easily cleaned and allows you to transfer the cake from the fridge to a pretty cake stand or plate. These boards are available in cake decorating stores, online, and in general-purpose craft stores.

Cake Turntable

Icing a cake well takes some practice. It is possible to do it on a plate or sheet tray or by rotating it in one hand and icing with the other. If you think you'd like to ice many cakes, having a rotating cake stand will make the process easier.

BREAD-BAKING TECHNIQUES

Many of us are unfamiliar with making yeasted baked goods. It's no longer a common home activity. To help, we've included this section on bread-baking terminology and techniques. It's important to refer to this section as you're making the recipes for a thorough understanding of how to proceed.

Water Temperature

Room-temperature water (68° to 72°F [20° to 22°C]) is best for mixing yeasted doughs. If you live in a very hot climate and your room has an ambient temperature above 80°F [27°C], you may want to chill your water to 55° to 60°F [13° to 15°C]. In general, cooler water is better, as it allows the bacteria to create more acids and thus more flavor. Warmer water stimulates the yeast, speeding up the process and therefore decreasing the time available for other flavor development.

If your tap water is highly chlorinated, allow it to sit for a couple of hours and the chlorine will dissipate. Using bottled or purified water is not necessary unless you are unhappy with the flavor or other qualities of your water source.

Room Temperature and Humidity

Ideal fermentation happens at about 78°F [25°C] and 80 percent relative humidity. This precise state is rarely available in most people's homes most of the year. Good bread can be baked in a variety of conditions, but you may have to adjust proofing times to suit your local conditions. Most of us can find a spot in our home that has a relatively stable environment. It might be the inside of a cool oven, on top of the refrigerator, or, if you're lucky, right on your counter. Just know that if your environment is cooler, your dough might require a longer fermentation or proofing time. Similarly, if it's warmer, the process might happen more quickly. For the most consistent results, try to keep the environment the same from one time you bake to the next.

Mixing

All the mixing is described in detail in each of the recipes in our book. It can be accomplished with a large bowl, a wooden spoon, and a little bit of effort. We have written most of the recipes to mix and then knead by hand, though it is possible to use a stand mixer as well.

Kneading

Wash your hands. Unless specifically instructed, turn your dough onto a work surface that is clean, not floured, and at or slightly below waist height. It's worth stating this again emphatically—the dough should be placed onto a work surface that hasn't been floured. All of the recipes are written with the proper weight of flour to make great-tasting bread. Placing flour on the work surface will alter the recipe some and actually prevent you from achieving the maximum flavor. Place your mass of dough about 3 to 4 in [7.5 to 10 cm] from the edge of the work surface. Hold a plastic scraper in one hand and, with the heel of the other hand, press firmly into the mass of dough and stretch it several inches in front of you. With your bare hand or the plastic scraper, fold the dough farthest from you back toward you, over the top of the dough. Rotate the mass 90 degrees and repeat. This stretching and folding technique is what will help align the gluten network in your dough. We suggest putting one foot in front of the other so you are in a comfortable position, and find a gentle rhythm to press the dough out in front of you, fold it over, rotate, and repeat. If the dough is sticky, use the plastic scraper to clean the dough from the work surface as well as off your hands.

Don't add any additional flour to the work surface. Some doughs are intended to be sticky, and if you can embrace the stickiness, you will be rewarded with an open crumb and a delicious loaf of bread. One hint for sticky doughs is to move your dough 6 in [15 cm] to the right or left to a "drier" spot on the work surface every couple of minutes. Then continue to knead the dough. If it begins to stick to the work surface again, move it back in the other direction. Each recipe will instruct you to knead for somewhere between six and nine minutes to develop the dough properly. After several minutes of kneading, your dough should begin to hold together in a consolidated mass. That said, it may very well continue to stick to the work surface and your hand.

Folding

Folding is a step we sometimes include in our yeasted dough recipes. We may recommend it intermittently during the bulk fermentation stage. Folding is necessary in high-hydration doughs (those with a high proportion of water relative to dry ingredients) as well as lightly mixed doughs. The process of folding helps build structure in the dough by organizing and aligning the gluten network. It's an amazing little step that has an enormous positive impact on the strength of the dough.

To fold the dough, turn it out onto a lightly floured surface. For very wet doughs, make certain to have enough flour on the work surface to keep the dough from sticking, but avoid using too much flour.

Shape the dough into a rectangle. From right to left, fold the dough as you would a letter, bringing one third of the dough toward the left and then pulling the remaining portion of the dough over the top. Now do the same vertically, by folding the top third toward the bottom and the bottom over the top.

Finally flip the "package" of dough back over (seam side down) into the proofing container.

Repeat as necessary in the recipe. After the final fold, allow at least 30 minutes before dividing and pre-shaping the dough.

The Windowpane Test

For doughs that won't be folded, use the windowpane test to check whether you have kneaded your dough sufficiently. After kneading for the recommended time, cut a 1-by-2-in [2.5-by-5-cm] section of your dough. Press it gently between both thumbs and index fingers and carefully and gently stretch it slowly in each direction. When a dough has been mixed sufficiently and the gluten matrix has developed, you will be able to take that small portion of dough and stretch it so thin that you could imagine reading a paper through it, hence the name "windowpane test." If the piece of dough rips dramatically or quickly while you are gently stretching it, this indicates a need for more kneading. If this happens, knead for another minute or two and then try the windowpane test again.

Bulk Fermentation

After the dough has been mixed or kneaded, it is left to rest relatively undisturbed in a covered container. This period is known as the bulk fermentation, sometimes called "proofing" or "rising." It can last anywhere between one and four hours, depending on the type of dough and the quantity of commercial yeast used. During this period enzymatic activity ramps up and the yeasts do their thing of feeding, reproducing, and giving off carbon dioxide. In general, the mass of the dough doubles in volume during this process.

Pre-Shaping and Resting

After the dough has been mixed and has completed its prescribed proofing or bulk fermentation time, it is ready to be divided. Most of the recipes call for dividing the dough into two pieces. While a family member won't reject a loaf that isn't exactly the same weight as the other, the loaves will bake most similarly if they are the same size. If you have a scale (which we strongly recommend), you can be precise in dividing the dough.

After the dough has been divided, it's time to gently round the piece of dough if making a round loaf or a batard (football shape), or into a cylinder shape if the final shape is to be a baguette. The purpose of this step is to add strength to the dough as well as to gently release some of the carbon dioxide that has been produced and to get those little microorganisms in the dough back in contact with their food.

After this pre-shaping step, we generally allow the dough to relax for a period of time (usually 30 to 45 minutes) before manipulating the dough into its final shape. The more the dough is allowed to relax, the easier it will be to get it into its final shape. The tighter the pre-shaped piece of dough, the longer the resting period required. Listen to the dough. It will tell you when it needs more time to relax. If it's loose in your hands, it has likely relaxed a bit too long. While not ideal, it can still make a good loaf of bread, though with perhaps less than ideal volume.

Pre-Shaping a Round Loaf or Batard

Lightly flour your work surface. Tap a portion of dough gently onto the floured surface. Hold the dough in both hands. With your right hand, stretch about a sixth of the dough away from you and tuck it under the rest of the dough. This tucked section should be facing away from you. Rotate the loaf 60 degrees and repeat the tucking motion. Continue to slightly rotate and tuck the dough until you have completed a full revolution or a bit more. At this point, place the piece of dough into the palm of your left hand with all of the tucks facing up. With the fingers of your right hand, gently press and seal all of the tuck sections together while continuing to rotate the round piece of dough. You can imagine allowing these tucked sections to take on a cone shape as you gather them together. When sufficiently sealed, place the dough on the work surface to rest with the tucked section facing down. The top of the round should be smooth and unblemished. Cover it with plastic and allow it to relax for the prescribed amount of time.

Pre-Shaping a Baguette

Place a portion of dough on a lightly floured work surface. Gently manipulate it into a rectangular shape, with the longer section facing side to side. Pat the dough gently. With the fingers of both hands, lift about 2 in [5 cm] of the dough farthest away from you, press it gently downward into the rest of the dough, and push it gently away from you. Don't let your piece of dough grow longer. Repeat this process a second time. Spin your piece of dough 180 degrees and repeat. At this point, you should have a nice log-shaped piece of dough with a seam running the length of the dough. Flip it over and place it seam side down. Cover it with plastic and allow it to relax for the prescribed amount of time.

Final Shaping and Final Fermentation

After your pre-shaped loaf has rested, it's time to give it its final shaping.

For a round loaf, uncover the pre-shaped round. Pick it up, turn it over, and tap the top surface gently onto a lightly floured work surface. Then follow the same instructions that you used for pre-shaping to get the final shape—no difference.

For a batard or football shape, uncover the pre-shaped round and place it with the top surface facing down onto a lightly floured work surface. Gently press it out with the flats of your palms. With the fingers and thumbs of both hands, lift up about 2 in [5 cm] of the dough farthest from you (at about 10:00 and 2:00 if you think of the dough round as a clock) and fold each toward the center to form a triangle. Keep the tips of your thumbs touching the tips of your index and middle fingers. Your hands should be slightly cupped, and you should see a triangle formed by your thumbs and fingers. Keeping your hands in this orientation will help you keep the batard from lengthening too much. Lift up about 2 in [5 cm] of the top of the triangle, fold it down, and gently press it into the dough and then away from you. Next take another 2 to 3 in [5 to 7.5 cm] of dough and repeat the motion of folding it and gently pressing it into the dough and then away from you. You should now be able to repeat this step one final time and you will have formed a slightly pointy cylinder. With the heel of your right hand, firmly pat the seam that you have formed. Place the cylinder seam side down. With your cupped hands forming the triangle, gently push the seam away from you, onto the work surface, with your thumbs and then pull the dough onto the work surface with your fingers. Repeat this two or three times until you have tightened up the batard.

Preparing the Oven

Preheat your oven and baking stone for at least 45 minutes prior to baking. Place your baking stone on a middle or lower rack at least 2 in [5 cm] from the front of the oven. If steam is required for your recipe, place a cast iron skillet on the bottom of the oven such that it is ½ in [1.5 cm] from the oven door. Have a large stainless steel bowl or aluminum roasting pan that is taller and larger than your loaves ready.

Knowing When the Bread Is Ready to Bake

Thirty minutes prior to the prescribed final proofing time, check on your loaves. Delicately uncover them. First use your eyes—are your loaves larger? Then gently touch your loaf with a fingertip. If you press your finger gently into your loaf and then lift it off, and the indentation immediately pushes back out, the loaf requires more time before it's ready to be baked. Give it another 15 minutes and check

again. The loaf is ready when the indentation made by your finger pushes back very slowly and doesn't completely fill back in. If you wait too long, your finger will leave an indentation that will just remain an indentation. There's nothing you can do at this point other than bake it right away: it's overproofed. If the recipe calls for the loaf to be scored prior to baking, score it very lightly if it is overproofed.

Transferring to the Oven

Lightly flour your peel or dust with coarse cornmeal. Gently lift your loaf and place it on the peel. Place the second loaf on the peel as well, making certain that both loaves will fit on the baking stone and are not touching. Score the bread before transferring it to the baking stone.

Scoring

Scoring the bread before baking is done for two purposes: one functional and the other aesthetic.

As bread bakes, it expands. By scoring the bread, we create more surface area for the bread to expand into. If the bread is not scored, it is possible that as it expands it may do so unevenly and cause tearing or sections of dough to pop out. The scoring allows a more controlled and even expansion of the dough. If your dough is young (not as proofed as it should be), but you're baking it anyway, we suggest that the scores be deeper than normal to allow for more oven jump. If the bread is more proofed than optimal, make the scores delicate, as the bread may not have much energy left to fill them out. If your bread is very overproofed, there is no need to score it, and scoring may actually cause it to lose any remaining gas and therefore completely ruin it.

Many artisan breads have a beautiful appearance, some of which is the result of artistic scoring. There are many patterns you can use to decorate your loaves. Choose one that you find appealing.

To score the bread, take a razor blade or sharp knife and make a cut through the top surface of the dough as directed in the recipe. In general, the blade should be held at an angle of about 30 degrees relative to the top surface of the loaf.

Baking with Steam

We use steam in our oven when we bake bread to keep the exterior of the bread supple as it has its oven jump and expands. Without steam, the crust of the bread may start to form before the crumb has expanded to its full capacity. The result will be a tighter crumb than is optimal.

Have several ice cubes ready. Holding the peel in one hand, open the oven door, carefully place the ice cubes in the cast iron skillet, and then slide the loaves onto the baking stone. Carefully place the stainless steel bowl or aluminum pan over the loaves, making certain that the edge of the bowl extends over the edge of the baking stone, allowing it to capture and contain the steam produced by the ice cubes evaporating. Close the oven door. Remove the bowl or aluminum pan after 10 minutes and continue baking.

Assessing When the Bread Is Done

Fifteen minutes before the lowest suggested baking time is up, put on an oven mitt. Open the oven door, rotate each loaf 180 degrees, and evaluate the loaves for color. While they should require more baking time, it is possible that they will be fully baked. Judge whether the loaves are baked based on their color and how they feel in your hand. A loaf that is fully baked will make a hollow sound when tapped on the bottom with your finger. Note that a loaf that is overbaked will also sound hollow when tapped with your finger. In general, we recommend developing a deep, rich, caramel-brown crust on the loaves.

We suggest baking nonenriched breads quite dark. Many artisan bakers prefer a dark bake, even though it can be a challenge to sell the loaves. Why do we like to bake the bread so dark that people might think it's burnt? There are three main reasons:

The crust has much more flavor, and it adds flavor to the internal crumb of the bread. Think of caramelized onions or darkly seared steak. A dark crust has the same positive effect on a loaf of bread.

Dark crusts have a wonderful texture that's a great contrast to the soft interior of the bread.

The crust protects the interior from drying out. This is especially helpful if you bake large, heavy loaves that you intend to eat for a week or two.

Removing the Bread from the Oven

When the loaves are baked, carefully slide the peel underneath them and remove them from the oven. Place the loaves on a cooling rack. Allow them to cool completely, preferably for several hours.

Nothing smells better than a warm loaf of bread fresh out of the oven. However, the flavors of the bread will take at least a couple of hours to fully compose, so it's best to allow several hours before eating.

Fermentation Method for Our Bread Recipes

Our bread recipes use three basic doughs—straight doughs, poolishes, and naturally leavened doughs—and each has its own fermentation style.

Straight doughs are yeasted doughs in which commercial yeast is added in the initial mixing of the dough. The quantity of yeast is relatively high compared to the other doughs we make, and the fermentation times are relatively short, three to five hours from the start to the oven. For this sort of dough, all the information you need is in the recipe. Often doughs made this way are very enriched with lots of flavor from fat and other ingredients like dried fruit. They may have a sweetener in them as well. Examples of recipes made with straight doughs are the Challah and Stollen.

Poolish doughs receive a large amount of their fermentation power and flavor from the creation of a pre-ferment, which we call a poolish. A poolish is made from flour, water, and commercial yeast (specifically, equal weights of flour and water and a very small amount of yeast) that we mix together hours before making the final dough. We then use this fermenting mixture as an ingredient in the dough.

The doughs themselves also include a relatively small amount of additional commercial yeast. By using a poolish, we are able to reduce the overall quantity of commercial yeast in the recipe. This extends the fermentation time, allows more flavor to develop naturally, and results in a chewier crumb with larger and more irregular holes. The bread develops better flavor from the grain and good bacterial cultures, rather than from fat, sweeteners, or flavorings that might be added. The fermentation time from start to finish, including for the poolish, is more like 13 to 17 hours. These breads are very doable at home. All the necessary instructions are in the individual recipes. They do require more planning than straight doughs, however. Examples of recipes that use a poolish are the Focaccia with Gorgonzola and Caramelized Onion and Sicilian Sesame Semolina Bread.

The final type of dough that we make is naturally leavened. This means that it is leavened using a sourdough starter that contains naturally occurring yeast. There is no commercial yeast in the recipe or the starter. The result is bread with complex flavor that is developed in the starter and from long fermentation times of the dough. The hole structure is also more open and irregular (as in poolish doughs). The fermentation time of these recipes ranges from 13 to 21 hours. Examples of naturally leavened bread recipes in this book are the Roadhouse Bread and Better Than San Francisco Sourdough Bread.

The actual making of naturally leavened breads is quite easy. They require planning, a couple of steps, and lots of elapsed time for fermentation and flavor development. The challenging part is creating your own sourdough starter and maintaining it for optimal flavor and strength.

The following recipe will help you create and maintain a starter and make a levain, which is an ingredient in some of the recipes. The first loaves you make with your starter will not be your best. It is our experience that the starter becomes optimal after several weeks of baking.

For those of you who already have a starter, converting your starter into our levain can be achieved by the following feeding: 1 part starter, 1 part water, and 2 parts all-purpose flour (one-fourth starter, one-fourth water, and one-half all-purpose flour).

SOURDOUGH STARTER

DAY 1 IN A ONE-TIME PROCESS:
CREATE THE SOURDOUGH STARTER

All-purpose flour	1 cup	140 g
Organic whole wheat flour	1 Tbsp	10 g
Water, room temperature	⅓ cup	77 g

1. In a small bowl, combine the flours and water. Stir until well blended, then scrape the mixture out onto a work surface and knead for a couple of minutes, until the dough is smooth. It will be rather firm. Place the dough in a container. Cover tightly with a lid or plastic wrap.

2. Let the dough ferment at room temperature (68° to 72°F [20° to 22°C]) for 24 hours (1 day).

DAY 2 IN A ONE-TIME PROCESS:
FEED THE SOURDOUGH STARTER

Sourdough starter	1⅓ cups	220 g
Water, room temperature	½ cup	115 g
All-purpose flour	1½ cups	215 g

3. Now that 24 hours have elapsed since the initiation of the starter, uncover the starter and transfer it to a large mixing bowl. Add the water to the starter and stir it in thoroughly. Add the flour and stir until well blended.

4. Transfer the fed starter to a work surface and knead by hand until it forms a smooth ball. This time it should be firm, but not too stiff.

5. Place the fed starter into a container and cover with a lid or plastic wrap.

6. Ferment the fed starter for 24 hours (1 day) at room temperature.

DAY 3 IN A ONE-TIME PROCESS:
FEED THE SOURDOUGH STARTER

Sourdough starter	1⅓ cups	220 g
Water, room temperature	½ cup	115 g
All-purpose flour	1½ cups	215 g

7. Now that 48 hours have elapsed since the initiation of the starter, uncover the starter and transfer 1⅓ cups (220 g) of it to a large mixing bowl. You can compost or discard the rest. Add the water to the starter and stir it in thoroughly. Add the flour and stir until well blended.

8. Transfer the fed starter to a work surface and knead by hand until it forms a smooth ball. This time it should be firm, but not too stiff.

9. Place the fed starter in a container and cover with a lid or plastic wrap.

10. Ferment the fed starter for 24 hours (1 day) at room temperature. After it has fermented for 24 hours, it will be ready to use to make Starter Farm Bread, which will yield "Put Away Farm" (as described in step 14).

DAY 4 IN A ONE-TIME PROCESS:
FEED THE SOURDOUGH STARTER AND USE TO MAKE STARTER FARM BREAD

Water, room temperature	2¼ cups	520 g
Sourdough starter	1⅔ cups	275 g
All-purpose flour	5½ cups	770 g
Whole wheat flour	½ cup	75 g
Sea salt	4 tsp	23 g

11. Now that 24 hours have elapsed since the last feeding (and 72 hours since the initiation of the starter), place the water in a large mixing bowl. Tear the fed starter (discard any extra) into pieces and add to the water. Add both of the flours and stir with a wooden spoon until combined. Add the salt and mix it in.

12. Scrape what is now starter farm dough out of the bowl onto a clean, unfloured work surface and knead for 6 to 8 minutes (page 34) until it forms a smooth ball. Place in a lightly oiled bowl and cover with plastic.

13. After 1 hour, turn the dough out onto a lightly floured work surface and fold (page 34). Return it to the oiled container and re-cover. After 1 hour turn the dough out onto a lightly floured work surface and fold it a second time. Return it to the oiled container. After 1 hour turn the dough out onto a lightly floured work surface and fold it a third time. Return it to the oiled container. Allow the dough to proof for 1 additional hour.

14. Cut off 1 cup [180 g] of the starter farm dough, which becomes "Put Away Farm." Place it in a tightly sealed container and refrigerate it for the next bake. Divide the remaining starter farm dough into two equal portions, pre-shape each into a round (page 35), and let relax for 45 minutes.

15. Shape each round into a batard and place seam side up in a lightly floured basket to proof for 3½ to 4 hours.

16. Preheat the oven with a baking stone and cast iron skillet (for creating steam) to 450°F [230°C] for 45 minutes before baking (page 38).

continued

17. Flip the loaves out of the baskets onto a lightly floured peel, score with a wheat stalk pattern (as detailed in the Farm Bread recipe, page 110), and bake with steam for 45 to 50 minutes, until the crust is dark brown.

note: *The "Put Away Farm" from Day 4 (step 14) of the sourdough starter is now used to make the levain, which in turn is used as an ingredient to make more Farm Bread, as well as the other sourdough breads in this book: Parmesan Pepper Bread (page 56), Roadhouse Bread (page 86), Farm Bread with Pepper and Bacon (page 174), 8 Grain 3 Seed Bread (page 176), Better Than San Francisco Sourdough Bread (page 203), Chestnut Baguettes (page 228), and True North Bread (page 227).*

ONCE A WEEK:
MAKE A LEVAIN

Water, room temperature	½ cup	115 g
Put Away Farm	½ cup	115 g
All-purpose flour	1½ cup plus 2 Tbsp	230 g

1. Place the water in a large mixing bowl. Tear the "Put Away Farm" into small pieces and add to the water. Add half of the flour and stir with a wooden spoon until combined. Add the rest of the flour and mix to combine until it becomes a shaggy mass.

2. Turn onto a clean, unfloured work surface and knead for 6 to 8 minutes (page 34), until it forms a smooth ball. Place in a lightly oiled bowl and cover. Put the bowl in a warm spot and allow the levain to ferment for 6 to 8 hours, until it doubles in volume.

3. After the levain is fermented, it can be used to make any of the sourdough breads in this book. When the Farm Bread final dough is ready for shaping, remember to save 1 cup [180 g] of it (which is now called "Put Away Farm"), and store it in the refrigerator for later use, per the Farm Bread recipe (page 110).

note: *The "Put Away Farm" can be stored in the refrigerator for up to 5 days before you feed it and turn it into levain. If you haven't used the "Put Away Farm" to make levain within 5 days, dispose of all but 115 g of it and feed as described in steps 1 through 5 above.*

getting started and CREATING OUR MISSION

FRANK: We baked our first Bakehouse loaf on September 13, 1992, but the idea for the Bakehouse germinated many months before. In early 1992, Ari spent a couple of weeks in San Francisco. At that time, while there were essentially no hearth-baked artisan bread bakeries in Michigan, there were many thriving bakeries in the Bay Area. During his trip, Ari was in heaven: one day he could enjoy a loaf from Acme, the next a baguette from Semifreddi's, followed by olive bread from Metropolis, and then Italian bread from Grace Baking. Near the end of his trip, he made a mental decision to find a way to start baking for Zingerman's Delicatessen.

During the ten years of the Deli's existence, Paul and Ari had traveled around the world searching for producers of traditionally made and really flavorful foods. The breads they found in Europe were superior to what they were buying for the Deli. Although they were buying the best bread available in Ann Arbor and Detroit, it didn't measure up to what they knew was possible. Ari returned from his time in San Francisco with "start a bakery" on his five-year planning list.

On the morning of March 12, 1992, I told Ari over coffee that I was starting a new job the following Monday, but I would love to do a project with him in the future. Ari's face lit up. "What about starting a bakery?" he said. I laughed. I'd never baked a loaf of bread in my life—except for zucchini bread in college. Ari said that he knew of a baker in upstate New York who was helping people get started in baking. "Put off starting to work for a week or two, enough to do some research and see what might be possible," he said. So that's what I did.

We contacted Michael London that week and had a half dozen loaves of bread flown in from Saratoga Springs, New York, where Michael had his bakery. Paul, Ari, and I gathered in the Deli and tore open that box. The loaves looked magnificently beautiful. We popped them in the oven for a few minutes to rejuvenate them and then had a bread tasting that changed our lives and our business (really!).

Prior to that day I'd never tasted bread so flavorful that it was satisfying to eat all by itself. Prior to tasting Michael's bread I thought bread was something that was intended to be part of a sandwich; spread with butter, peanut butter, or jam; dipped in olive oil; used to soak up soup or a sauce—in other words, a vehicle for other things. I thought, "Wow, if I can learn to bake this I'll be the happiest man on Earth."

While that bread tasting made a significant impression on us, we had been in the food business long enough to know that people can have moments of inspiration, but that true greatness is much more elusive. We needed to meet this man, look him in the eye, and see if we might share any values with him.

So we flew Michael to Ann Arbor. As we got to know him, we found that he wanted to make the best bread that he possibly could and valued the people who actually did the work. And he had a background that would make him a good teacher for us: born in Brooklyn, he was Jewish and had a real love and knowledge of challah, onion rye, and pumpernickel—breads we would need to bake for the Deli. In turn, he fell in love with the Delicatessen and admired what Paul and Ari had built. We were a great match.

But could I learn to bake and love the work of baking? Paul, Ari, and I flew to Albany, rented a car, and drove up to Saratoga Springs to spend a couple of days in Michael's bakery, Rock Hill Bakehouse. I needed to get my hands in the dough. I worked side by side with a sarcastic, bandana-wearing baker who was really good at assessing my lack of shaping skills and giving me humorous and cynical feedback. He reminded me of someone I had worked with years before, and I found this comforting. Either from foolishness or some sense of confidence, I came away from those two days excited. For the first time, I really allowed myself to think, "Maybe I could do this."

We came back to Ann Arbor with a lot more information about what it would take to start up this bakery—an oven from France, a mixer or two, a bread molder, some benches for shaping, proofing baskets for the loaves. We made some calls and found out that it would likely cost over $100,000 for the equipment and another $100,000 to get a space outfitted, buy ingredients, find and hire a crew of a half dozen people, and get us all trained.

I began to write a business plan that we could present to a bank. We were looking for a loan of $225,000. I'd never written a business plan before, but I knew I needed to be both realistic about the story I told the bank and also dreamy enough (not my strength) to paint a picture of a future they'd want to participate in. We got the money. The plan must have seemed good enough and was possibly helped by some of Michael's breads that we flew in and served to the loan committee before they met to make a decision.

With the loan secured, I was able to write the largest check I'd ever written for a 40 percent deposit to get the oven and mixer ordered from France. The oven would take 10 to 12 weeks to arrive, and we spent this time looking for a location. Every baker I spoke to either said that they were in too small a space or that they were just moving into a larger space. So while I was told that 1,600 to 2,000 square feet would do, we opted for a 3,200-square-foot space that we thought would be big enough to last us forever. (We now occupy more than 25,000 square feet.)

The real challenge was to learn to bake. I made two visits of five days each to Saratoga Springs in July and August, and spent those weeks learning all that I could about baking bread. We started mixing each morning at 2 a.m. and ended the baking between 4 and 5 each afternoon. The night before the first day I was so excited that I barely slept. Then, after 14 hours, I was a bit woozy and Michael took me outside in the shade and starting speaking about baking. He looked to the heavens, raised his arms, and said that someday he hoped to bake a bread that rose with the power of the rising sun. I blinked and waited to see him laugh at his joke, but he didn't. He was serious, and suddenly I was scared that I was learning from a crazy man. The rational engineer in me didn't relate easily to Michael's more spiritual side.

The oven arrived on the Friday before Labor Day, and that day was a blur of activity as Paul, Tammy Chew (Zingerman's Deli's maintenance person), Mike Dvorin (Paul's nephew and one of our first employees), myself, and two technicians from Europe put together our first deck oven. Much to my dismay, at the end of the day the technicians left to fly back to New Jersey.

We resumed working on Tuesday, got the oven hooked up, fired it up, and started the slow process of bringing it up to temperature and burning off all the grease and oil that the parts were packed in for shipping. Over the next five days I kept the oven running at 450°F for eight hours each day. Then it was ready to use.

That weekend, I picked up Michael London from the Detroit Metro Airport. He walked off the plane with a Coleman cooler under his arm with 5 pounds of starter from his bakery. At the Bakehouse, we fed the starter, mixed some poolish, and started a rye sour, and the next day we began to mix our first bread doughs ever. That first day was a blur, filled with an incredible amount of running around in a very hot bakery (the temperatures were in the 90s). The rest of the week and much of the following month were also quite challenging. We created an order of production that still serves as our basis for basic breads. Each day we made a couple dozen loaves of each type, attempting to get enough repetitions in to gain some level of proficiency before taking over as the primary supplier of bread to the Delicatessen on October 12.

While all this was happening, I was also in the process of hiring a team. I felt fortunate to have the eight-person crew that we started with. Amy Emberling was one of them. Jeff Stopa was hired to do the important job of early morning mixing, a position that enabled me to be present for nearly all the other work that was done each day. Mike Dvorin had just moved to town and was looking for something interesting to do while he took a couple of college classes. He ended up staying for eight years.

After about two weeks I realized what a huge process this was going to be. I asked Ari in desperation if he thought that we could close one day each week. Detroit bakeries were traditionally closed on Wednesdays. Now I understood why. However, we had already advertised that we would bake seven days per week, so that idea fell to the wayside. We just had to continue to learn and get better at what we were doing.

After our first Christmas baking season, I met with Ari to discuss the progress we'd made. He mentioned the idea of baking pastries. At this time the Delicatessen was baking a dozen or two scones each morning, one or two coffee cakes a few days each week, a few dozen cookies each week, and a tray of brownies whenever they could schedule the oven. Ari wondered what I thought of the idea of us taking over the pastries. Didn't I agree that it would make much more sense for us to do the baking at the Bakehouse?

I don't like to disappoint people, but I was pretty exhausted and overwhelmed by the past five months, so I probably said that it might be an idea I could get behind someday. Paul and Ari immediately started planning to bake pastries at the Bakehouse.

In February 1994 we began building our pastry bakery. We cut a hole in the wall to connect the bread bakery with the pastry space. Our first baking project was to make 150 hamantaschen for a Delicatessen catering event, and we officially opened the pastry kitchen of the Bakehouse in March 1994.

The next significant addition to the bakery was a retail shop. We're located in an industrial complex on the south side of Ann Arbor, about four miles from the Delicatessen. We chose this location for the affordable rent and its proximity to my home, the Deli, and the interstate. I never considered that we might have a store here; we were starting up a wholesale bakery to bake bread for one customer, the Delicatessen.

But a wonderful and funny consequence of baking bread is that at a certain point we open the damper to allow the steam to escape from the baking chamber. When this happens, along with the steam goes the amazing aroma of whatever type of bread we're baking. And so for the first year and a half that we were open, each morning at 10 a.m. the aroma of rye would escape into the complex, followed by the aroma of Italian bread at 12:30, and sourdough and Farm Bread throughout the afternoon.

Early on, neighbors would follow their nose to our door, politely knocking to ask what was going on. Soon we had a very local clientele who would drop in on their way home after work to buy a loaf for the road. After we opened the pastry bakery, we'd put an assortment of pastries on a tray, adding other breads as they came out of the oven. One thing led to another, and soon we had an informal "bake shop" inside our bread bakery. We operated that way for about two and a half years until, needing additional space, we expanded the bread bakery into the suite next door, walling off an 800-square-foot retail space in the process. That little shop is still our Bakeshop, only now it sells thousands of pastries and loaves of bread each week. I pinch myself whenever I reflect on this; I never dreamed that customers would come out to our industrial setting.

This all happened over the course of four years. We morphed from a very challenging bread baking business into an increasingly complex bakery business with several different operations—bread, pastry, and retail. Amy was playing an increasingly important role by growing our pastry kitchen while streamlining the offerings and improving the consistency of the baking. Her contribution ended in August 1996 when her husband, Geoff, got a job in Copenhagen, and off they went. What a loss for the Bakehouse. This was before e-mail, the Internet, and cell phones, so we stayed in touch the old-fashioned way, by exchanging postcards and letters. Mine would beg Amy to come back and run the pastry kitchen. Amy's return postcard would describe how delicious the yogurt was in Denmark. Next Geoff got a job in Manhattan and the script was the same—Amy come back. No thanks, I'm going to grad school.

Between 1996 and 2000, the Bakehouse continued to grow in size, staff, and complexity. We were now beginning to have people working around the clock, and I no longer felt like I could support all of my managers in the manner that I wanted. I realized that I didn't need another manager but really a partner to help guide and support this incredible endeavor. By 2000 Amy had gotten her MBA and had spent part of a year as a consultant. She came back to Ann Arbor for a weekend in the summer and met with Paul, Ari, and me and . . . you know the rest. Amy came back, and what's followed have been nearly two decades of innovation, growth, and fun.

We've expanded our baking; increased our customers; and invited a former baker, Mary Kalinowski, who had left to start her own soup business, to help us make a small selection of humble but tasty lunch offerings for our neighbors in the complex. Amy loves celebration cakes, so we started to make decorated cakes, and in 2006 we opened a small school for home bakers, BAKE!

Creating a thriving bakery, the kind that I wanted to own, required a focus not only on the baking but also on the workplace culture. One of the first formal steps we took in this area was to create a mission statement. It has been the foundation of our culture ever since. Amy has a more vivid memory of how we created it than I do, so I'm going to let her tell you about it.

OUR MISSION STATEMENT

AMY: An important part of the Bakehouse story is our mission statement. We created it in 1994, and it's been a solid guide through years of opportunities and challenges. What is it exactly? It's a written statement that answers these questions:

- Who are we?
- What do we do?
- Why do we do it?
- Who do we do it for?

When done well a mission statement encompasses the most important values of a business and is a shorthand expression of the organization's purpose. It is general enough that it never needs to be revised. It's essentially timeless. We think mission statements are most effective when they are created by many people in an organization (not handed down from on high) and are relatively short so that people can actually commit them to memory and recite them. No worries about keeping them top of mind when they're in everyone's mind. We created ours one afternoon with the twenty-some employees of the Bakehouse at the time and have used it to keep us on track with the choices we've faced ever since.

at zingerman's bakehouse we are passionately committed to the relentless pursuit of being the best bakery we can imagine.

We created this as a group after brainstorming the positive characteristics of our work, and then we voted. The bolded words in the statement won the most votes. It has shaped our culture.

"Passionately"! You bet. This was and is an intense and dedicated work environment (sometimes cited as "not for everyone" in our staff surveys), not one that tolerates apathy and low engagement. We're focused and engaged in what we're doing, committed to making super-flavorful, traditional foods for our guests with the best service we can conjure.

"The relentless pursuit" is shorthand for our dedication to continuous improvement and was really a reference to Frank's natural approach to work. He is never done with making something better or doing something in a more effective way.

"Best bakery" means that we're a culture of excellence and we're not going to settle for good but rather are always aiming for great. We recognize that we don't always achieve it, but this doesn't mean we aren't going to try.

Finally, the phrase "we can imagine" is an indication of our dedication to visioning. We are not so much market driven but rather purpose and vision driven. We create a bakery that we imagine is great—the food, work environment, customer experience, and community engagement. We try not to be limited to the generally accepted beliefs about how things can be.

The recipes in this chapter are some of our most beloved by customers and probably considered our most iconic. They are all good examples of us living our mission. Many of them are from our earliest years.

reLentLess tasting

One way that we actively live our mission statement at Zingerman's Bakehouse is with something we call "tastings." Simply put, tastings are where the makers and bakers of our food critically sample that food. It's different than eating a cinnamon raisin bagel for breakfast, snacking on a ham and cheese croissant at lunch, or enjoying a slice of cake for dessert. Tastings are something that our bakers, cooks, and decorators are trained to do as a part of their work. It includes all of the food we make at the Bakehouse. Each day, the tasting scores are recorded, tracked, and then talked about at our staff huddles (weekly meetings). We know this practice is one of the reasons our great food keeps getting greater.

Because tastings are such an important part of our work, we have a recipe for them. We grade our food in three different areas: visual appearance, texture, and flavor. For us, every item has a specific way we want it to look, a texture we desire, and a taste profile we strive for. These standards are agreed upon and documented. We train the staff on these standards and then taste and score our food against these standards. So while it's certainly a fun dream job to eat samples in a bakery, this is some serious business.

The visual score pertains to how the food looks on the outside. It includes everything about the food's appearance, like color, shape, size, and volume. Is the Boston Cream Pie's chocolate glaze smooth and shiny? Is the True North Bread's crust dark enough? Since we are an artisanal bakery and use our hands to make our food, some variation in appearance is expected.

The score for texture involves the inside of the food. Are the holes inside the Rustic Italian Bread the right size? Is the Cheddar Ale Soup just the right thickness? Does the cross section of a butter croissant show an open honeycomb structure? These are the types of details we're looking for when we grade the texture of our food. Also contributing to the texture score is the way the food feels in your mouth. Is the Buttermilk Cake the right density when you bite into it? Does the sourdough bread have a crisp, crackly crust with a moist and chewy interior? Is the sugar on the palmiers caramelized, or are there granules of sugar that are noticeable in your mouth?

Flavor is our final tasting criterion. After all, we are known to say, "You really CAN taste the difference!" Does the food taste like it is supposed to? This is different from whether the food tastes "good" or whether today's taster likes it. Each food has a clearly defined flavor profile, and the taster compares the taste to that desired goal. We have dozens of staff, all with different tastes, so we need to have an agreed-upon standard we can all work with.

Each item tasted gets three scores of 1 to 10, one each for its visual appeal, texture, and taste. The item's final tasting score is the average of the three scores. A score of 9 means the item is ideal. A score of 7 to 8 means the food is good but not quite hitting the desired mark. Any score below a 7 is something we won't sell. This food just doesn't live up to the Zingerman's name. On the rare occasion that all the stars are in alignment and the baking gods have smiled down upon us, we get an item that is the absolute best that we can imagine it to be. This is a 10! Our goal is to have our tasting scores average no lower than 8.8.

What exactly gets tasted at the Bakehouse? The quick and simple answer is everything. Between Monday and Sunday, nearly every item that we make and sell gets formally tasted. With over 25 varieties of bread, 75 different pastries offered each season, at least 10 different kinds of cake, and 10 seasonal selections of soup, we do a lot of formal tasting.

Over the years, we have improved our recipes or techniques many times based on the data we collect from the tasting scores. Recent improvements have included updating the Sicilian Sesame Semolina Bread recipe to 100 percent semolina flour, hand-rolling our French Baguettes and Farm Bread rather than using a molding machine, adding to the richness of our cinnamon roll dough, and tweaking the ratios of our Funky Chunky Cookie, Hot Cocoa Cake, and New Deli Crumb Cake recipes for better texture. Some of these changes were relatively small; others were quite involved and resulted in significant changes in the way we work. They all had one thing in common, though: we made them because we believed the food could be better. We're confident that there's room for improvement in everything we do. So we go to work to take those recipes from really good to great.

nina PLasencia
Zingerman's Bakehouse baker

In order to open the Bakehouse, we had to be able to bake great Jewish rye bread for Zingerman's Delicatessen, which was our first (and at the beginning our only) customer. It's not possible to have a superb Reuben sandwich without authentic Jewish rye bread. We wanted our Jewish rye to be an essential part of the sandwich, not just a structural element that didn't really add to the flavor. So right from the beginning, we used and further evolved the excellent recipe and techniques we learned from our first teacher, Michael London.

What makes this a great Jewish rye?

First, we use a sour starter, which is unusual these days. It adds a little bit of leavening to the recipe, but mainly it provides depth and complexity of flavor. We created the starter in the fall of 1992, and we've been feeding it every day since to keep it healthy, with just the right amount of tang. This version of rye bread was the one made most often by the Polish Jewish bakers in New York and was called sour rye. It later became known as Jewish rye.

Second, we use "Old"—rye bread from the previous day's bake that we slice and soak in water and then add to the dough. It adds a layer of texture, flavor, moisture, and color to the bread. It's also a tradition for Jewish bakers to take something from yesterday and put it in today's recipes, representing the continuity and interconnectedness of life.

Third, there's actually some rye in the recipe. Many rye breads are made from white-wheat flour with a touch of rye added. We use lots of medium rye (rye flour that has some of its bran) in our sour starter.

Finally, we create a real crackly crust. We brush each loaf with water before it goes into the oven and then again when it comes out. The contrast of the cool water on the hot

JEWISH RYE BREAD

makes 2 Loaves

Day-old bread, preferably rye, torn into pieces	¼ cup	95 g
Rye sour (page 55)	2¼ cups	420 g
Water, room temperature	¾ cup	175 g
Instant yeast	1½ tsp	5 g
Ground caraway	½ tsp	
All-purpose flour	3½ cups plus 1 Tbsp	500 g
Sea salt	1 Tbsp	20 g
Cornmeal for dusting		

Mix the Dough

1. Prepare the "Old." Take some bread—really of any age, preferably rye, but an unflavored white bread will work—break it into pieces, and moisten it with ½ cup minus 1 Tbsp [105 g] water. Let sit for 15 minutes. Measure out ¼ cup [95 g].

2. In a large, wide mixing bowl combine the rye sour, water, Old, instant yeast, and ground caraway. Stir with a wooden spoon until well blended. Add half of the flour and stir until the mixture looks like thick pancake batter. Add the salt and remaining flour and stir until it starts to form a shaggy mass.

3. Scrape the dough out of the bowl onto a clean, unfloured work surface and knead for 6 to 8 minutes, until it forms a smooth ball (page 34). If the dough begins to stick, use a plastic scraper to clean the surface. Rye has a different chemical makeup than wheat flour and tends to be sticky. Don't be alarmed if that's the case, and resist the temptation to add flour. Keep gently kneading and the dough will come together.

4. Lightly oil the mixing bowl, place the dough in the bowl, and cover with plastic. Allow it to ferment for 1 hour. It will increase in size by about 50 percent.

Shape and Bake the Dough

1. After 1 hour, uncover the dough and turn it out onto a lightly floured work surface. Divide the dough into two equal pieces. Pre-shape both pieces into rounds (page 35) and cover with plastic. Let rest for 30 minutes.

2. Shape the rounds into loaf shapes. Place on a cornmeal-coated board and cover with plastic.

3. Preheat the oven with a baking stone and cast iron skillet (for creating steam) to 450°F [230°C] for 45 minutes before baking (page 38). Ferment the loaves for 40 minutes to an hour. Use the touch test (page 38) to see if the dough is ready for the oven.

continued

loaf causes the crust to crack in a distinctive way that is characteristic of Jewish rye.

But how does it taste? Jane and Michael Stern, in their 2011 article "Bread Alone: In Search of the Best Rye Bread in America," sing its praises:

> America's very best deli rye? No contest. We found it in Ann Arbor, Michigan, when we noticed that the bread that Zingerman's Deli used to construct our Diana's Different Drummer sandwich (brisket, Russian dressing, coleslaw, and horseradish) was sensational. It comes from Zingerman's Bakehouse, which makes loaves of rugged rye that are dense and springy, laced with the taste of hearth smoke. (Saveur, March 2011)

This recipe takes some planning because you need to prepare the sour the day before. Nothing is hard, other than it not being instantaneous. The inconvenient aspects of many recipes are the steps that take a food from good to great. The rye sour is an example of this.

4. Uncover the loaves and spray heavily with water. Place the loaves on a cornmeal-dusted wooden peel. With a razor blade or sharp knife, score the tops of the loaves with five uniform slices perpendicular to the length of the loaf (page 38).

5. Slide the loaves onto the hot baking stone. Bake for 8 minutes with steam (page 38), uncover, then bake for an additional 32 to 35 minutes, or until the desired color has been achieved. Baking times will vary depending on the size of your loaves.

6. Remove from the oven, place on a cooling rack, and spray heavily with water. Let cool completely before cutting.

more on rye bread and rye flour

Rye flour has four basic grades—light, dark, medium, and pumpernickel. Light contains no bran and is pale in color. Dark contains all the bran and is just that, dark. Medium is a mix of light and dark rye, and pumpernickel is dark rye with added extra bran. All of the recipes in this book call for medium rye.

In Eastern Europe rye grew easily and was readily available and relatively inexpensive. For these reasons it became the daily bread of the relatively poor Jewish communities. Korn in Yiddish means "rye," so it was called kornbroyt. It often had rye and varying amounts of wheat in it. Sometimes in the United States you'll see a loaf called corn bread or corn rye. This has nothing to do with New World corn. It is just a misspelling of the Yiddish word for rye. Another commonly eaten bread was called schwarzbroyt, or "black bread." This was dark rye bread with little or no wheat in it. A tall, round loaf was called tsitsel ("breast") rye. We make it from time to time, and when we do we leave out the caraway, for those who enjoy rye bread but don't love caraway. Another common version of rye bread that we make several times a year has nigella or chernushka seeds in it. This small, dark seed can easily be confused with black sesame. It's often used in Middle Eastern baking and in Indian cooking.

Rye bread was eaten as part of every meal in combination with butter or chicken fat and often with raw onions and herring. Chopped liver was also a favorite treat with it. Its use for sandwiches is an American innovation.

The foundation of some of the great rye breads, including Jewish rye, is an acidic "sour," or starter. The sour may be kept alive and well in the refrigerator forever if it is fed regularly. The chopped onion and whole caraway seeds should be removed and discarded after the first day and not used in future feedings. Once the mixture has fermented all night, the helpful organisms and flavor boosters will have moved off the onions and seeds and into the mixture you have created. If you are going to make this recipe infrequently, just make fresh sour each time. There's no need to keep your sour alive for weeks or months in between uses. If you are going to bake weekly, feed your sour at least once between baking sessions.

important notes

- If you are not baking weekly, only feeding, you will end up throwing away or composting some rye sour.

- If you use most of the rye sour to make bread and you are left with less than 1 cup, you can still use the steps in "Maintain the Rye Sour" to feed whatever amount you have left. Even if all you have left is a tablespoon, that is enough. Just feed it as directed, and in a matter of hours you'll have a cup of rye sour bubbling away.

RYE SOUR

Day 1: Make the Rye Sour

Medium rye flour	1 cup	110 g
Water, room temperature	¾ cup	175 g
Instant yeast	⅛ tsp	
Coarsely chopped onion	½ cup	70 g
Caraway seeds	1½ tsp	

Day 2: Feed the Rye Sour

| Water, room temperature | ¾ cup | 175 g |
| Medium rye flour | 1 cup | 125 g |

Once a Week: Maintain the Rye Sour

Rye sour	1 cup	205 g
Water, room temperature	¾ cup	175 g
Medium rye flour	1 cup	125 g

Day 1: Make the Rye Sour

1. In a medium bowl, mix the rye flour, water, and yeast. Stir until the mixture is completely smooth.

2. Tie the onion and caraway seeds together tightly in cheesecloth (like a homemade tea bag), then sink the whole package completely into the flour mixture.

3. Cover the bowl tightly with plastic wrap and put it in a nice warm spot (70° to 75°F) [21° to 24°C] overnight.

Day 2: Feed the Rye Sour

1. Remove the onion/caraway bag and scrape the sour off the bag and back into the bowl. To the sour add the water and rye flour, and mix until smooth. Cover with plastic. Let it ferment for 3 to 4 hours more, until it is visibly fermented and frothy.

2. The rye sour can now be used in your rye bread recipe, with plenty left over to put in the fridge until the next feeding. Store it in a tightly sealed container. Any subsequent feedings need to ferment at room temperature for only 3 to 4 hours.

Once a Week: Maintain the Rye Sour

1. To the sour add the water and rye flour, and mix until smooth. Cover with plastic wrap and let ferment at room temperature for 3 to 4 hours, until it is nice and frothy and full of fermentation bubbles. Use the sour to make more rye bread, or put it back in the refrigerator, where it will be okay for another week. Feed the sour at least once per week and you will be able to use it indefinitely.

FRANK: *In the winter of 1993, after we had been baking for six months, we added about six new varieties of bread to our repertoire. Our partner Ari suggested that we make bread with the combination of Parmigiano-Reggiano cheese and Tellicherry black pepper.*

Zingerman's Delicatessen was a great source for both of these ingredients. We purchase 80-pound wheels of this king of cheeses and split and trim them each week to make what is still one of our most popular specialty breads. During our busiest days in December, we'll bake more than 300 of these loaves daily for several consecutive days, which means that we use more than one wheel of cheese each day. Because of the generous amount of cheese in each loaf, these are very delicate to shuffle in the oven with a large peel. Occasionally while unloading we'll "stab" a loaf and it will be unsellable. While this is unfortunate, the loaf doesn't go to waste. It gets placed on the rack next to the oven, where we keep our baking tools, and is usually there for no more than an hour. I should film our staff walking past this damaged loaf, looking at it, and then grabbing a chunk of warm and delicious savory goodness. I personally go for the melted chunks of cheese that make their way to the surface of the loaf.

PARMESAN PEPPER BREAD

makes 2 Loaves

Water, room temperature	1¾ cups	400 g
Levain (page 42)	¾ cup	114 g
Whole wheat flour	¼ cup	35 g
All-purpose flour	3¾ cups	525 g
Sea salt	2 tsp	14 g
Cubed Parmesan cheese (¾ in square [2 cm square])	1 cup	114 g
Shredded Parmesan cheese	2¼ cups	114 g
Coarsely ground black pepper	1 Tbsp	9 g
Cornmeal for dusting		
Coarsely ground black pepper for sprinkling tops		

1. Place the water in a large mixing bowl. Tear the levain into small pieces and add to the water. Add the whole wheat flour and half of the all-purpose flour. Stir with a wooden spoon to combine and break up the levain. Add the remaining all-purpose flour and the salt. Mix until the dough is rough and shaggy.

2. Turn the dough out onto a clean, unfloured work surface, scraping any bits of flour or dough out of the bowl. Knead the dough for 6 minutes (page 34) to develop the gluten. Be sure to stretch and fold the dough over and over again, so that gluten strength is developed.

3. Spread out the dough and gently form it into a rectangle. Sprinkle the cheese and pepper onto the rectangle. Carefully gather up the edges of the dough, keeping the cheese and pepper inside. Knead for another 3 to 4 minutes, or until the cheese and pepper are both uniformly distributed in the dough.

4. Place the dough in a lightly oiled container and cover with plastic. Ferment for 3 hours. The dough will grow in volume by about 50 percent.

5. Uncover and place the dough on a lightly floured work surface. Divide into two equal portions, and pre-shape each piece into a ball (page 35). Allow to rest for 30 minutes, covered with plastic.

6. Uncover and reshape each piece again into a round. Place the rounded loaves on a cornmeal-covered surface with the seam side down. Cover with plastic. Allow the shaped rounds to proof for 3 to 3½ hours. Use the touch test (page 38) to see if the dough is ready for the oven.

7. Preheat the oven with a baking stone and cast iron skillet (for creating steam) to 450°F [230°C] for 45 minutes before baking (page 38).

8. Uncover the rounds and brush the top of each with water. Sprinkle some coarsely ground black pepper on top. Place the rounds side by side onto a lightly floured peel. With a razor blade or sharp knife, make a single diagonal slice on the top of each round loaf (page 38).

9. Slide the loaves onto the baking stone and add steam to the oven (page 38). Keep covered for about 8 minutes, uncover, and bake the loaves for an additional 22 to 28 minutes, or until they are nicely browned and sound hollow when tapped on the bottom.

10. Remove the loaves from the oven and cool on a wire rack. Cool completely before slicing.

SICILIAN SESAME SEMOLINA BREAD

makes 2 loaves

FRANK: *Centuries ago, durum wheat was grown primarily in southern Italy, Sicily, and North Africa. In Puglia (the southeastern tip of Italy), durum flour has been used to bake bread since the 13th century. I had a chance to bake there in the town of Altamura one night in 2007. Throughout Sicily, hundreds of different types of bread are baked using primarily durum flour. This bread, our homage to Sicily, has been one of my favorites since we opened. It's now made with nearly 100 percent durum wheat in its two different forms—both the coarser ground semolina and the more finely ground durum. The beautiful and rich yellow color of the crumb comes from the natural yellow color of durum and semolina flour.*

This bread is fantastic grilled and takes a typical bruschetta to a new level. It's also good just plain a couple of hours after being baked. The flavor of the toasty crust, the toasted sesame seeds, and the durum crumb is super rewarding.

Poolish

All-purpose flour	¾ cup plus 1 Tbsp	114 g
Water	½ cup	114 g
Instant yeast	⅛ tsp	

Final Dough

Water, room temperature	2½ cups plus 1½ Tbsp	608 g
Poolish	all	
Instant yeast	½ tsp	5 g
Durum flour	2 cups	300 g
Sea salt	1 Tbsp plus ¼ tsp	23 g
Semolina flour	4¼ cups	681 g
Sesame seeds, for coating	2 cups	280 g

Make the Poolish

1. Place the all-purpose flour, water, and yeast in a medium mixing bowl and mix together until incorporated. Cover the bowl loosely with plastic wrap and allow the poolish to ferment for 8 hours. It can now be used, or it can be refrigerated and used within the next 24 hours. For the best results, do not use it after 24 hours.

Mix the Dough

1. In a large bowl, add the water, poolish, and yeast and combine thoroughly with a wooden spoon. Add the durum flour and mix with the spoon. The dough will look like thick pancake batter. Add the salt and semolina flour and mix thoroughly. You may use your hands. When the mixture comes together and starts to just barely form a ball, scrape the dough out of the bowl onto a clean, unfloured work surface.

2. Knead the dough for 6 to 8 minutes (page 34). Do not add any extra flour. Place the dough in a lightly oiled bowl and cover with plastic wrap. Ferment for 4 hours. The dough will nearly double in volume.

3. Remove the dough and place it onto a lightly floured surface. Divide the dough into two even pieces and gently pre-shape each one into a ball (page 35).

continued

4. Place the pre-shaped loaves on the lightly floured counter or workbench and cover loosely with plastic wrap. Allow them to rest for 45 minutes before final shaping.

5. Once the dough has relaxed, shape both loaves into a round (page 35). Using a pastry brush, wet the tops with water and cover completely with sesame seeds by rolling the loaves, wet side down, in a tray covered with the sesame seeds.

6. Preheat the oven with a baking stone and cast iron skillet (for creating steam) to 450°F [230°C] for 45 minutes before baking (page 38).

7. Cover the loaves and allow them to proof for 1 to 1¼ hours. Use the touch test (page 38) to see if the dough is ready for the oven.

8. Place both loaves on a floured or cornmeal-dusted peel. Score the top surface of each loaf (page 38) to encourage rising and discourage ripping, and place them on your baking stone. Bake with steam for 8 minutes (page 38), uncover, and then bake for an additional 30 minutes, until the bread is nicely browned. Remove from the oven, place on a wire rack, and cool completely.

Making a pie crust is one of the most anxiety-provoking baking tasks we teach our students at our baking school, BAKE! Although the process is exacting, our professional pastry bakers don't suffer from this high level of anxiety, and there's no reason we can't all get to their level of calm proficiency.

Why are we so anxious about making a pie crust? We've all eaten tough pie crusts in our lives, so we know that failure is a real possibility. We also keep hearing that it's difficult to make a flaky and tender pie crust. Between what we've been told and what we've experienced, we're primed to be anxious and insecure about our pie crust–making abilities. Let us show you that a good pie crust is completely achievable.

The recipe and process given here have been taught successfully to at least 2,000 home bakers at BAKE! None of them had pie crust–making super powers. You can learn too!

We asked Anna, Frank's oldest daughter, who had never made a pie crust before, to test our recipes for pecan and chocolate chess pies. Here's what she said about making the crust: "I really liked your description and instructions of the various steps. I've never made a pie dough from scratch before and was somewhat intimidated, and this was empowering and well-written." We hope you have the same experience.

PIE DOUGH

makes two 9-in [23-cm] crusts

Unsalted butter, cold	1 cup	227 g
All-purpose flour	2½ cups plus 1 Tbsp	363 g
Sea salt	1 tsp	
Water, cold	⅓ cup	73 g

Mix the Pie Dough

1. Cut the cold butter into ¼-in [6-mm] cubes. In a large mixing bowl, mix the flour and salt with a fork. Add three-fourths of the cold butter to the bowl. Cut the butter into the flour mixture using a pastry blender, or two butter knives, or your fingers. Cut or work the butter into the flour until the mixture looks like coarse cornmeal. If using your fingers, break the butter chunks down and rub the butter and flour together. Pick the mixture up between your hands and rub your palms together as if they're cold. This will break down the butter and rub it all over the flour.

   The flour will take on a creamy yellow color during this step. When you pick the mixture up in your hand, it should be possible to squeeze it into a mass that will hold together. When you see the color change, and the mixture holds together when squeezed, you know that you've worked the butter in enough. Work quickly so that the butter doesn't become warm.

   The goal of this step is to cover the flour with fat so that the gluten strands are not able to develop. This will allow the dough to be short and tender. It is much more problematic to not break down the butter enough in this step than it is to break it down too much. Most of us don't incorporate it enough. Try not to be hesitant in this step.

2. Add the remaining one-fourth of the butter and cut it into the mixture as before. These butter pieces should be left pea sized. The chunks of butter will create flakiness in the final pie crust—when they melt during baking, they will create steam, which separates layers of the coated flour, making flakes of crust.

3. Create a well in the center of the mixture. Add the chilled water. Using a fork, blend the water into the flour mixture. The mixture will still be crumbly in the bowl, but it should look moist. If it still looks dry, add an additional 1 to 2 Tbsp of water, until the mixture looks moistened but still crumbly.

4. If the butter has been rubbed into the dough adequately in step 1, the amount of water specified should be adequate. More water is usually necessary only when the butter has not been adequately distributed. It's not desirable to add more water, because it tends to make a tougher crust.

continued

5. Turn the mixture out onto a clean, unfloured work surface, form it into a mound, and push out sections of dough across the work surface with the heel of your hand. We call this "schmearing." Push each section of dough once, not twice. Make sure to schmear enough so that the dough loses its dry, crumbly appearance. At the end of the schmearing, all of the pie crust will be pushed out flat on the work surface.

6. Fold the dough back onto itself with a bench scraper. Gather it into a ball, pressing it firmly so it holds together.

7. Cut the dough into two equal pieces, shape each into a disk, and wrap with plastic wrap. Chill for at least 1 hour before rolling it out.

tip: *The dough can stay in this form in the refrigerator for up to 5 days. It can also be frozen, well wrapped and preferably in an airtight container, for up to 3 months.*

Roll Out a Single-Crust Pie Shell

1. Remove one piece of the chilled dough from the refrigerator. While the dough is still in the plastic wrap, firmly but gently tap on it with the rolling pin until it is flexible but still cold. Lightly dust the work surface with flour. Place the disk of unwrapped dough on the surface and lightly flour the top of the disk with flour.

2. Using a rolling pin, start rolling the dough from the center to the edge, away from you. Do not use too much pressure or the dough will crack.

3. Stop and give the dough a one-eighth turn. This rotation will prevent the dough from sticking to the work surface and will help make a perfect circle.

4. Reflour the work surface and the top of the dough to prevent the dough from sticking. Continue to roll and rotate the dough until it's about ⅛ in [4 mm] thick and about 1 in [2.5 cm] bigger than the pie plate you will be using. Flour is your friend in this process. Use it liberally to avoid sticking.

5. When the crust has reached the correct size, use a pastry brush to brush away any extra flour from the top of the pie dough. Turn the dough over and brush off any extra flour from the bottom. One way to do this is to roll the dough up on your rolling pin and then unwind it with the bottom surface now facing up.

Fit the Dough into the Pie Plate

1. Using a rolling pin, gently roll the dough loosely around the rolling pin. Position the edge of the dough over the edge of the pie plate and unroll the dough. Gently ease the dough down into the pie plate, making sure not to stretch the dough.

2. To finish the edge of the pie shell, trim the edge, leaving ½ in [1.5 cm] of dough over the edge of the pie plate. Turn this extra dough under to make a neat thickened border.

continued

3. Create a decorative edge with this border as you choose. A simple finish is to press the tines of a fork all around the edge or to press a spoon into the edge to make semicircles.

4. Now follow the directions in the specific pie recipe. The crust will either be used raw or blind baked. Blind-baking instructions are given next.

tip: *If you are not going to use the crust right now, wrap the unbaked crust well and it can stay in this form in the refrigerator for up to 5 days or in the freezer for 3 months.*

Blind-Bake the Crust

1. Preheat the oven to 375°F [190°C].

2. Roll out a single pie crust and fit it into the pan, as just described. Dock the dough all over. This means to make tiny holes in the bottom and sides of the dough with a fork. All of these holes will allow the gas from the melting butter to escape without forming large air bubbles in your crust.

3. Refrigerate or freeze the pie shell for at least 20 minutes before baking. Remove the chilled pie shell from the refrigerator. Line the chilled crust with parchment paper, pressing it snugly against the bottom and sides. Fill with dried beans or pie weights to hold down the parchment.

4. Bake the crust for 25 minutes, or until the edge begins to color. Remove the parchment and the beans. Bake for another 5 minutes. At this point the pie shell is considered partially blind baked. For a fully blind-baked crust, bake for another 12 to 15 minutes after removing the parchment.

Make a Double-Crust Pie

1. Using one of the two pieces of pie dough, follow the directions given earlier for rolling out a single-crust pie shell and fitting it into the pie plate. However, trim the edge of the dough so at least 1 in [2.5 cm] of excess is hanging over the edge of the pie plate.

2. Follow the directions for creating the filling in the specific pie recipe you are making. Put the filling into the bottom crust. Brush the edge of the bottom crust with water.

3. Using the second piece of pie dough, roll the top crust out slightly larger than the top diameter of the pie plate, so that it will comfortably be able to cover your filling.

4. Roll up the top crust onto your rolling pin and, starting at one side of the pie, gently unroll the crust over the filling. If you do not place the crust perfectly, just move it gently with your hands to make it as evenly placed as possible. Trim the crusts, leaving 1 in [2.5 cm] of excess to form the border.

5. Now it is time to seal the edges. Fold the excess dough from the bottom crust over the edge of the top crust and seal by lightly pressing both layers together with your fingers against the top of the pie pan. Decorate the edge as you like. There are many different decorative edges to choose from. You can do a simple one by pressing the tines of a fork all around the edge of the pie. You can also press a spoon into the edge to make semi-circles. Or you can pinch the dough with your fingers to make the classic fluted edge. Now cut at least four 2-in [5-cm] vents in the top of the crust at even intervals to allow the steam to escape as the pie bakes. Follow the directions for baking in the recipe of your choice.

which fat should i use in my pie crust?

Bakers have strong feelings about the kind of fat used in pie crusts—some use vegetable shortening, some use lard, and some use butter. And some use a combination.

We're fans of butter and lard. Generally we use butter because we think it gives better flavor to the crust and lard because it gives great texture. Lard has lots of flavor, but many of us are not used to it in our pie eating, so it's not always enjoyed or it's problematic for some of our customers to eat. Setting aside religious considerations, mixing butter and lard can be a fantastic choice. The butter and lard flavors blend well, and the crust gets a combination of crispness from the butter and flakiness from the lard.

If you are going to use lard, try to find unrendered leaf lard. Leaf lard is the fat that surrounds the kidneys of pigs, and it tends to be the most pure. Unrendered lard is preferred because it still contains the molecular structure of the fat, which contributes to the flakiness of the crust. Rendered fat destroys the crystals by melting them. If you do find unrendered leaf lard, remove any extra membranes and fascialike material, and then cut it into cubes just as you would butter.

Why not use vegetable shortening? Basically, shortening has less flavor than either butter or lard and doesn't color as nicely as butter, so we avoid it because we're all about flavor. Shortening also contains a high amount of trans fats, which many of us don't want to eat. Shortening does have its advantages, though. It's less expensive relative to other fats and has a long shelf life, and it definitely makes a nicely textured crust. It is also easier to use, so it may be a good fat to use when you're learning to make a crust. Shortening is often used in Jewish baking because the baked good can be eaten with a dairy or meat meal.

It's your pie, so you choose! If you make a lot of pies, try experimenting with different fats and assess the result.

PECAN PIE

makes one 9-in [23-cm] pie

AMY: *This is my favorite Bakehouse pie, just because I enjoy it and also because it fits our mission perfectly— full flavored and traditional. Mention of pecan pie is first found in the late 1880s with recipes in southern news-papers and magazines. It became really popular, especially in the South, in the 1930s, when Karo brand corn syrup began promoting it in ads and recipe books.*

The pie filling, clearly the star of this dessert, is not difficult to make. What makes the difference between a good and a great version is the quality of the ingredients and their proportions. This filling is special because of the muscovado brown sugar, which has exponentially more flavor than standard American brown sugar. Real vanilla extract and flavorful butter are also critical. Finally, not all pecans are the same. The variety and how they are grown, harvested, and stored makes a differ-ence in the intensity of their flavor and the crispness of their texture. We use what are called mammoth halves (big ones! avoid chopped pieces) and include them generously. The vari-eties we use are Western Schley and Pawnee, both of which are known for their good flavor.

Although the filling is the star of this pie, the crust is an important partner in the deliciousness. Its crisp-ness is a nice contrast to the smooth filling, and the toasty butter flavor is a good complement. Every star needs a strong supporting actor, right?

Large eggs	3	
Muscovado brown sugar	1 cup plus 3 Tbsp (packed)	230 g
Sea salt	½ tsp	
Vanilla extract	1 tsp	
Unsalted butter, melted	9 Tbsp	132 g
Corn syrup	9 Tbsp	186 g
Pecan halves	1½ cups	173 g
9-in [23-cm] single pie crust, unbaked (page 61)		

1. Preheat the oven to 350°F [180°C].

2. In a mixing bowl, combine the eggs, muscovado brown sugar, salt, and vanilla. Beat until well combined. Add the melted butter and corn syrup and mix to combine. Spread the pecans evenly in the bottom of the unbaked pie crust. They will float to the top, so there's no need to arrange them precisely.

3. Pour the filling over the pecans. Bake the pie for 1 hour. The center of the pie should be set and the pecans will be a golden brown. Remove the pie from the oven and cool before serving. You can store this pie at room temperature for 5 to 7 days. It has an incredible shelf life if you can resist eating it.

BIG O COOKIES

makes 21 cookies

Unsalted butter, room temperature	1 cup plus 2 Tbsp	250 g
Brown sugar	¾ cup plus 2 Tbsp (packed)	154 g
Maple syrup	½ cup plus 1 Tbsp	172 g
Large egg	1	
Vanilla extract	1 tsp	
All-purpose flour	1¾ cups plus 1 Tbsp	255 g
Baking soda	1⅛ tsp	
Sea salt	1⅛ tsp	
Ground cinnamon	1 tsp	
Ground nutmeg	¼ tsp	
Old-fashioned rolled oats	3 cups	300 g
Flame raisins	2¾ cups	390 g

1. Preheat the oven to 350°F [180°C].

2. In a large mixing bowl, with a wooden spoon, cream the butter with the brown sugar until it is light and fluffy. If using an electric stand mixer, use the paddle attachment and mix on medium speed. Add the maple syrup in thirds to the butter and brown sugar mixture, beating well after each addition. If too much syrup is added at once, it will be more difficult for the butter to absorb it all, and the mixture will look permanently curdled. Add it slowly and it will blend in easily. Add the egg and vanilla extract and mix until thoroughly incorporated.

3. In a separate large bowl, combine the flour, baking soda, salt, cinnamon, and nutmeg. Mix the ingredients with a spoon to evenly distribute the spices, salt, and leavening in the flour. Add the flour mixture to the butter mixture and stir by hand with your wooden spoon until evenly combined. If using an electric mixer, combine on low speed. Add the oats and raisins and mix until they are distributed evenly throughout the batter.

4. Using a 1½-oz [48-ml] portioner, or scooping up about 3 Tbsp of dough with a spoon, form the cookies into round balls and place on a baking sheet lined with parchment paper. Gently press the balls to slightly flatten them out to ½-in-thick [1.5-cm-thick] disks. Since the cookies will double in size, leave plenty of space between them to give them room to spread.

5. Bake the cookies for 15 to 17 minutes, until golden brown around the edges and just set in the middle. Cool the cookies to room temperature.

tip: *This dough can be refrigerated raw and kept for a week. Bake the cookies right from the refrigerator. Expect to bake them for 2 to 3 minutes longer because they are cold.*

FRANK: *This is my favorite Bakehouse cookie and also our most popular. "Big O's" had their start at Zingerman's Delicatessen long before the bakery opened, and my appreciation for them started when I spent a summer working there.*

I was taking a break from the restaurant world and decided to be a stay-at-home dad to my eldest daughter, Anna, while her mother, Kathy, taught school. (It was a great year, even though I had moments of trauma, such as singing "Head, Shoulders, Knees, and Toes" at play group.) To make a little extra money, and to get out of the house, I worked at the Deli for a couple of shifts every week. On each shift I managed to eat a Big O cookie. More than two decades later, I still love them.

What makes them so good? The basics of real butter and real vanilla extract are certainly part of their appeal. The star ingredients, though, are the Michigan maple syrup, the old-fashioned rolled oats, and the super-plump Flame raisins that we use. The maple syrup adds an interesting and unexpected complexity of flavor, and the shape of the oats creates an appealing chewiness and a pleasing visual texture. The raisins are big and juicy, allowing them to be a major contributor to the cookie's character. If you're not a fan of raisins, substitute dried cherries or chopped dates.

Wondering about the name? Our tag line was originally "orgasmically good." We had a complaint from a customer, though, so now you just have to use your imagination.

AMY: *Our brownies are iconic Zingerman's treats. Many Deli Reuben sandwiches are followed by one of these fudgy, rich brownies. They were first developed at Zingerman's Delicatessen by Connie Gray Prig before the Bakehouse started and were simply referred to as Connie's brownies. They made them Deli big, each a quarter pound. Just as popular as the brownies were the brownie trimmings—the crispy edges that the Deli bakers cut off and sold in bags.*

The Bakehouse later took over baking a handful of items that were being made at the Deli, brownies being one of them. I was confused by the brownie trimmings—I didn't see a reason to have this "waste," which was the result of baking brownies on sheet trays rather than in proper baking pans. If we just baked them in an appropriate pan, we could eliminate the unattractive edges. (I also prefer interior pieces, so I couldn't imagine that anyone really liked the edges.) We made that change in 1995, and some customers still reminisce about the brownie edges!

We soon developed other brownie flavors—coffee, raspberry, ginger—but simpler versions proved to be most popular. Here are our recipes for our biggest sellers.

BAKEHOUSE BROWNIES—
BLACK MAGIC, MAGIC, AND BUENOS AIRES

makes 12 deli-big brownies

Black Magic Brownies

Chopped unsweetened chocolate	1 cup plus 1 Tbsp	195 g
Unsalted butter	¾ cup plus 2 Tbsp	195 g
Pastry flour	1½ cups	218 g
Baking powder	1 tsp	
Large eggs	4	
Granulated sugar	2¾ cups	540 g
Sea salt	1 tsp	
Vanilla extract	2 tsp	

Magic Brownies

Walnut pieces	1¼ cups	150 g

Buenos Aires Brownies

Dulce de leche	3 cups plus 6 Tbsp	546 g
Demerara sugar for sprinkling top		
Sea salt for sprinkling top (optional)		

1. Preheat the oven to 350°F [180°C]. Spray a 9-by-13-in [23-by-33-cm] pan with nonstick cooking spray.

2. In a double boiler, melt the chocolate and butter. Set aside.

3. In a medium bowl, combine the pastry flour and baking powder. Mix with a whisk to eliminate any lumps of flour and to distribute the baking powder evenly.

4. In a large mixing bowl, combine the eggs, sugar, salt, and vanilla. Beat with a whisk until well combined and aerated, about 5 minutes. If you are using a stand mixer, use the whisk attachment on medium speed for this step. Add the melted chocolate/butter mixture to the egg mixture and whisk to combine evenly. Stir in the dry ingredients, using a rubber spatula. If using a stand mixer, use the paddle attachment for this step and mix on a low speed.

continued

5. If you are making Black Magic Brownies, you are done mixing and can move to step 6. If you are making Magic Brownies, toast the walnuts. Place the walnuts on a sheet tray in a 325°F [165°C] oven for 10 to 15 minutes, or until they're a deep golden brown. Let cool. Add the toasted walnuts to the batter and mix gently simply to distribute them evenly, then go to step 6. For Buenos Aires Brownies, see the directions that follow.

6. Pour the batter into the prepared pan. Carefully spread it to the corners of the pan in an even layer. Bake for 40 to 45 minutes, or until a toothpick inserted in the center is clean.

7. Remove from the oven and cool on a cooling rack for at least an hour. Cut into 12 squares, using a sharp knife to avoid crushing the top. Chilling the brownies before cutting may help the squares look more beautiful, but they taste better at room temperature.

Buenos Aires Brownies

1. Warm the dulce de leche slightly, on the stove or in a microwave. This will make it more spreadable. Place two-thirds of the brownie batter in the pan and spread evenly to cover the bottom. Spread the dulce de leche out evenly over this layer of batter. Top with the remaining brownie batter and spread to cover the dulce de leche. Sprinkle the top with Demerara sugar. If you like sweet and salty desserts, also sprinkle with a little sea salt.

2. Bake for 45 to 55 minutes. Cool and then enjoy. These cut more easily if they are refrigerated.

duLce de Leche

Unfamiliar with dulce de leche? It is a staple sweet spread, like a milk jam, used in South America in baking and as a condiment on things like bread and ice cream. It literally means "sweet of milk" and is made by slowly heating milk, sugar, and vanilla. The mixture thickens and then the sugars caramelize and it turns a butterscotchy color. There are many recipes available to make it yourself.

Prefer to purchase it? Our favorite brand is La Salamandra from Argentina. They make it with only milk, sugar, and vanilla, no additives or preservatives. La Salamandra is located near the historic towns of Lujon and Capilla del Señor (50 miles from Buenos Aires). They use milk from their own grass-fed herds.

The first version of this cake was created in the late '80s at Zingerman's Delicatessen. Then as today, the Deli version is a whopping 7-pound cake! It's a four-layer, 9-inch round cake that can easily satisfy 30 people, but the Deli serves big pieces, so this cake is cut into 16 slices for individual sale. The cake itself is a fudgy, solid butter cake with a lusciously smooth chocolate buttercream. For extra goodness try to find high-fat cocoa to use in the cake recipe.

The recipe we provide here is for a more modest-sized cake that is great for birthdays or just everyday enjoyment. Serve it at room temperature for the best experience. This means letting it come to room temperature for 3 to 5 hours before eating.

HUNKA BURNIN' LOVE CAKE

makes one 8-in [20-cm] two-layer cake

Cake

All-purpose flour	1 cup plus 2 Tbsp	163 g
Unsweetened cocoa powder	⅔ cup	54 g
Sea salt	¾ tsp	
Baking powder	½ tsp	
Baking soda	½ tsp	
Unsalted butter, room temperature	1¼ cups	281 g
Granulated sugar	1⅓ cups plus 1 Tbsp	281 g
Large eggs	3	
Vanilla extract	1½ tsp	
Buttermilk (4% milkfat if available)	½ cup	114 g

Chocolate Buttercream

Large egg whites	5	
Sea salt	½ tsp	
Granulated sugar	1¼ cups	250 g
Chopped chocolate (56% cacao)	1½ cups	272 g
Unsalted butter, room temperature	1⅔ cups	367 g
Vanilla extract	½ tsp	

Make the Cake

1. Preheat the oven to 300°F [150°C]. Spray the sides and bottoms of two 8-in [20-cm] diameter round cake pans with nonstick cooking spray. Set aside.

2. In a medium bowl, combine the flour, cocoa powder, salt, baking powder, and baking soda. Whisk together until well blended. Set aside.

3. In the bowl of a stand mixer fitted with the paddle attachment, place the butter and sugar and cream on medium speed until light and fluffy. Scrape down the sides of the bowl as needed to make sure there are no unincorporated chunks of butter. Add the eggs, one at a time, to the butter mixture, beating to incorporate each egg completely before adding the next one. Add the vanilla extract. Mix until the batter is light and creamy.

4. On low speed, add the dry mixture in three parts, alternating with the buttermilk. Begin with dry ingredients and end with the buttermilk, mixing after each addition.

continued

5. Divide the batter equally between the two pans. Spread it evenly to cover the entire bottom of the pan. The more evenly you spread the batter, the more even the cake layers will be.

6. Bake for 40 to 45 minutes. When done, the cake will spring back when lightly pressed in the center and will have begun to pull away from the sides of the pan. If you stick a toothpick in it, it should come out clean.

7. Cool on a rack for 10 minutes. Run a small knife or metal spatula around the sides of the pans, and invert the cakes onto a cooling rack. Cool completely before icing.

Make the Buttercream

1. In a medium mixing bowl, combine the egg whites, salt, and sugar and stir to combine. Place over a pan of simmering water and heat the egg white/sugar mixture until the sugar is completely dissolved and the temperature reaches 180°F [82°C]. Use a candy or meat thermometer to assess the temperature. Stir occasionally.

2. In the meantime, melt the chocolate in a small pan, stirring constantly, or in a double boiler, and let it cool to room temperature.

3. Transfer the egg white mixture to the bowl of a stand mixer. Using the whisk attachment, whip the mixture on high speed until it doubles in volume, becomes thick and shiny, and has cooled to room temperature. Touch the bottom of the mixing bowl to assess the temperature. The next step is to add the butter. If the egg mixture is too hot, the butter will melt and ruin the buttercream.

4. When the egg white mixture is at room temperature, put the mixer on medium speed and add the soft butter, a piece at a time, until all is incorporated. The butter should be approximately the same temperature as the egg mixture to ensure easy incorporation and a smooth texture.

5. Add the vanilla and the melted chocolate and mix to incorporate. Beat on high speed for 1 minute to ensure that all the butter is combined with the whipped egg white and sugar mixture. Scrape the sides of the bowl and mix briefly to make sure the buttercream is homogeneous.

6. Use the buttercream immediately or place in an airtight container and refrigerate for up to a week or freeze for up to 3 months. If you refrigerate it, let it come to room temperature before using. This could take at least 6 hours, so we recommend removing it from the refrigerator the day prior to using it. You'll want to rewhip the buttercream before using.

Assemble the Cake

1. Place one cake layer upside down on a 9-in [23-cm] cake board or on a serving tray. If it has domed dramatically, remove the domed top with a serrated knife so that the layer is level. Take enough buttercream to make a ½-in [1.5-cm] layer of filling and spread it evenly over the surface.

2. Place the second cake layer upside down on top of the buttercream, removing any dome first, if necessary. Use the remaining buttercream to ice the exterior of the cake. Ice the sides and top smoothly if you're planning to pipe a border on the edges. Ice rustically, swirling the buttercream with your spatula, if you prefer not to have a border.

3. If you choose to make a border, reserve some of the buttercream and put it in a pastry bag with a star tip. Pipe a border around the top and bottom edges.

choosing names is fun, even for food

AMY: *In the '90s the Hunka Burnin' Love Cake was named Voodoo Love Cake. It is a rich, dark, and compelling cake, as we imagined voodoo love might be.*

I left the bakery in 1996 to get on with my life. When I returned four years later, I was in the pastry kitchen baking when a voice bellowed over the intercom, "Can you make another 9-inch Hunka Burnin' Love Cake?" I called to Patti, a longtime pastry and cake baker who was icing cakes that day, "Patti, can we make another 9-inch Hunka Burnin' Love?" I laughed after the name rolled out of my mouth—it sounded pretty racy! I thought to myself, "We gotta change that name."

The following day I said to Frank, "We gotta change the name of the chocolate cake. It's really too explicit." He laughed. Literally the month before I returned, they had run a contest to change the name from Voodoo Love. (I had totally forgotten the original name.) A customer had complained about the reference to voodoo, thinking that we were being disrespectful to the religion, so we renamed it. The name Hunka Burnin' Love had won the contest! Needless to say, we never changed the name of the cake—and none of our customers have complained about it.

This is our most popular coffee cake and possibly our most popular sweet item. It is adored as a daily treat and is definitely a Deli standard. Many Ann Arborites enjoy it regularly and send it to friends and family all over the country for holiday gifts.

Our cake is unassuming in appearance yet deeply satisfying in flavor. As you can see, it's full of tasty fat—half a pound of butter, half a pound of sour cream, and three whole eggs—which yields a mellow and moist cake crumb. Contrasting this mellowness is the distinctive flavor of the cinnamon nut swirl created with Indonesian Korintje cinnamon, brown sugar, and freshly toasted walnuts. Consider grinding your own cinnamon for this recipe to get unmatchable cinnamon flavor.

Why is the sour cream coffee cake considered a Jewish dessert? Yeasted coffee cakes, baked in kugelhopf pans, were somewhat common in Eastern European Jewish baking, as was the use of sour cream. Without refrigeration, most milk was consumed in some fermented form. Sour cream, along with buttermilk, became an element common to their baking.

Fast forward to 1950 Minnesota, when a group of Jewish women wanted to bring back some of the old Jewish recipes. To be successful they needed the right fluted pan with the tube in the center, which wasn't available in the United States. They approached a local pan-making company and asked the owner to create one. He generously obliged, and that first version was the inspiration behind the classic Bundt pans we are now all familiar with, branded as Nordic Ware. The ladies, thinking the European yeasted cakes were too time consuming, transformed them into a more American pound cake style, and the sour cream coffee cake as we know it was born.

SOUR CREAM COFFEE CAKE (OR LEMON POPPY SEED)

makes one 9-in [23-cm] bundt cake

Walnut halves	1 cup plus 2 Tbsp	132 g
Brown sugar	3 Tbsp (packed)	41 g
Ground cinnamon	2 tsp	
Granulated sugar	2 cups	395 g
Unsalted butter, room temperature	1 cup	227 g
Large eggs	3	
Sour cream	¾ cup plus 3 Tbsp	227 g
Vanilla extract	1½ tsp	
All-purpose flour	2⅓ cups	336 g
Baking soda	½ tsp	
Sea salt	1 tsp	

1. Preheat the oven to 325°F [165°C]. Spray a 9-in [23-cm] Bundt pan with nonstick cooking spray, coat with flour, and set aside.

2. Toast the walnuts on a sheet tray for 10 to 15 minutes, or until they're a deep golden brown. After they are done, turn the oven down to 300°F [150°C].

3. In a small bowl, mix together the toasted walnuts, brown sugar, and cinnamon. Set aside.

4. In a large mixing bowl, combine the sugar and butter. Cream by hand or with the paddle attachment of an electric mixer on medium speed. Mix until the color lightens. Add the eggs, one at a time, creaming thoroughly after each egg until the mixture is homogeneous. Add the sour cream and vanilla. Mix briefly until light and creamy. Scrape the sides of the bowl to make sure all of the ingredients are evenly incorporated.

5. Combine the flour, baking soda, and salt in a separate medium bowl. Mix to combine. Add the flour mixture gradually to the creamed mixture and mix by hand or with a mixer on low speed until smooth and homogeneous.

6. Scoop one-third of the batter into your prepared pan. Smooth it evenly over the bottom of the pan with a spoon. Sprinkle one-half of the nut mixture evenly over the batter. Cover with another third of the batter. Smooth it evenly over the nut mixture and to the edges of the pan. Sprinkle the remaining nut mixture evenly over the batter. Spread the remaining batter evenly over the nut mixture.

continued

7. Bake for 60 minutes, or until a skewer comes out clean. Cool for 15 minutes. Do not leave the cake in the pan for much longer than this. The brown sugar in the nut filling might stick to the sides of the pan and make it difficult to release the cake.

8. Put a wire cooling rack on top of the Bundt pan and then invert the pan to release the cake. Cool to room temperature before eating.

Storage: *This cake is so rich that it keeps very well at room temperature for at least two weeks, if wrapped well. It also freezes nicely. Wrap it carefully in plastic wrap and then put it in a plastic freezer bag or airtight container. It will hold well for up to three months in your freezer.*

Variation:
LEMON POPPY SEED COFFEE CAKE

The second coffee cake we made was lemon poppy seed. If you're a fan, simply make the sour cream coffee cake batter and add 1 tsp of lemon oil and 1 cup [130 g] of ground poppy seeds at the end of the mix. Bake at the same temperature and for the same length of time as the sour cream coffee cake. The nut filling is not a part of this version.

Lemon Oil

At the Bakehouse, we love intense flavors and are always looking for ways to increase the flavor in our recipes. With citrus flavors it's not always possible to get the intensity we want with only fresh juice or zest. Fortunately, many years ago we discovered a line of citrus oils from a company called Boyajian. According to Boyajian, they are "natural essences that are cold pressed from the rind of the fruit." They are considerably more intense than extracts and are used in small quantities. Boyajian suggests starting with ½ tsp per cup of dry ingredients, plus ¼ tsp per cup of liquid ingredients. We often use some fresh juice and zest and then a little oil just to bump up the flavor.

AMY: *Scones were first made in the 1600s in the British Isles, and people have been refining and improving them ever since, all over the world. They can be delicate and tender or heavy and dense, all depending on the proportion of fat to flour in the recipe and on the mixing method. Our scones are remarkably tender and delicate because of two things: (1) the large, unapologetic quantity of fat in them—lots of butter and cream, and (2) the mixing method, which makes them short. Short doughs are tender doughs rather than chewy doughs because of how the fat is combined with the flour, keeping the gluten strands short. When gluten strands are long, they give a chewiness to bread or pastry. If you follow our recipe, you'll create scones that are so tender and light that you'll surprise friends and family when you serve them. You may even convert some scone skeptics into scone lovers.*

Our scones are particularly popular as a breakfast sweet on holidays and for Mother's Day. We make so many on these occasions that we refer to them as "scone-age," our mass noun for scones. Special thanks go to Saul Wax, who introduced currant scones to the Deli many, many scones ago.

The recipe is written to make ginger scones. They happen to be my favorite. We also give directions for two variations.

GINGER SCONES
(OR LEMON OR CURRANT)

makes 12 scones

Unsalted butter, cold	½ cup	114 g
Pastry flour	3 cups plus 1½ Tbsp	436 g
Granulated sugar	⅓ cup	64 g
Baking powder	1 Tbsp	14 g
Sea salt	1 tsp	
Ground ginger	½ tsp	
Diced crystallized ginger	½ cup	82 g
Heavy cream, cold	1½ cups	341 g
Egg Wash		
Large egg	1	
Egg yolk	1	
Water	1 Tbsp	

1. Preheat the oven to 400°F [200°C]. Dice the cold butter into ¼-in [6-mm] cubes.

2. In a large mixing bowl, with a fork, stir together the pastry flour, sugar, baking powder, salt, and ground ginger. Mix until well combined. Add the diced butter to the dry mixture. Working quickly, cut the butter into the flour mixture, using a pastry blender. Work until the mixture looks like coarse cornmeal with pea-sized pieces of fat. If you do not have a pastry blender, you can use two butter knives or your hands. If using your hands, break the pieces of butter up in your fingers and then pick up some butter and flour and rub it together in the palms of your hands. Add the crystallized ginger to the bowl and stir until it is evenly distributed.

3. Next make a well in the center of the dry ingredients. Pour the heavy cream into the well and, using a fork, gently mix it into the dry ingredients. The dough will look rough.

4. Gently knead the dough in the bowl, 6 to 8 times, using your hand or a plastic scraper. The goal is to evenly distribute the moisture from the cream and to bring the dough together. By the end of the kneading, there should be no loose flour remaining in the bowl.

5. Turn the dough out onto a lightly floured surface, divide into two pieces of equal size, and gently shape into round balls.

6. Lightly sprinkle the work surface, as well as the tops of the dough, with flour. Place the balls of dough on the flour and pat or roll out the dough into disks that are ½-in [1.5-cm] thick and 7 in [17 cm] in diameter.

7. Using a bench knife or a chef's knife, cut each circle into six triangular wedges. Place the scones on a parchment-lined baking pan with at least 2 in [5 cm] between them.

8. Make the egg wash by beating together the egg, egg yolk, and water in a small bowl, and brush the tops of the scones with the egg wash.

9. Bake the scones for 18 minutes, or until the tops and bottoms are golden brown. Serve warm or at room temperature.

tip: *If you don't have any pastry flour and you don't want to buy a bag that will sit in your cupboard for a long time, go ahead and use all-purpose flour. The scones will be slightly less delicate but still plenty tender and light. They will probably get a little better loft with the all-purpose flour as well.*

Variations:
LEMON OR CURRANT SCONES

For different flavors, omit the ground ginger and crystallized ginger and replace with the following:

Lemon Scones: ⅓ cup plus 1 Tbsp [64 g] of chopped candied lemon peel and 1 Tbsp [14 g] of lemon zest.

Currant Scones: ½ cup plus 1 Tbsp [64 g] of dried currants.

chapter 3

creating a
GREAT PLACE TO WORK—
PEOPLE matter!

AMY: People matter! Both Frank and I simply enjoy people and care about people, so we are naturally inclined to prioritize the experience of working at the Bakehouse in our decision making. We want work at the bakery to be great—rewarding, interesting, and fun—for everyone. We believe that the joyful, creative engagement of people is the core of a successful organization. Recipes, systems, and equipment all matter, but it's people who really make it happen in the moment, and who bring the innovation for the future. Providing an inspiring and supportive environment for people is therefore critical to our success. And it just feels good.

Unfortunately, in general, the food service industry is not known for providing great work environments. Jobs in our field are often just jobs, with little opportunity, low pay, few benefits, physically challenging environments, and strict social hierarchies. Both of us know about that uglier side of our industry from personal experiences many years ago. The combination of our early positive experiences and challenging negative ones inspired us to want to stay in the food business and to consider doing some things differently in our own bakery, including implementing a management style called "Servant Leadership," which we learned from Paul and Ari.

Soon after Paul and Ari started hiring other people to be managers, they realized that they needed to define their basic approach to management and to teach it, because it wasn't natural to everyone. They saw managers relating to staff in unpleasant ways that they knew were not modeled after their own behavior. They realized that the greater culture had given people many ideas about how a boss behaved, and that if they wanted their ideas to be the leadership style used at Zingerman's, they'd have to make it explicit and teach it. They set out on a multiyear process to create the foundation of management classes and recipes that we use to train our managers today. Thirty-five years later, Paul, Ari, and many others of us are still refining and expanding on it.

To get started, Ari and Paul delved into leadership literature and discovered that their natural approach had been articulated, described, and named by others: Servant Leadership, Stewardship, and Open Book Management. We have relied most on the work of Robert Greenleaf, who wrote a seminal book called *Servant Leadership*. For Stewardship we are grateful for the work of Peter Block, and our knowledge of Open Book Management began with Jack Stack and *The Great Game of Business*. For explicit descriptions of how we've evolved these approaches and adapted them for our environment, I recommend Ari's series of books *Zingerman's Guide to Good Leading*.

These approaches resonate with me and Frank because they are based on ideas that are fundamental to our world view. We believe that people are good and want to do good. If given clear expectations, training, and resources, we believe people will aim to do a good job. Everyone in the workplace has something of value to contribute. Diversity of perspective yields better results. Front-line people are often more in touch with the food and customers than leaders are. Their participation in decision making is necessary for the successful management of the business. Sharing information will allow people to do a better job. People will use the information in the service of their work. We believe that our food, service, and finances are all made better by working in this collaborative and transparent environment. It is our strongly held belief that an interesting and open work environment leads to greater creativity and innovation.

PRACTICING SERVANT LEADERSHIP TODAY

When it all works well, what does it look like? It looks like a thriving business filled with engaged, high-energy people doing work that they find interesting, challenging, and enriching. According to Greenleaf, the test of Servant Leadership is "Do those served grow as persons? Do those being served become healthier, wiser, freer, more autonomous, more likely themselves to become servants?" Throughout this chapter we've included the stories of people for whom this approach has been enriching. These stories illustrate the very concrete ways that people have thrived.

The Challenges

Creating an organization like this isn't simple. There are some challenges. The biggest that I've experienced is getting everyone to first understand how we're trying to work together and then to actually buy in. This takes time, effort, lots of educating, positive experiences, practice, reflection, and conversation. It also requires setting up systems and rewards that are aligned with the philosophy, so that it's baked into the culture. (Yes, that's a pun.) It doesn't happen overnight.

Another challenge is helping people overcome their fears and lack of confidence. Many people who work with us have had other experiences in which their opinions weren't valued. They were basically taught not to share and at times to stop thinking. Through practice and participation, we try to show them that that isn't the case here. So first they have to believe that they've been invited to truly participate, that it's their place to comment, actually their responsibility, and then they have to believe that they're worthy of being on the team.

Once we've overcome these obstacles, there's often the realization that with this opportunity to participate comes more responsibility, not just status and higher pay. The more traditional approach to work often minimizes participation, and by extension minimizes responsibility. In the Bakehouse, we get to carry out some of our suggestions and bear responsibility for the results. We think the personal growth and development and full engagement in work are worth the added responsibility.

Being an effective servant leader isn't easy. It doesn't just happen overnight after being presented with the material. We may try hard and be fully committed, but sometimes we're unsuccessful. We have made decisions that in the moment were well reasoned but that on reflection years later I now think were wrong, and I regret them. I think we could have been more patient or more creative or more inclusive in the problem solving.

Zingerman's Bakehouse isn't a utopia, and more often than we'd like, we have conflict, disappointment, and frustration. Why does this happen? We're human, and sometimes we apply our principles clumsily. We're all at different places in our lives, personal development, and leadership development, which means we act imperfectly. We aim not to repeat our errors, though, and to improve our skills. We reflect and try to do better next time.

In general, however, I think our workplace is joyful and participative. Every day in the bakery we hear laughter and chatter and see people smiling. Creative work is done by individuals and groups of people. Ideas for change and improvement come from many different directions and are usually activated by teams. Individuals find their way along many different career paths.

This chapter celebrates people and a positive work environment. The recipes are examples of the creativity that can happen when people are free to think, play, and experiment, when they are believed in and respected. I think we make better food when we can be our best selves in the bakery.

I appreciate that my managing partners actually care about me as a person. Over the many years that I've worked at the Bakehouse I've had really great days and some crummy days and I've never taken for granted that my managers understand I'm human & some days my customer service game is not as on point as it should be. They've also demonstrated time and time again that they're committed to my & my coworkers' success in this organization through classes, opportunities, and simply talking to me about it.
—Anonymous, Feelin' Groovy Survey 3/16

While I personally LOVE working in the Zingerman's Community of Businesses, I don't think the culture meshes with 100 percent of personalities. It's a very interactive, committed atmosphere which requires everyone to participate. Some people might prefer a less "involved" workplace.
—Anonymous, Feelin' Groovy Survey 3/16

FRANK: *In 2003 our organization prepared to open Zingerman's Roadhouse, a restaurant specializing in really good American food. Alex Young, the managing partner, asked us to develop a signature bread for the opening. At the time Shelby Kibler was leading our bread bakery, and Shelby and I began researching old American bread recipes. Our research brought us to a recipe for "thirded bread" or "Injun bread." It was made with a combination of corn, wheat, and rye and sweetened with a bit of molasses. We played around with it, varying the grain ratios and struggling to get it right, until we came up with the initial step of making the mush, which stabilized the corn. The bread has been served at the Roadhouse ever since.*

An important key to getting the most flavor out of this bread is to bake it truly dark, as a super-dark crust makes the tang of the sour starter and the slight sweetness of the molasses sing. In the past few years this has become our partner Ari's favorite bread.

ROADHOUSE BREAD

makes 2 loaves

Cornmeal Mush

Water, boiling	2 cups	455 g
Coarse cornmeal	1⅓ cups	195 g

Final Dough

Water, room temperature	½ cup plus 2½ Tbsp	130 g
Molasses	2 Tbsp plus 1 tsp	45 g
Levain (page 42)	1⅓ cups	195 g
Cooled mush	all	
Medium rye flour	1 cup plus 3 Tbsp	155 g
All-purpose flour	3 cups plus 1 Tbsp	430 g
Sea salt	1½ Tbsp	27 g
Cornmeal for dusting		

Make the Mush

1. Put the water in a saucepan, bring to a boil, and then turn off the heat. Weigh out or measure the water and pour it into a bowl. Add the coarse cornmeal to the boiling water and stir for a few minutes to completely hydrate the cornmeal. Make a thin layer of mush by pushing it up the side of the bowl. Place the bowl, uncovered, in the refrigerator until it comes to room temperature.

Make the Bread

1. In a large bowl, add the water, molasses, and levain, tearing the levain into small pieces. Combine thoroughly with a wooden spoon. Add the cooled mush and rye flour, and stir to mix. Add the all-purpose flour and salt and stir together. Continue mixing until the dough becomes shaggy and starts to just barely form a ball. Turn the dough out onto a clean, unfloured work surface.

2. Knead the dough for 6 to 8 minutes, using a plastic scraper to scrape the dough off the work surface (page 34). Place the dough in a bowl that has been sprayed with nonstick cooking spray or oil, and cover with plastic. Ferment for 1 hour.

continued

3. Uncover and place the dough on a lightly floured work surface. Fold the dough (page 34). Place back into the bowl and cover with plastic. Ferment for 1 hour. Uncover and place the dough on a lightly floured work surface and fold it a second time. Put it back in the bowl and cover. Ferment for 1 hour. Uncover and place the dough on a lightly floured work surface. Divide into two equal pieces. Pre-shape into rounds (page 35), and lightly dust with flour. Cover with plastic and let relax for 1 hour.

4. Lightly flour a work surface. Turn a dough round over and place it top down onto the floured surface. Gently pat down and shape it into a batard (page 35). Place seam side down onto a cornmeal-covered baking sheet. Repeat for the second loaf. Dust the tops of the loaves with flour, and cover with plastic. Proof for 1½ to 2 hours, until the loaves have nearly doubled in volume. Use the touch test (page 38) to see if the loaves are ready for the oven.

5. One hour before baking, preheat the oven with a cast iron skillet (for creating steam) and baking stone to 450°F [230°C] (page 38). Carefully remove the plastic cover; avoid tearing the surface of the loaves.

6. Place the loaves side by side onto a peel that is lightly covered with cornmeal. Brush the top surface of the loaves with water, then generously dust the top of each loaf with cornmeal.

7. With a razor blade or very sharp knife, make three cuts on the diagonal in the top of each loaf (page 38). The cuts should be 3 in [7.5 cm] long and should overlap by about 1½ in [4 cm]. The first cut should start 2 in [5 cm] from the top of the loaf, and the third cut should end 2 in [5 cm] from the bottom of the loaf.

8. Slide the loaves onto the preheated baking stone and bake for 8 minutes with steam (page 38). Uncover, then bake for an additional 42 to 47 minutes, or until the loaves are a very dark brown color. (Note: It is important for the flavor of this bread to allow it to bake until it's really dark brown.)

9. Remove the loaves from the oven, place on a wire rack, and cool completely.

tips for placing the cuts on your loaf: *With the tip of your knife, gently scratch in the cornmeal a 1½-by-7-in [4-by-17-cm] rectangle centered on the top of the loaf. Your three cuts should be completely contained in this rectangle. The first cut should start in the upper right corner of the rectangle, and the third cut should end in the lower left corner of the rectangle.*

Dan Centurione, our third BAKE! principal, is a native Detroiter, and he has a long list of Michigan-based dishes loved by Detroiters. With fond memories from his childhood, loyalty to the city, and a desire to celebrate its resurgence, Dan created a class to teach this pizza and other Detroit favorites. Detroit-style pizza? Really? There's New York and Chicago, but how many Americans have heard of this unique Detroit style? It's a thick, rectangular pizza, distinctive in that it has the sauce on top of the cheese, has particularly crispy edges, and is sometimes twice baked. It was first created after World War II in Buddy's Rendezvous, which later became Buddy's Pizza and is still open today.

This pizza is intimately related to the Detroit car industry. It's made in distinctive blue steel pans that were used by the automobile industry as containers for hardware on the assembly line. The steel provides superior heat conductivity and caramelization of the crust (the mark of a great Detroit-style pizza). These pans are available from various manufacturers online.

Another Midwest-specific quality to this pizza is brick cheese. This is a simple, pragmatic cheese made in the tradition of the washed-rind abbey cheeses of Europe. Many immigrants brought this cheese-making process with them. We buy ours from the Widmer family of Wisconsin. They use large, rectangular, brown heavy bricks from Ohio to weigh down the cheese curd overnight, hence the name of the cheese. The young version is particularly good for melting. If you can't find brick cheese, substitute mozzarella.

If you don't have an authentic Detroit pizza pan, you can use a 9-by-13-in [23-by-33-cm] pan instead.

DETROIT-STYLE PIZZA

makes 1 pizza

Pizza Dough

Water, 100°F [38°C]	1 cup	230 g
Sea salt	1 tsp	
All-purpose flour	2 cups plus 1 Tbsp	290 g
Instant yeast	¾ tsp	

Pizza Sauce

Crushed tomatoes (canned)	28-oz can	795 g
Granulated sugar	3 Tbsp	44 g
Dried oregano, crushed	1 tsp	
Dried basil, crushed	1 Tbsp	
Finely minced garlic	1½ tsp	
Sea salt	1 tsp	
Ground black pepper	½ tsp	

Topping

Shredded Parmesan cheese	¼ cup	45 g
Pepperoni (optional)	8 slices	
Shredded mozzarella cheese	2 cups	230 g
Shredded brick cheese	2 cups	230 g
Dried oregano	pinch	
Sea salt	pinch	
Pizza sauce, warm	1 cup	230 g

Make the Dough

1. In the bowl of a stand mixer, add the water and sea salt and stir to dissolve the salt. Add the flour and yeast and mix with a wooden spoon until the dough becomes a shaggy mass. Make sure that all of the flour is hydrated. Using the dough hook attachment, mix on medium-low speed for 4 minutes. Scrape the sides of the bowl and release the dough from the hook. Mix for an additional 4 minutes. It will now hold a round shape.

2. Spray a bowl with nonstick cooking spray or brush lightly with olive oil. Place the dough into the bowl and cover with plastic. Let the dough relax for 15 minutes, and then shape the dough.

continued

Shape the Dough

1. Lightly oil or butter the inside surfaces of a 9-by-13-in [23-by-33-cm] baking pan or Detroit pizza pan.

2. Place the dough into the pan and use your fingertips to spread the dough out to the corners and sides of the pan. The dough will be sticky, so lightly dip your fingertips in oil to make stretching it easier. Set the pan aside, cover with plastic, and let rise in a warm area for 1½ to 2 hours, or until the dough is approximately ½ to ¾ in [1.5 to 2 cm] tall in the pan.

Make the Sauce

1. Combine the tomatoes, sugar, oregano, basil, garlic, salt, and pepper and stir together in a medium saucepan. Bring to a simmer over medium heat, stirring periodically. Using an immersion blender or food processor, purée the sauce until smooth. Place it back over medium heat. Simmer the puréed sauce until slightly thickened, 5 to 10 minutes, stirring periodically.

2. Keep the sauce warm for ladling over the pizza, or cool and refrigerate for up to a week. This recipe makes about 3 cups [710 ml] of sauce and it can also be frozen for up to 3 months, if desired. You will have more sauce than you need for one pizza.

Top and Bake the Pizza

1. Preheat the oven to 475°F [240°C].

2. Sprinkle the Parmesan cheese around the edge of the pizza where the dough touches the sides of the pan. This cheese will form a crispy, cara-melized edge on the crust. If desired, place pepperoni in two rows of four down the length of the pizza, directly on top of the dough. Gently push the pepperoni into the dough.

3. Sprinkle the mozzarella and brick cheeses over the surface of the pizza, spreading them all the way to the edges where the dough meets the sides of the pan. This cheese will also contribute to the crispy, caramelized edge on the crust. Season the top of the pizza with a pinch each of oregano and salt.

4. Place in the oven and bake for 15 minutes. Look for an amber-colored top and crispy edges.

5. After removing the pizza from the oven, use a small offset spatula or knife to loosen the sides of the crust from the pan. Slide the pizza out of the pan onto a cooling rack. At this point, if a crispier bottom is desired, you can put the pizza (out of the pan) directly onto the oven rack or a sheet tray and bake for an extra 5 minutes for a slightly more browned finish on the bottom of the crust.

6. After you remove the pizza from the oven, top it with the warm sauce. Traditionally, it is ladled into two rows down the length of the pizza. Serve warm.

Storage note: *This pizza can be kept in the refrigerator for up to 3 days and reheated on a lightly oiled sheet tray at 475°F [240°C].*

Michigan is a big state with several distinct cultural areas. The Upper Peninsula, five hours north of Ann Arbor by car, known to Michiganders as the UP (its residents are "Yoopers"), is a beautiful, primarily rural and remote area. Its long winters make agriculture not very productive, so the economy is based on logging, and in the past it was a big mining area.

Many European immigrants populated the UP to work in the mines in the early 19th century, Cornish miners being one of the cultural groups. These miners had a tradition of bringing pasties (hand-held meat pies) to the mines every day for their lunch. Although most of the mines are closed, pasties are still a living tradition.

Every year Zingerman's Community of Businesses gives out several scholarships to employees who want to study something related to our work. It could be to study food or a software package, or it could be to study leadership. One year a former Bakehouse employee named Anne Good decided that she wanted to learn to make Cornish pasties in Cornwall, England. She won the scholarship and set off.

Boy, did she learn. She returned to the bakery and started the somewhat painstaking activity of translating a recipe from one environment to another. None of the ingredients tasted quite the same and the flour performed differently, so it took many trials to adjust the recipe for the desired outcome. Anne was persistent and determined to make it authentic.

Now pasties are a Bakehouse standard. We have our own Cornish pasty season. It runs from October through March, our coldest months, when a warm and filling pasty is just the thing. Guests look forward to the beginning of the season, often asking impatiently when the first batch will be out.

CORNISH BEEF PASTY

makes 4 meal-sized pasties

Pasty Dough

All-purpose flour	2 cups	281 g
Sea salt	½ tsp	
Lard, cold	5 Tbsp	73 g
Unsalted butter, cold	5 Tbsp	73 g
Water, cold	6 Tbsp	91 g

Filling

Diced beef sirloin tip (½ in [1.5 cm])	1¼ cups	227 g
Finely diced beef suet	⅓ cup	36 g
Dried thyme	1 tsp	
Diced potato (¼ in [6 mm])	¾ cup	59 g
Finely shredded rutabaga	¾ cup	141 g
Diced onion (¼ in [6 mm])	¾ cup	118 g
Sea salt	¾ tsp	
Ground black pepper	½ tsp	

Egg Wash

Large egg	1
Egg yolk	1
Water	1 Tbsp

Prepare the Dough

1. In a large mixing bowl, combine the all-purpose flour and salt and blend together. Add the lard and cut in with a pastry blender until it is pea-sized pieces. Once it reaches this point, use your hands to rub the lard into the flour until it isn't visible. The flour should no longer look white and dry.

2. Cut the butter into ½-in [1.5-cm] pieces and add to the bowl. Cut in with the pastry blender until the butter is broken down into smaller, pea-sized pieces. Make a well in the center of the flour mixture. Add the water and blend the flour mixture and water with a fork until a dough forms.

3. Scrape the sides of the bowl and knead the dough in the bowl 8 to 10 times. Knead until the dough holds together and all of the flour is incorporated. Do not knead more than necessary, however, or the dough will become tough.

The dough in this recipe is flaky and flavorful because of the mix of lard and butter. If you're not a lard lover, just replace it with an equal amount of butter. The other key "secret" ingredient is the beef suet, simply beef fat. Any butcher should be able to provide it. It is a critical element of the filling, adding a distinctive richness. The miners certainly needed that fat, and we can enjoy it too.

4. Remove the dough from the bowl and cut it into four equal pieces, shape into disks, and wrap with plastic wrap. Chill the dough for at least 30 minutes before rolling it out. The dough can be kept refrigerated for a week or frozen for several months.

Make the Filling

1. In a large bowl, mix together the beef, suet, thyme, potato, rutabaga, and onion. Do not add the salt and pepper until just before filling the pasties.

Assemble and Bake the Pasties

1. Preheat the oven to 375°F [190°C]. Make the egg wash by beating together the egg, egg yolk, and water until well combined.

2. Remove the dough from the refrigerator and roll each piece into an 8-in [20-cm] disk about ⅛ in [4 mm] thick. Brush the edge of each disk with a light amount of egg wash. Add the salt and pepper to the filling mixture and stir to combine.

3. Divide the filling evenly among the disks of dough. Place it in the center of the disk. Fold the far edge of the dough over to reach the near edge, enclosing the filling. Press the edges together to seal, then crimp them as you would a pie crust or press them with the tines of a fork held flat.

4. Brush each pasty with egg wash. This will give them a nice golden color. Place the pasties on a baking sheet and bake for 45 to 50 minutes, until they are deeply golden brown. Let cool for at least 10 minutes before serving. Serve warm or at room temperature.

These are intensely flavored cookies that practically make us jump up when we eat them!

Karen Lucas, our pastry kitchen leader in the mid-1990s, introduced the first versions we created to our repertoire. She had made them for her brothers and then her own children and wanted to share them with more people.

Karen left, but the cookies stayed. We continued to experiment to make them even more tempting. We replaced regular American brown sugar with muscovado brown sugar from Mauritius. It's more complex in its flavor. Nowadays it's available in many grocery stores, so try using it in place of brown sugar in your recipes. We increased the quantity of ground ginger and added pieces of candied ginger that really pop when you bite into them. (One of our secret indulgences is eating candied ginger as an afternoon sweet treat. Very satisfying.) With all this flavor we gave the cookie a more appropriate name—Ginger Jump-Up.

tips

- If you'd like bigger cookies, make them bigger! In the bakery we make 3-oz [96-ml, about ⅓ cup] cookies regularly, and they're wonderful. These will need to bake for closer to 18 minutes. The critical point about size is that it's best if all the cookies on a baking tray are the same size, so that they will all bake at the same rate.

- If you don't want to bake all of your cookies at the same time, you can form them and refrigerate them for a week in a closed container. You'll need to add a couple of minutes to the baking time.

GINGER JUMP-UP COOKIES

makes 2 dozen cookies

Unsalted butter, room temperature	½ cup	110 g
Muscovado brown sugar	¾ cup (packed)	150 g
Molasses	⅓ cup	110 g
Large egg, room temperature	1	
All-purpose flour	2 cups plus 3 Tbsp	310 g
Baking soda	1 tsp	
Ground cinnamon	1 tsp	
Ground ginger	1 tsp	
Ground cloves	¼ tsp	
Chopped crystallized ginger	½ cup	110 g
Demerara sugar for sprinkling tops		

1. Preheat the oven to 350°F [180°C].

2. In a large mixing bowl, cream the butter, muscovado sugar, and molasses with a wooden spoon until well blended. If you are using a stand mixer, use the paddle attachment on medium speed. Add the egg and mix until the mixture is light and creamy.

3. In a separate bowl, combine the flour, baking soda, cinnamon, ground ginger, and cloves. Stir with a fork until evenly combined. Add all of the dry ingredients and the crystallized ginger to the creamed butter mixture and mix until completely incorporated. If using an electric mixer, use a low speed.

4. Portion the cookie dough using a ¾-oz [22-ml] portioner, or shape it by hand into balls, using about 1½ Tbsp of dough for each. Place onto a sheet tray lined with parchment paper, leaving space for the cookies to spread. With the palm of your hand, press each cookie down to a thick disk. Top each cookie generously with Demerara sugar. For the best coverage, dip the cookie's top surface into the sugar to completely cover it. This is easier to do when the cookies are chilled.

5. Bake the cookies for 12 to 14 minutes. Overbaking will make the cookies too firm. You want them to be fairly soft. It is a little difficult to know when they are done because they are so dark to start with that the color change is not dramatic. Look for firm edges, and avoid a visibly wet center. Also remember that they will continue to bake after you remove them from the oven.

Charlie Frank, the creator of this recipe, arrived unannounced at the bakery in August 2001, sort of looking for a job. We didn't have an opening and Charlie wasn't sure he wanted a job, but neither of us was too concerned about that, so we sat and talked.

We try to speak with anyone who approaches us at the bakery on their own, not responding to a job posting, because it is often the sign of someone who really fits.

After our talk, we agreed that Charlie would come and work on a trial basis, a couple of weeks, to see what he thought and what we thought. In the end he stayed for nine years, managing the pastry kitchen, and has since opened up his own Zingerman's business, Zingerman's Candy Manufactory.

But what about the blondies? Zingerman's Mail Order was eager for new versions of brownies. We were making a blondie that was essentially a cookie studded with hazelnut-flavored chocolate. It was popular and people still reminisce about it, but it was good the first day and then dried out quickly. It was also tricky to bake properly—it was either dry or raw. So Charlie got to work on creating a new recipe, and it's now one of our standards. This pecan blondie is moist, butterscotchy, and full of chunks of our own salty pecan praline.

The pecan praline is the super-special part of this recipe. The biggest challenge is not eating the praline before it gets mixed into the batter. We often say that we're going to sell it on its own, but we haven't gotten there yet. Maybe Charlie will at the Candy Manufactory.

BAKEHOUSE PECAN BLONDIES

makes one 9-by-9-in [23-by-23-cm] pan of blondies

Praline

Unsalted butter	2 Tbsp	57 g
Pecan pieces	1 cup	115 g
Sea salt	½ tsp	
Vanilla extract	½ tsp	
Water	2 Tbsp	27 g
Granulated sugar	½ cup plus 1 Tbsp	115 g

Blondies

Muscovado brown sugar	1 cup plus 3 Tbsp (packed)	230 g
Unsalted butter, melted	1 cup	230 g
Large eggs	2	
Vanilla extract	1 tsp	
All-purpose flour	1½ cups	200 g
Sea salt	½ tsp	
Baking powder	1 tsp	

Make the Praline

1. Preheat the oven to 325°F [165°C]. Spray a 9-by-9-in [23-by-23-cm] square baking pan with nonstick cooking spray.

2. Brown the butter as follows: Place the butter in a medium saucepan over medium heat. It will melt and then begin to sizzle—this is the water cooking out. Once it stops sizzling, the milk solids in the butter will begin to brown. Swirl the pan often, and remove it from the heat when it smells nutty and there are golden brown speckles in the pan. Err on the side of browning too little, because the butter will continue to cook in the pan after you remove it from the heat. Add the pecan pieces, salt, and vanilla extract to the browned butter and toss to coat the nuts.

3. Toast the pecans on a sheet tray at 325°F [165°C] for 12 minutes until they are toasty brown. Start checking after 8 minutes. Set aside. Leave the oven set at 325°F [165°C] to bake the blondies.

continued

4. Next, caramelize the sugar: Stir together the water and sugar in a small saucepan. Cook the mixture over medium-high heat without stirring until it is caramelized to a rich, reddish brown color. Once it has taken on the correct color, immediately add the pecans. Stir to combine, and then spread the praline evenly in the prepared 9-by-9 in [23-by-23-cm] baking pan to cool. (You can cool it on the baking tray if you'd like, but spray the tray with nonstick cooking spray first.)

5. When cool, remove the praline from the pan and, with a chef's knife, chop it into irregular ¼- to ½-in [6- to 12-mm] pieces. The praline can be made up to a week ahead and stored in a cool, dry place.

Make the Blondies

1. In a large bowl, using a whisk, combine the muscovado sugar, melted butter, eggs, and vanilla extract. Whisk until the mixture is homogeneous and thick.

2. In a separate medium bowl, combine the flour, salt, and baking powder. Stir to combine. Add the dry ingredients to the butter and sugar mixture and mix until homogeneous. Add the cooled chopped praline to the mixture. Stir to combine.

3. Pour the batter into the 9-by-9-in [23-by-23-cm] pan, spread it out with a spatula, and bake for 45 minutes, until puffed in the middle and golden brown and a toothpick comes out clean. Cool on a wire rack.

staff stories—katie "swanky" janky

AMY: *Another important person who arrived at the bakery on her own initiative and who ended up making a significant positive impact was Katie Frank, formerly Katie Janky. Frank's nickname for Katie is Swanky Janky.*

Although Katie loves all things baked and had actually managed retail bakery shops in Nashville, Tennessee, her first application to our organization was to be a trainer at ZingTrain, our business training organization. Our partner at ZingTrain, Maggie Bayless, saw Katie's bakery experience and encouraged her to consider working for us instead. We were so impressed with Katie when we met that we created a manager-in-training position and hoped that within six to nine months we would find a more permanent spot for her. Sure enough, Katie ended up managing our retail shop for five years.

Near that five-year mark, Maggie let us know that she was going to hire a new trainer and that the position was posted. Even though we didn't want Katie to leave, we sent her the posting. She was now ready for this position. We try to work with an abundance mentality. If Katie did well, the organization would benefit. Doing the right thing is never wrong, we tell ourselves.

Katie applied for the position. In the meantime, unbeknownst to most of us, she was dating Charlie, who was then the Bakehouse pastry chef. In the end, she got the job, she and Charlie got married, and now she's thriving at ZingTrain. Our shop is going strong and still enjoying the foundation Katie built.

People in the bakery are important, and so are our relationships with people we work with outside of the bakery. A particularly appealing aspect of our work is having the opportunity to work with artisanal producers from all over the world and learning how to make their traditional recipes. Sometimes we even get to host them in Ann Arbor. The Mahjoub family from Tunisia makes olive oil, couscous, harissa, and a variety of Mediterranean vegetable and fruit spreads. Their couscous is so fantastic that we regularly order a 10-kg (22-lb) container of it and share it among ourselves.

On one visit, Majid Mahjoub and his wife, Onsa, taught a class at BAKE! featuring Tunisian specialties. For dessert Onsa prepared this simple but characterful cake featuring their olive oil, fresh oranges, and sesame seeds. It's perfect with coffee or mint tea.

TUNISIAN ORANGE AND OLIVE OIL CAKE

makes one 9-in [23-cm] round cake

Seedless orange	1 large	320 g
Large eggs	2	
Granulated sugar	1 cup	200 g
Extra-virgin olive oil	½ cup plus 1 Tbsp	130 g
All-purpose flour	2 cups plus 1 Tbsp	290 g
Baking powder	1 Tbsp	14 g
Sea salt	½ tsp	
Sesame seeds	1 Tbsp	

1. Preheat the oven to 350°F [180°C]. Spray a 9-in [23-cm] round cake pan with nonstick cooking spray.

2. Wash the orange and cut off both ends. Cut the orange into quarters and put into a food processor, peel and all. Process until the orange is a pulp.

3. In a large bowl, crack the eggs and add the sugar. Use a whisk to combine, and then beat until light and smooth, about a minute. Add the orange pulp and olive oil and whisk to combine.

4. In another bowl, combine the flour, baking powder, and salt. Sift the dry ingredients into the orange mixture and stir gently until all the ingredients are combined. All the dry ingredients should be moistened.

5. Spread the cake batter into the pan and sprinkle it with the sesame seeds. Bake for 35 minutes, or until a toothpick inserted into the middle comes out clean. Remove from the oven and let cool completely before removing from the pan.

AMY: *This cruller recipe of fried pâte à choux dough came about during a casual conversation with Alejandro Ramon (former longtime employee, BAKE! instructor, and great baker) while we taught a class together many years ago. Alejandro loves to cook and bake, and he's really talented. He's the middle of nine children and began his baking career at age 10 with a Betty Crocker book. He's been working on his craft ever since, and it's obvious.*

Whenever Alejandro taught a BAKE! class, he'd give the students ideas about how to use the recipes we were teaching and how to make them a part of a great meal or party. They were always mouth-watering descriptions. We'd be oohing and aahing and before long a student would invite Alejandro to be his or her private chef. Oh, and occasionally a phone number and name would be left on his workbench at the end of a class. He's an irresistible guy!

During our "Who Are You Calling a Cream Puff?" class, where we teach the pastry for cream puffs, I mentioned how much I love French crullers, which are made with the same dough. Well, before I knew it, Alejandro was making French crullers for us!

This was the beginning of our Bakehouse tradition of French crullers every Saturday morning.

Many people have never had a real, non-doughnut-chain cruller before. Let me describe them to you. They are a complex mix of textures and flavors—crisp exterior, moist

FRENCH CRULLERS

makes 12 crullers

Vanilla Glaze

Water, warm	3 Tbsp	45 g
Unsalted butter	1½ Tbsp	23 g
Vanilla extract	1 tsp	
Corn syrup	1 Tbsp	23 g
Powdered sugar	1¾ cups plus 2 Tbsp	230 g

Crullers

Water	½ cup	115 g
Whole milk	½ cup	115 g
Unsalted butter	½ cup	115 g
Sea salt	½ tsp	
Granulated sugar	1 tsp	
All-purpose flour	1⅓ cups	180 g
Large eggs	4	
Vegetable oil for deep-frying		

Make the Glaze

1. In a small saucepan, combine the water, butter, vanilla extract, and corn syrup. Warm over medium heat until the butter is melted. Stir intermittently. Once the butter is melted, bring the mixture to a boil and then remove from the heat.

2. Set up your stand mixer with the paddle attachment. Put the powdered sugar in the mixer bowl and stir on low speed to break up the lumps in the sugar. With the mixer running, pour in the melted mixture. Mix for 5 minutes on low speed.

3. The glaze coats the crullers best when it is warm. It can be heated gently on the stove or kept in a double boiler when you are ready to use it.

Make the Dough

1. Put the water, milk, butter, salt, and granulated sugar into a medium saucepan. Set over high heat and bring to a full rolling boil. Melt the butter completely. Remove from the heat and add the flour while stirring with a wooden spoon. Stir until completely combined.

2. Return the saucepan to medium heat and continue stirring with the wooden spoon. This process is removing some of the moisture from the mixture. Cook and stir the paste until a film forms on the bottom of the pan.

continued

but light interior, lightly sweet, eggy, vanilla-ey. Mmh, so good!

Try them. They are pretty simple to make, and there's no elapsed time for proofing because the leavening comes from the flour and the eggs, not yeast. You don't need to wait until the last minute to make them, either. They are just as good a few hours later. I've even eaten them the next day and they are still decent, especially if you're a cruller addict like me.

3. Once there is a visible film on the bottom of the pan, remove the pot from the heat and spread the paste along the bottom and up the sides of the pan. Let cool for 3 to 4 minutes before incorporating the eggs. The eggs may cook if the paste is too hot.

4. Add the eggs, one at a time, stirring until each is completely incorporated before adding another. This can be done by hand or in a mixer with the paddle attachment. Once all of the eggs have been mixed in, the paste should be thick and smooth. Each time an egg is added the paste will initially look curdled. This is normal. Stir with some force and the egg will become incorporated. Then you can add another egg. After the eggs are incorporated, the paste is ready to use.

Fry and Glaze the Crullers

1. Heat 3 in [7.5 cm] of vegetable oil to 375°F [190°C] in a deep pan. As you fry the crullers, check the temperature of the oil periodically, because it will drop during the process. You may need to stop frying to let the oil come back to the proper temperature.

2. Prepare a pastry bag with a ½-in [12-mm] star tip. Fill the bag with about half of the paste. Do not overfill the bag; it will make it more difficult to pipe your crullers. You can put less paste in the bag if you are concerned about having adequate strength to pipe.

3. On 4-in [10-cm] square pieces of parchment paper, pipe out rings of dough 3 in [7.5 cm] in diameter. For best results, hold the tip 2 to 3 in [5 to 7.5 cm] above the parchment paper. This will help you get a good thickness to your cruller and an even circle.

4. Use a slotted spoon or skimmer to gently lower one cruller, parchment and all, into the hot oil. Use your spoon to submerge the cruller in the oil. The parchment paper will release and you can remove it from the oil with tongs. Depending on the space you have available in your fryer, repeat with more cruller rings, but be careful not to overcrowd the pot. The crullers will swell considerably as they fry.

5. Fry them for only 20 seconds and then flip them. If they fry too long on their first side they lose the distinctive cruller ridges. The next flip comes when you see cracks forming on the surface of the crullers. Turn again and then fry until they are a nice tan color, slightly darker than golden. Lift the crullers out of the oil with a slotted metal spoon, and drain on a wire cooling rack placed over a sheet tray. Repeat with the remaining crullers.

6. Use a large ladle to generously pour the warm vanilla glaze over the crullers. We pour almost five times as much glaze on each cruller as actually stays. This ensures even coverage. The excess glaze will collect on the sheet tray. You will need to reuse the glaze that lands on the sheet tray to complete the process for all of the crullers. Only one side of the cruller is glazed.

tip: *There are other ways to garnish your crullers if you'd prefer something different than vanilla glaze. When they are cool enough to touch but still warm, toss them in a bowl of granulated sugar or cinnamon sugar. For a little adventure you can flavor the sugar with other spices you may prefer. Cardamom, ginger, or even a curry mixture with the sugar are all interesting and surprising.*

AMY: *Chocolate-covered doughnuts are an American classic. I particularly love this version because it is first covered with vanilla glaze and then iced with chocolate. The glaze keeps them fresher longer and adds a bit of sweetness, and the chocolate ganache is full flavored and a world apart from what we're used to eating.*

Some of what happens at our bakery is about team and timing. When the timing was right for us to venture into the world of fried dough, a team emerged. We needed a few things before we could really get going:

1. Leadership support: I love to eat and make doughnuts. Frank's always a willing taster.

2. The tools for the job: We had bought a small fryer to try making cannoli. This allowed us to experiment with doughnuts without making much of an investment.

3. Confidence-building small steps: Alejandro Ramon, one of our former BAKE! instructors, had been making doughnuts since he was a child, and we created a BAKE! class for him to teach how to make them.

4. Bold entrepreneurial steps: Shelby Kibler, our BAKE! principal, created a daring bacon-apple doughnut to honor a book Ari wrote about bacon. Nina Plasencia, our pastry kitchen manager, had built a great team and they were game to have the kitchen make doughnuts on Saturday mornings.

CHOCOLATE-COVERED GLAZED DOUGHNUTS

makes 8 doughnuts

Doughnuts

Unsalted butter, room temperature	¼ cup	65 g
Granulated sugar	½ cup	100 g
Whole milk	¾ cup plus 2 Tbsp	205 g
Instant yeast	4 tsp	13 g
All-purpose flour	3½ cups	510 g
Large egg	1	
Egg yolk	1	
Spirytus vodka or other neutral, high-proof alcohol	2 Tbsp	27 g
Sea salt	1 tsp	

Vanilla Glaze

Water, warm	3 Tbsp	45 g
Unsalted butter	1½ Tbsp	23 g
Vanilla extract	1 tsp	
Corn syrup	1 Tbsp	23 g
Powdered sugar	1¾ cups plus 2 Tbsp	230 g

Chocolate Ganache

Finely chopped semisweet chocolate	1¼ cups	230 g
Heavy cream	1 cup	230 g
Vegetable oil for deep-frying		

Mix the Dough

1. In a stand mixer with the paddle attachment, cream the butter and sugar until smooth. Add the milk, yeast, half the flour, and the whole egg and egg yolk. Mix on low speed until a smooth batter forms. Add the vodka and mix until combined completely. Add the rest of the flour and the salt. Mix until a dough is formed.

continued

5. Expert knowledge and enthusiasm: Randy Brown, our sales guy, grew up working in bakeries and had spent many hours frying doughnuts. He was super excited to teach us what he knew. The stars came into alignment, and off we went into the world of doughnuts.

Note that the vodka keeps the dough from absorbing too much oil. We use Spirytus (see page 166), but any neutral, high-proof alcohol will do.

2. Turn the dough out onto a clean, unfloured work surface and knead by hand for 6 to 8 minutes. The dough will be tacky but smooth. If you prefer to use your mixer, switch to the dough hook attachment and mix on medium speed for 6 minutes. You may need to scrape the dough from the sides of the bowl intermittently.

3. Place the dough in a lightly oiled bowl, cover with plastic wrap, and ferment for 1½ to 2 hours, or until doubled in size.

4. While the dough is fermenting, prepare the vanilla glaze and chocolate ganache.

5. After the dough has doubled, uncover it and turn onto a lightly floured work surface. Fold the dough (page 34) and place it back into the oiled bowl. Ferment for 1 more hour, or until doubled in volume.

Make the Vanilla Glaze

1. In a small saucepan, combine the water, butter, vanilla extract, and corn syrup. Warm over medium heat until the butter is melted. Stir intermittently. Once the butter is melted, bring the mixture to a boil and then remove from the heat.

2. Set up your stand mixer with the paddle attachment. Put the powdered sugar in the mixer bowl and stir on low speed to break up the lumps in the sugar. With the mixer running, pour in the melted mixture. Mix for 5 minutes on low speed.

3. The glaze coats the doughnuts best when it is warm. It can be heated gently on the stove or kept in a double boiler when you are ready to use it.

Make the Chocolate Ganache

1. Place the chopped chocolate in a mixing bowl.

2. In a small saucepan over medium-high heat, bring the cream to a full boil. Remove the cream from the heat and pour over the chocolate. Let stand for 3 minutes and then whisk until the chocolate is completely smooth.

3. If using right away, let the ganache thicken enough that it covers easily but doesn't pour right off the doughnut. If you make it ahead of time, warm the ganache gently until it is the perfect thickness for coating. Use a double boiler or be very attentive to it in a pot on the stove, stirring frequently.

Roll and Cut the Doughnuts

1. After the second fermentation, lightly flour the work surface and turn the dough out from the bowl. Lightly flour the top of the dough and pat it out to ½-in [1.5-cm] thickness with flat hands, or roll out with a rolling pin. Brush off excess flour after the dough is the desired thickness.

2. With a 3½-in [9-cm] doughnut cutter (one that makes a hole), cut out the doughnuts. Place on a lightly floured surface. Cover lightly with plastic wrap so that the exterior of the doughnuts does not dry out and proof for 30 minutes.

3. The doughnut holes and scrap dough can be proofed and fried. Do not attempt to rework the dough because it will become tough.

Fry and Finish the Doughnuts

1. Heat 3 in [7.5 cm] of vegetable oil to 375°F [190°C] in a deep pan.

2. To fry the doughnuts, carefully lower the proofed pieces of dough into the hot oil. The number of doughnuts you fry at once depends on the size of your fryer. Do not crowd the frying pot.

3. Fry the doughnuts on the first side for 1 to 2 minutes, or until golden brown. With tongs, turn the doughnuts over and fry on the second side for 30 to 60 seconds, or until golden brown. Remove the doughnuts from the fryer and drain on a wire cooling rack placed over a sheet tray. Fry all the doughnuts before glazing.

4. To glaze the doughnuts, ladle a large quantity of warm vanilla glaze over each doughnut so that it will cover evenly. When you run out of glaze, recover what has dripped onto the sheet tray and reuse it. If it has cooled too much to pour easily, reheat it gently in a microwave and start the process over. Glaze only one side of the doughnuts.

5. When the glaze is set, ice the doughnuts with the chocolate ganache. Once again, place the doughnuts on cooling racks set on a clean sheet tray. Use a ladle to pour a generous amount of warm ganache over each doughnut. If necessary, use a butter knife to spread the ganache evenly. As with the glaze, if you run out of ganache, reuse some that has dripped onto the sheet tray.

chapter 4

the flow of
OUR DAYS

AMY: What is it like to be a professional baker? Does it always involve working through the night? Is it a solitary and lonely life, or is it peaceful, spiritual, and sensuous? Many baking enthusiasts are curious about the ins and outs of a professional baker's day. In the next few pages, we'll describe the flow of work in our bakery, which is similar to some and entirely different from others.

By design, most days at our bakery have a similar schedule and flow. We joke that it's like the 1990s movie *Groundhog Day*, because although there's remarkable consistency, there's always something that's just a little different—the temperature dropped 10 degrees, a new shipment of flour has arrived and it's performing differently, or an unexpected staffing challenge comes up. It's just enough change to keep us engaged and clear that it is actually a different day.

Our work, staff, and energy come in and leave the Bakehouse in waves. The flow of the day almost seems tidal, with the energy starting low, building, finally reaching full capacity, and then receding. Then it starts again with the night shift and ends with the delivery drivers leaving the building in the early morning—high tide, low tide, and high tide over and over again.

We now work 24 hours a day. It's so continuous that it's not obvious what moment to call the start, but I'll choose one anyway. In a way, the beginning of our work each day is when the first bread mixer arrives at 2 a.m. to begin mixing the doughs. The remaining crew of 10 or so bread bakers arrive at staggered times, 5, 6, and 7 a.m., and the oven crew arrives last, at 9 a.m.

While the bread bakery is getting going, much is going on in the rest of the Bakehouse. Shop folks and their teammates who make soup and sandwiches arrive between 5 and 6 a.m. By 7 a.m. the cake decorators, one person in our service office, and the bread sorters all arrive. By 8 a.m. another wave of people comes in: our admin team, more shop help, pastry managers, and the maintenance crew. Customers are coming to the shop for their morning treat and coffee. The bakery is beginning to hum. Lights are on everywhere and work is happening in every room.

The pastry bakers come in at a seemingly leisurely 9 a.m., and start with a group stretching session. Their start intersects with the return of the night delivery drivers who've brought yesterday's baking to our customers. Yesterday and today connect! By 10 a.m., yesterday is done, and by 11 a.m. the last of today's crew is in with the shop closers, who will be here until about 8 p.m. At this point,

we usually have about 60 people working and we're in full swing. It's high tide.

There are little changes in energy as the day goes on. Teams stop to have lunch at different times. Their work spaces empty out, while the lunchroom becomes noisy. The shop picks up for lunch as workers in the area take their breaks and come to buy some soup or a sandwich or both.

Then the tide starts to recede. The bread bakers begin to wind down their day with cleaning tasks. The flow of people out of the building is like inventory—first in, first out. Early-morning bread mixers and bakers are leaving. Savory cooks leave. Early-morning shop staff leave, more bread bakers leave. By 3 p.m. we receive customers' orders for the next day and start to plan. For the day staff, mentally we're leaving today and are on to tomorrow.

Then the flow back into the bakery begins, with evening bakers for bread and pastry starting to arrive between 4 and 5 p.m. We experience slowing-down energy and just-getting-started energy all at the same time. By 5 p.m. the crews have completely changed and the night is getting going. The shop is ready for the after-work rush and then closing duties.

Nighttime has an entirely different feel in the bakery— no customers, phones are quiet, no admin staff, and few meetings being held. It feels much more like many of us imagine a bakery would feel—quiet, cocoonlike. Usually only half as many people are working. The center of the bakery is busy, while the peripheries are quiet and dark. The one thing that remains the same is that there's plenty of work and lots of hustle. Energy is high. The night bakers have a very clear deadline. The delivery drivers will be in by 1 a.m., and everything has to be ready for them to load onto their trucks. The wholesale customers will be waiting in their stores to put pastries in their cases for early-morning coffee customers and bread on their shelves for shoppers.

The arrival of the cleaning crew at 10 p.m. is another indication of time passing. The cleaners spread throughout the quiet areas, cleaning where the work has stopped and preparing to get into the pastry kitchen and bread bakery, the toughest areas to clean every day. Between midnight and 1 a.m., the bread and pastry bakers and sorters are performing their final tasks and closing down. The energy starts to slow down and people begin to leave. It's getting very quiet at the bakery. We're down to perhaps 15 people.

At 1 a.m., four night drivers come in to perform the last but critical part of our day—delivering our day's work. Soon after, our first bread mixer arrives to start the flow all over again. It's one big predictable, continuous cycle.

OUR APPRECIATION OF WORK HABITS AND ROUTINES

Our days are designed to be the same. Why? This predictability helps all of us do our work well. At any time of the day we have a clear sense of what ought to be happening, at least in our own areas, and if it's not, we know we need to make some sort of adjustment to get back on track.

Just as the day has this consistency, so too does the way we work within the day. Clear systems and defined work habits give the work itself a predictable character. Doing the same thing over and over again, in the same way and at the same time every day, is our version of work heaven. It's our experience that schedules, consistency, repetition, and well-chosen work habits help us be successful. This quote from the 17th-century British poet John Dryden resonates with us: "First we make our habits and then our habits make us." If we want to be excellent, we must have the behaviors that will take us there.

Does working this way sound boring to you? We get that it might. It's not for all contexts, all times, or all people. In our American culture that prioritizes the future, novelty, and the next new thing, our work approach may seem unimaginative and rigid. In the bakery, though, we actually find it liberating. What we've learned is that by maintaining schedules and systems, the environment and ingredients, we're able to learn more and feel freer to be creative.

Consistency, routine, and repetition—when done with intention and attention—all help us learn and improve. Frank says that we never know a bread until we've made it at least a hundred times. Done mindlessly, endless repetition is just boring and emotionally draining. Studies show that jobs that have high burnout rates are characterized by high-intensity repetition without a sense of purpose. We want to avoid that.

Supporting our daily schedule are work habits. When we follow them, our bread and pastries usually taste great.

Here are our top habits in the bakery:

Timeliness. Our attention to time dates back to the early days, when we were making only bread, when being on top of fermentation times was critical to success. We have since found that the habit of timeliness everywhere else in the bakery is also helpful.

Adherence to recipes and systems. We have hundreds of food recipes and operational systems. The expectation is that we all follow them. We might prefer to do things our own way, but we work hard to align ourselves to common systems. Changing systems and recipes is certainly okay. How else can you get better? But it's important to follow the process of change. The decision makers are expected to discuss the change, test it, and then to agree to make it or not.

Attention to detail. We want to deliver what we promise. To achieve that goal, we emphasize accuracy. People often think that it takes too long to do what it takes to be accurate. We think that overall accuracy, no matter how painstaking the steps are to get there, actually saves time. If we mess it up, we'll be remaking it or redelivering it. That takes time. That's time not well spent.

Daily tasting. In each area of the bakery we select a variety of items that we taste and score every day. This helps us make sure that we haven't strayed from the results we initially defined.

Working with intention. We encourage everyone to have a goal in mind when working, with an eye to gaining knowledge, skill, or speed or to improving the method in order to make our food better.

Taking time to learn and explore. With all this order, we need to balance it out with some exploration, creativity, and spontaneity. Schedule it in. Now that's a paradox to embrace!

The recipes in this chapter are representative of our schedules. They are key placeholders in our days, helping us to be aware of the time in a tasty way.

FRANK: *This has been far and away my favorite bread since we started baking. I especially love the flavor of this bread when we bake it nice and dark—the color that only about 1 percent of our customers like. I feel a great affinity with that 1 percent, and it's because of them that I implore our bakers to put the Farm Bread back in the oven and let it get dark. I realize that the 99 percent want their preference too, so we aim each day to bake a range of darkness, so everyone can get the loaf that they want.*

When a loaf is four different shades of brown, including one that approaches black, you know that you've baked something special. This bread has a nice sour flavor that is complemented by the caramel flavor that a dark brown crust contributes. Bake it light and the loaf has a distinctly sour flavor—that's okay, but it's much improved when sour is one of many flavor components and not the dominant one. Give it a try! Bake your Farm loaf really dark one day and taste the difference. Ari is part of the 1 percent and orders his own super dark. He believes that the flavors are out of balance otherwise.

FARM BREAD

makes 2 Loaves

Water, room temperature	2½ cups plus 1 Tbsp	580 g
Levain (page 42)	⅔ cup	145 g
Whole wheat flour	½ cup	72 g
All-purpose flour	6 cups plus 3 Tbsp	865 g
Sea salt	4 tsp	23 g

1. Place the water in a mixing bowl. Tear the levain into small pieces and add to the water. Add the whole wheat flour and half of the all-purpose flour. Stir with a wooden spoon to combine and break up the levain. Add the remaining all-purpose flour and salt. Mix to combine until the dough is rough and shaggy.

2. Turn the dough out onto a clean, unfloured work surface, scraping any bits of flour or dough out of the bowl. Knead the dough for 6 to 8 minutes (page 34).

note: *At this time 1 cup of dough can be cut off to use as the "Put Away Farm" (page 41). Allow it to ferment in a covered, oiled container for 4 hours, then refrigerate for future use to make one of the other sourdough breads in this book.*

3. Lightly oil a container and place the dough into the container. Cover with plastic. Let the dough ferment for 1 hour.

4. Place the dough on a lightly floured work surface and fold for the first time (page 34). Place it back into the container and cover with plastic. Ferment for 1 hour. Place the dough on a lightly floured surface and fold for the second time. Place it back into the container and cover. Ferment for 1 hour. Place the dough on a lightly floured surface and fold for the third time. Place it back into the container and cover. Ferment for 1 hour.

5. Lightly flour the work surface and place the dough on the surface. Divide the dough into two equal portions. Pre-shape each into a round (page 35), cover, and let relax for 45 minutes.

6. Prepare two proofing baskets by lightly flouring each basket. If you have round baskets, you will be shaping the dough into rounds. If you have long baskets, you will shape it into the batard shape.

7. Shape each round into the desired final shape (page 35) and place into the baskets with the seam side up. Let ferment for 3½ hours at room temperature. Use the touch test (page 38) to see if the loaves are ready for the oven.

8. Preheat the oven with a baking stone and cast iron skillet (for creating steam) to 450°F [230°C] 45 minutes before baking (page 38).

continued

9. Turn the loaves out of the basket onto a lightly floured baking peel. If making long loaves, with a razor blade or sharp knife, make six cuts to create a wheat stalk pattern (page 38). Trace a 4-by-9-in [10-by-23-cm] rectangle onto the top of the loaf. Working lengthwise, in one half of the rectangle, make three cuts, starting at the outside of the loaf and extending at a 30-degree angle toward the center, each 3 in [7.5 cm] in length. Start the second and third cuts at the edge of the rectangle, about 1 in [2.5 cm] up from the bottom of the previous cut. Make the next three cuts in a mirror image in the other half of the rectangle. The cuts should be about 1½ in [4 cm] apart at their closest point. If making round loaves, with a razor blade held at a diagonal to the dough, make a single long cut along the top and center of the round. Then add two angled 3-in [7.5-cm] long cuts on each side of the center cut as mirror images.

10. Slide the loaves onto the preheated baking stone and bake for 8 minutes with steam (page 38), uncover, then bake for an additional 35 to 40 minutes, until the loaves are dark brown. Remove the loaves from the oven and cool on a cooling rack. Cool completely before cutting.

A few of the breads and pastries that we make are like little miracles, and French baguettes are one of them. Our baguettes have both a buttery and a slightly sweet flavor (although there's no butter or sugar in the dough) that lingers in the mouth and evolves for many minutes after a bite. They actually have so much flavor that no condiments are necessary to enjoy them. This method also creates the quintessential baguette texture: crispy exterior and diaphanous, holey interior.

Part of our process is the long fermentation of the poolish: 12 hours. So this recipe is usually best made over a two-day period. Mix your poolish the night before you want to bake. Twelve hours later you can start mixing your dough or refrigerate the poolish until you're ready to start. While refrigerating your poolish for a few hours doesn't hurt it, don't hold it for more than a day or two.

None of this is truly hard. It just takes a little planning and lots of waiting.

Baguettes are one of the few breads that we bake twice every day. They are a modern urban bread made for city dwellers to consume entirely in a day, so they are best eaten soon after they're baked.

OUR FRENCH BAGUETTE

makes 4 baguettes

Poolish

All-purpose flour	1 cup plus 3 Tbsp	170 g
Water, room temperature	¾ cup	170 g
Instant yeast	⅛ tsp	

Final Dough

Water, room temperature	¾ cup plus 1 Tbsp	185 g
Poolish	all	
Instant yeast	¼ tsp	
All-purpose flour	2⅓ cups plus 1 Tbsp	340 g
Sea salt	2 tsp	12 g

Make the Poolish

1. In a medium mixing bowl, use a fork to stir together the flour, water, and instant yeast until everything is incorporated.

2. Cover the bowl with plastic wrap and allow the poolish to ferment at room temperature for 12 hours. After 12 hours, use the poolish immediately or refrigerate and use within 24 hours for best results.

Make the Baguettes

1. In a large bowl, add the water, poolish, instant yeast, and half of the flour. Mix thoroughly with a wooden spoon until the ingredients are well combined. The mixture will look like a thick pancake batter. Add the remaining flour and the salt and stir the mixture to incorporate the dry and wet ingredients. Continue mixing the dough until it becomes a shaggy mass. Scrape the side of the bowl with the spoon to pick up any dry bits.

2. Using a plastic scraper, remove the dough from the bowl and place on a clean, unfloured work surface. Knead the dough for 6 to 8 minutes (page 34). This is a very sticky dough. Do not add more flour! It will ruin the texture of the baguette. Initially you can knead it in the bowl if you like. As it comes together, you can move to kneading it on your work surface.

3. Spray your mixing bowl with nonstick cooking spray or brush with oil. Put the dough into the mixing bowl and cover with plastic. Ferment for 1 hour.

continued

4. Dust the work surface with flour. Uncover the dough and turn it out onto the floured surface. Fold the dough (page 34). Turn the dough over and return it to the oiled bowl and cover. Ferment for another hour.

5. Lightly dust the work surface with flour and turn the dough out onto the floured surface. Fold the dough again. Leave the dough on the surface, cover with plastic, and let rest for 30 minutes.

6. With a bench scraper, divide the dough into four equal pieces. Gently form the pieces of dough into loose rounds. Place them on a lightly floured work surface and cover with plastic. Let rest for 30 minutes.

7. After 30 minutes, uncover the dough and lightly dust the tops with flour. Follow the instructions for Final Shaping and Final Fermentation (page 38) to roll each piece into the final baguette shape, approximately 11 in [28 cm] long. Place the baguettes in a linen couche (page 33), seam side up and separated by pleats, then cover with the couche. Let them proof for 45 minutes to an hour at room temperature. Use the touch test (page 38) to see if the baguettes are ready for the oven.

8. Preheat the oven with a cast iron skillet (for creating steam) and baking stone to 450°F [230°C] for 45 minutes before baking.

9. When ready to bake, use a transfer peel or baguette board (page 33) to transfer the baguettes to a peel covered with a piece of parchment paper. Use a razor blade or a very sharp knife to score each baguette with three cuts (page 38).

10. Slide the parchment paper onto the preheated baking stone, and bake the baguettes with steam for 8 minutes (page 38). Remove the cover and bake for an additional 12 minutes, or until golden brown. You may need to rotate them for even browning halfway through. Remove from the oven, place on a cooling rack, and cool completely before eating.

This bread is our homage to the rustic country bread of Puglia (the southeastern tip of Italy). It's coated in a bit of our coarse-ground cornmeal and has a beautiful open, diaphanous crumb full of big, irregular holes. Although it is made up of some of the simplest ingredients that exist, its high hydration and long bulk fermentation give it a surprisingly complex flavor and glistening, moist crumb. It has been both a customer and staff favorite since we started baking it in 1993. We've made it 363 days each year since then.

With our large bread kneaders here in the Bakehouse, we develop the open crumb structure with a relatively long period of intense mixing. For our home recipe, we've used a series of four folds punctuated by periods of rest to get that same highly desirable crumb structure. Don't fear the stickiness of the dough as you initially begin to knead it. Have a plastic scraper in your free hand to help scrape the dough from the bench as you go. Remember, "the wetter, the better"!

PAESANO BREAD
makes 2 loaves

Poolish

All-purpose flour	¾ cup plus 1 Tbsp	114 g
Water, room temperature	½ cup	114 g
Instant yeast	⅛ tsp	

Final Dough

Water, room temperature	1¾ cups	400 g
Poolish	all	
Instant yeast	½ tsp	
All-purpose flour	3¾ cups plus 2 Tbsp	545 g
Sea salt	2½ tsp	14 g
Cornmeal for dusting		

Make the Poolish

1. In a medium mixing bowl, use a fork to stir together the flour, water, and instant yeast until everything is incorporated.

2. Cover the bowl loosely with plastic wrap and allow the poolish to ferment at room temperature for 8 hours.

Make the Bread

1. In a large bowl, add the water, poolish, and yeast and combine thoroughly with a wooden spoon. Add half of the flour and mix until the mixture resembles a thick pancake batter. Add the remaining flour and salt and stir the dry and wet ingredients together. Continue mixing until the dough becomes shaggy and starts to just barely form a ball. Turn the dough out onto a clean, unfloured work surface.

2. Knead the dough for 6 to 8 minutes (page 34), using a plastic scraper to scrape the dough off the table. Place the dough in a bowl that has been sprayed with nonstick cooking spray or oil and cover with plastic. Ferment for 1 hour.

3. After 1 hour, lightly flour the work surface and turn the dough out of the bowl. Fold for the first time (page 34). Return it to the bowl and cover. Ferment for 1 hour. After the second hour, lightly flour the work surface, turn the dough out of the bowl, and fold it a second time. Put it back in the bowl and cover. Ferment for 1 hour. After the third hour, lightly flour the work surface, turn the dough out of the bowl, and fold it a third time. Put it back in the bowl and cover. Ferment for 1 hour. After the fourth hour, lightly flour the work surface, turn the dough out of the bowl, and fold it a fourth time. Put it back in the bowl and cover. Ferment for 1 final hour.

4. Turn the dough out onto a floured work surface. Divide it in two and shape each into a round loaf (page 35). Place seam side down onto a corn-meal-covered sheet tray. Top with a dusting of cornmeal and cover the dough rounds with plastic. Proof for 1 to 1½ hours.

5. Preheat the oven with a baking stone to 450°F [230°C] for 45 minutes before baking. The loaves are ready when they've relaxed into disks 9 in [23 cm] in diameter by about 2 in [5 cm] tall. The top surface should be shiny with a few large bubbles visible.

6. When the loaves are fully proofed (page 38), gently flip one of the rounds onto a peel (with the bottom side now up) that has been lightly sprinkled with cornmeal, and slide it onto the baking stone in the preheated oven. Repeat for the second round. Bake for 35 to 40 minutes, until the loaves are a rich, deep brown. Remove from the oven, place on a wire rack, and cool completely.

Lemon Clouds are one of the first pastries made by the pastry bakers during our evening shift. We know the night is getting off to a good start when the baker who's making all the laminated doughs is preparing these light and tender morning pastries.

Lemon Clouds are a Danish dough that surrounds a thin layer of lemon curd. Making them gives you the opportunity to learn to laminate, which is the process of folding butter into dough to create distinct light layers after baking. It's the process that creates flaky croissants, tender Danish, and the incredible layering in the classic French cookie called a palmier.

To laminate well requires some important information, practice, and patience. We're going to give you the information and suggest that you try this on a day when you have lots of time. Our experience is that rushing never helps in baking. What about practice? Well, we encourage you to try this more than once. It's one of those skills that improves after mindful repetition. With that said, when our recipe testers made these, they came out very well on the first try, and the testers found the process easier than they had anticipated.

This recipe makes more lemon curd than you'll need for your clouds. It can be kept in the fridge for several days and is tasty on toast or ice cream or mixed into buttercream if you're making a cake.

LEMON CLOUDS

makes 12 pastries

Lemon Curd

Water	¼ cup	60 g
Cornstarch	2 Tbsp	20 g
Unsalted butter	½ cup plus 2 Tbsp	135 g
Large eggs	3	
Granulated sugar	1⅓ cups	270 g
Lemon juice	½ cup plus 2 Tbsp	140 g
Lemon oil	½ tsp	

Butter Block

Unsalted butter, room temperature	1½ cups	340 g
Lemon juice	¼ tsp	

Dough

Whole milk	⅔ cup	160 g
Large egg	1	
Instant yeast	2 tsp	8 g
Granulated sugar	1½ Tbsp	23 g
Sea salt	1½ tsp	9 g
All-purpose flour	2¼ cups	310 g

Finishing

Unsalted butter, melted	½ cup	115 g
Granulated sugar	1 cup	205 g

Make the Lemon Curd

1. Mix the water and cornstarch together in a small bowl to make a smooth mixture. Combine the butter, eggs, and sugar in a medium saucepan. Cook over low heat, stirring constantly, making sure to touch all spots on the bottom of the pot to ensure that there is no sticking or burning. Do not allow the mixture to boil because it will cause the eggs to cook. Cook until the butter is melted. Add the lemon juice and lemon oil and cook for 2 minutes. Add the cornstarch and water mixture and turn the heat to medium. Stir constantly and cook until the curd begins to bubble around the edges. Be careful to not overcook it because it will turn rubbery.

2. Pour the curd through a strainer into a storage container. This removes any small pieces of cooked egg that may have formed. Cover the curd with plastic wrap, pushing the plastic directly onto the surface, and then refrigerate until firm. It will keep for at least 5 days in the refrigerator if you wish to make it in advance.

Make the Dough

1. Prepare the butter block. Soften the butter by hand or in an electric mixer and add the lemon juice. Form the butter into a rectangle that is 8 in [20 cm] long and 6 in [15 cm] wide. Chill for at least 1 hour before starting the laminating process.

2. Now prepare the dough. Combine the milk, egg, yeast, sugar, salt, and flour in the bowl of a stand mixer. Using the paddle attachment, mix on medium speed for 5 minutes. The dough will be wet and sticky. Wrap the dough in plastic wrap and chill for 30 minutes.

3. Place the chilled dough on a floured work surface. Flour the top and roll the dough to approximately 8 in [20 cm] long and 12 in [30 cm] wide. Brush away excess flour with a pastry brush.

4. Place the butter block onto half of the dough and fold the other half on top of it. It should now look like a book. Turn the "mouth" toward you. The mouth is the side that is open, not the folded edge. Roll the dough out until it is 24 in [60 cm] wide and still 8 in [20 cm] long. Fold the dough as you would a letter—take one third and fold it onto the middle third. Take the remaining third and fold it over the center.

5. Take the mouth, the open edge of the letter, face it toward you, and repeat the previous step. Wrap in plastic and refrigerate for 30 minutes.

6. After 30 minutes, do two more folds as you did in steps 4 and 5. Wrap the dough in plastic wrap and chill for 1 hour.

Shape, Proof, and Bake the Lemon Clouds

1. After the dough has rested in the refrigerator, place it on a floured work surface. Flour the top and roll the dough to approximately 12 in [30 cm] long, 16 in [40 cm] wide, and ¼ in [6 mm] thick. Brush off any excess flour with a pastry brush.

2. Measure 4-by-4-in [10-by-10-cm] squares and cut with a pizza cutter. Place ½ Tbsp of lemon curd into the center of each square. Bring all four of the corners of the square to meet in the center, holding them in the air above the lemon curd. Pinch along all of the seams to seal the dough around the lemon curd. This forms an X shape. Then bring the four new corners into the center and pinch together.

3. Place the Lemon Clouds with the seam facing down onto a sheet tray with a 2-in [5-cm] space between them. Loosely cover with plastic wrap and proof at room temperature for 2½ hours.

4. Preheat the oven to 375°F [190°C].

5. Bake for 18 to 20 minutes. The clouds should be a golden brown color when they are done. Allow to cool before finishing them. To finish, brush the Lemon Clouds with melted butter, then roll them in sugar.

In the summer, we know that the pastry kitchen is getting close to the end of their day when we see the biscuits being made. The day bakers mix and portion them and the night bakers do the final baking hours later, so that they are as fresh as possible for morning delivery.

We make lots of complicated breads and pastries, but sometimes it's the simplest items that we crave the most. These biscuits are basic and relatively straightforward to make, a favorite of our summer menu. People eat them plain for breakfast or an afternoon snack and use them to make strawberry shortcake for a dinner dessert. Flavorful cream and butter are the shining ingredients in this recipe, so feel free to indulge in the best you can find.

SWEET CREAM DROP BISCUITS

makes 12 biscuits

All-purpose flour	3 cups plus 2 Tbsp	440 g
Granulated sugar	¼ cup	55 g
Baking powder	2 Tbsp	28 g
Sea salt	½ tsp	
Unsalted butter, cold	½ cup plus 2 Tbsp	145 g
Whole milk, cold	1 cup	235 g
Heavy cream, cold	1 cup	245 g
Demerara sugar for sprinkling tops		

1. Preheat the oven to 375°F [190°C].

2. In a large mixing bowl, combine the flour, sugar, baking powder, and salt. Mix with a wooden spoon to combine evenly.

3. Dice the cold butter into ½-in [1.5-cm] pieces and add to the dry ingredients. Using your fingers or a pastry blender, work the butter into the flour mixture until it's reduced to pea-sized pieces. It also helps to pick up the mixture and rub it together between your palms. This step is important for creating tender biscuits. The butter coats the grains of flour, making it less possible to form long gluten strands that would give the biscuits a chewy rather than tender texture.

4. Make a well in the center of the ingredients, and pour in the milk and heavy cream. Use a fork to gently mix the wet and dry ingredients together until homogeneous. Let the mixture sit in the bowl for 15 minutes. This will allow the dry ingredients to fully absorb the wet ingredients without overmixing.

5. Using a 2-oz [59-ml] portioner or a ¼-cup measure, drop level scoops of biscuit batter onto a sheet tray lined with parchment paper. Leave at least 3 in [7.5 cm] between the biscuits to allow for spreading during baking. Sprinkle Demerara sugar on the tops of the biscuits.

6. Bake the biscuits for 13 to 15 minutes, or until golden brown on the bottom and edges. Let cool to room temperature before serving.

We went through a period of nostalgia in the pastry kitchen, making flavorful versions of our childhood favorites. This graham cracker recipe is from that period. Our tastes have changed since childhood, so we made an adult version that is quite gingery.

Wednesdays are Graham Day in the pastry kitchen, and these crackers rule the day. The pastry leaders make their plans around the hundreds of graham crackers that need to be made. First the dough is made and portioned, and then it's rolled out super thin (no small job when we're making so many) and marked and scored and then finally baked. When 30 trays of grahams come out of the oven at one time, the toasted wheat, honey, and ginger aroma is fantastic.

This is a good recipe for practicing your dough-rolling skills. Make it when you're feeling patient, calm, and up for a little challenge. It's good to do this in a cool environment.

GRAHAM CRACKERS

makes twenty-four 4-by-4-in [10-by-10-cm] squares

Unsalted butter, room temperature	1 cup	225 g
Granulated sugar	½ cup plus 1 Tbsp	115 g
Brown sugar	½ cup plus 2 Tbsp (packed)	115 g
Large egg	1	
Honey	1 Tbsp	
All-purpose flour	2¼ cups	315 g
Whole wheat flour	½ cup	75 g
Baking soda	1 tsp	
Ground cinnamon	1 tsp	
Ground ginger	1 tsp	

1. In a mixing bowl, combine the butter, granulated sugar, and brown sugar. Beat with a wooden spoon to cream the mixture well. If you prefer to use a stand mixer, use the paddle attachment and a medium speed. Add the egg and honey, and beat until light and creamy.

2. In a separate bowl, combine the all-purpose flour, whole wheat flour, baking soda, cinnamon, and ginger. Mix until evenly combined. Add the dry ingredients to the creamed mixture and stir to combine completely. All the dry ingredients should be fully incorporated into the butter mixture.

3. Once the dough comes together, scrape it out of the bowl onto an unfloured work surface and knead it for a minute or two, until it is well mixed and holds together.

4. Divide the dough into four pieces. Form each piece into a 6-by-8-in [15-by-20-cm] rectangle. Wrap each rectangle in plastic wrap and chill the dough in the refrigerator for at least 30 minutes. It can be stored in this form for up to a week.

5. When you are ready to begin rolling out your crackers, preheat the oven to 350°F [180°C].

6. After the dough is chilled, remove it from the refrigerator and begin rolling out the crackers. Firmly tap on the wrapped dough with the rolling pin to make it more flexible. Flour your work surface. Unwrap one block of dough at a time and roll it out into a rectangle that is 12 in long by 8 in wide [30 by 20 cm]. As you are rolling the dough, move it often to ensure that it's not sticking to the work surface. The dough should be about ⅛ in [4 mm] thick.

7. Trim off any uneven edges of the dough to make nice straight sides, and mark the dough all over in an organized pattern with a fork to give it that characteristic look of graham crackers.

continued

8. To turn the dough into crackers, mark the dough every 4 in [10 cm] across the top, bottom, and sides. Using a ruler and pizza cutter, connect the marks to divide the dough into 4-in [10-cm] squares. Using a paring knife, lightly score each square down the middle with a line from the top to the bottom.

9. Transfer the squares with a spatula to a parchment-lined baking sheet. Leave ½ in [12 mm] between the squares to allow them to spread during baking. Bake the graham crackers for 10 minutes, until the edges are slightly browned and the dough has puffed up and set.

10. While the crackers are baking, prepare the next piece of dough. Continue the process until all of the crackers have been baked. When stored in an airtight container, these keep for several weeks.

AMY: *Every morning we make coffee cakes in the pastry kitchen. We start with sour cream and move through our repertoire. It's a constant. The making of coffee cakes is a sign that all is right in the world, at least in the Bakehouse world.*

The New Deli Crumb Cake is the most recent addition to our repertoire. It's a fun twist on a classic American crumb cake. We love crumb cake and wanted to make our own version. We also love Indian spices, hence the name New Deli (Delhi, get it?). Soon after we developed this cake, we met a fantastic family from Montreal, Canada, who own a spice company, Épices de Cru. They travel the world to find the most flavorful spices available. We use their spices for this cake, grinding them the day we make the cake to get the most intense and fresh flavors possible. You may not have access to Épices de Cru spices, but you can buy whole spices and grind them rather than using preground spices. It will make a remarkable difference in your crumb topping.

We like to serve this cake with a little fresh fruit and an appropriately flavored gelato or ice cream, like mango, coconut, or ginger. It's great as an afternoon treat with hot tea too.

For the best results with this cake, make the crumb topping the night before and let it air-dry on a sheet tray. Pressed for time? Dry the topping out in the oven a little before using it. If you put it on the cake without any of these adjustments, it will sink into the batter more than is optimal. Still tasty, just not as pretty.

NEW DELI CRUMB CAKE

makes one 9-in [23-cm] round cake

Topping

Topping		
Coconut oil	1 Tbsp	14 g
Unsalted butter, melted	3 Tbsp	45 g
All-purpose flour	⅓ cup plus 1 Tbsp	60 g
Muscovado brown sugar	5 Tbsp (packed)	60 g
Sea salt	½ tsp	
Ground cardamom	½ tsp	
Ground ginger	½ tsp	
Ground cloves	⅛ tsp	
Sweetened flaked coconut	½ cup	30 g
Coarsely chopped pistachios	½ cup	50 g

Cake

Cake		
Granulated sugar	1¼ cups	260 g
Unsalted butter, room temperature	½ cup plus 3 Tbsp	150 g
Large eggs	2	
Sour cream	½ cup plus 2 Tbsp	150 g
Vanilla extract	1 tsp	
All-purpose flour	1½ cups	220 g
Baking soda	½ tsp	
Sea salt	½ tsp	

Make the Topping

1. If possible, make the topping the day before and let it dry overnight. Doing so makes it less heavy, and it will be less likely to sink into the batter.

2. Melt the coconut oil and butter together in a small skillet. In a small mixing bowl, combine the flour, brown sugar, sea salt, cardamom, ginger, and cloves. Add the melted coconut oil and butter to the dry ingredients and combine with a fork until well mixed and crumbly. Take care not to overmix it, or it will turn into a paste. Add the coconut and pistachios and mix with your fingers to combine. Spread the topping on a sheet tray and let it dry.

continued

Make the Cake

1. Preheat the oven to 300°F [150°C]. Prepare a 9-in [23-cm] round cake pan by spraying the sides and bottom with nonstick cooking spray. Set aside.

2. Combine the sugar and butter in the bowl of a stand mixer. Cream with the paddle attachment on medium speed until the color lightens. Add the eggs, one at a time, creaming thoroughly after adding each one until the mixture is homogeneous. Add the sour cream and vanilla. Mix until light and creamy.

3. Combine the flour, baking soda, and salt in a separate bowl. Mix to combine. Add the dry ingredients gradually to the creamed mixture and mix until smooth and homogeneous.

4. Pour the batter into the prepared cake pan and use a spatula to spread the batter evenly. Evenly distribute the topping over the cake batter. Make sure to put topping along the edge.

5. Bake the cake for 55 minutes. The topping should be golden brown, and a toothpick or small knife inserted in the center of the cake should come out clean. Set aside to cool to room temperature before serving.

Looking for a tasty, very approachable, easy-to-make dessert for a potluck or picnic? This is it. The list of ingredients is long, but it's a one-bowl wonder. The pecans and the coconut can easily be left out if you prefer.

We started baking Hummingbird Cake for Zingerman's Roadhouse when it opened in 2003. At that time, we made a variety of American desserts, but we had not actively focused on southern baking. The Roadhouse features classic American dishes from around the country with a strong emphasis on barbecue and southern cuisine, and this cake seemed like a natural fit. It has since become a customer favorite in our own shop and at the Delicatessen, and it is a common choice for wedding cakes.

What does this have to do with the flow of our day? Well, the cake decorators have a precise order for their icing work. They start with vanilla Swiss buttercream and always end with cream cheese, which is what we put on this cake. We know that they're at the end of one part of their day when cream cheese frosting is in the mixing bowls.

HUMMINGBIRD CAKE

makes one 9-by-13-in [23-by-33-cm] cake

Cake

Pecans	¾ cup	85 g
Granulated sugar	1½ cups	305 g
All-purpose flour	2½ cups	355 g
Baking soda	1 tsp	
Sea salt	1 tsp	
Ground cinnamon	1 tsp	
Large eggs	2	
Vegetable oil	1¼ cups	230 g
Mashed bananas, very ripe	1½ cups	320 g
Vanilla extract	1 tsp	
Coconut extract	½ tsp	
Sweetened flaked coconut	¾ cup	70 g
Crushed pineapple	¾ cup	160 g

Frosting

Cream cheese, room temperature	½ cup	115 g
Unsalted butter, room temperature	½ cup	115 g
Vanilla extract	½ tsp	
Lemon juice	1 tsp	
Powdered sugar, sifted	2½ cups	230 g
Toasted, chopped pecans for decoration (optional)		

Make the Cake

1. Preheat the oven to 325°F [165°C]. Spray a 9-by-13-in [23-by-33-cm] cake pan with nonstick cooking spray and set aside.

2. Toast the pecans on a sheet tray. If you will be removing the cake from the pan and decorating the sides with chopped pecans, add more pecans for that purpose. Though the toasting typically takes 10 to 12 minutes, start checking them after 8 minutes. The browning happens suddenly when the nuts are heated to the point that their oil comes to the surface, and they can burn quickly. Use your nose while you bake! You will notice a toasty aroma when they are nearly ready. When they are done, remove them from the oven, let them cool completely, and then chop them into ¼-in [6-mm] pieces. Turn the oven down to 300°F [150°C].

continued

3. In a mixing bowl, combine the sugar, flour, baking soda, salt, and cinnamon. Add the eggs, vegetable oil, and bananas to the dry ingredients. Stir well to moisten the dry ingredients. Add the vanilla extract, coconut extract, coconut, pineapple, and pecans (reserving some for decoration if desired) and stir until everything is well incorporated.

4. Pour the batter into the prepared pan. Bake for 60 minutes, until the cake bounces back in the middle when pressed gently and a toothpick comes out clean. The cake will release from the sides of the pan. Let the cake cool before frosting. It can be iced in the pan or out, depending on your preference.

Make the Frosting

1. While the cake is baking, make the frosting. In the bowl of a stand mixer fitted with the paddle attachment, lightly beat the cream cheese until there are no lumps remaining. Add the butter and combine until smooth. Add the vanilla extract and lemon juice. Stir. Slowly add the powdered sugar until it is moistened, and then stir until completely smooth.

2. Spread the frosting on the cooled cake. Make a decorative pattern if you feel inspired. If you've removed the cake from the pan, put a small amount of icing on the sides and then coat the sides with toasted, chopped pecans.

3. Store this cake in the refrigerator because of the frosting. Remove it from the fridge an hour or two before serving for the best flavor and texture.

doctor bird cake

Hummingbird cake is so named because it is sweet enough to attract hummingbirds. In Jamaica, though, where the recipe originated, it's called doctor bird cake. Doctor bird is a nickname for Jamaica's national bird, the Red-billed Streamertail, which is a type of hummingbird. Jamaicans call the bird the "doctor bird" because of the similarities between a hummingbird probing flowers with its beak and a doctor prodding a patient during an examination.

How did this cake get to America? In 1968, Air Jamaica began flying from Kingston and Montego Bay to Miami and New York. The icon on the tails of the planes was none other than Jamaica's national bird. To increase interest in travel to the country, Jamaica's tourist board put together some promotional kits to send to the United States. The kits included recipes for some local foods, among which was doctor bird cake.

The cake quickly gained popularity in the South. There are numerous references to the cake in county fair reports and baking competitions throughout the 1970s, although not always under the same name. Variations of the name include Doctor Byrd cake after a familiar regional name dating back to early Virginia and then finally the more generalized name of hummingbird cake. The first printed recipe for the cake appeared in Southern Living *magazine in February 1978. Hummingbird cake has since become the most requested recipe in* Southern Living's *history.*

Adapted from a blog post written by Bakehouse baker Nina Plasencia.

Palóc leves (pal-OWTS lev-esh) *is a rich soup commonly made in northeastern Hungary. It is named after the Palóc tribe that lived in that area and is flavored with the most commonly used Hungarian spices—caraway, marjoram, and paprika. It also uses the favorite fats of Hungary—sour cream and lard.*

Hungarian soups are thickened in a variety of ways. The most distinctive is the method used in this recipe. We combine flour with sour cream, which we add to the base of the soup before cooking. This soup is unusual because of its use of lamb, which is not very common in modern Hungarian cooking but was more popular prior to World War II, particularly in this region. In Communist times, many indigenous breeds of animals were lost in favor of breeds that could be raised on industrial-sized farms. In today's Hungary, the heirloom breeds like gray cattle and Mangalica pigs are slowly making a comeback.

On one of our trips to Hungary, we drove to a small village three hours northeast of Budapest and cooked with a family in their home. They made this soup with us. They used wild ram, which the husband hunted himself on their property two days before our arrival. What an experience! We started serving palóc leves *in our shop soon after, using domestic lamb—no hunting involved and it is just as tasty. This soup is particularly good with* Pogácsa *(page 231).*

PALÓC LEVES
HUNGARIAN LAMB VEGETABLE SOUP
makes 4 to 6 servings

Canola oil	¼ cup	50 g
Diced lamb (½ in [1.5 cm])	2 cups	410 g
Sea salt	2 tsp	12 g
Lard	¼ cup	64 g
Finely chopped onion	1 cup	240 g
Caraway seeds	1½ tsp	
Fresh marjoram	½ tsp	
Sweet paprika	2 Tbsp	18 g
All-purpose flour	¼ cup	36 g
Sour cream	2 cups	410 g
Water	5 cups	1,182 g
Diced potato (½ in [1.5 cm])	2 cups	250 g
Diced carrot (½ in [1.5 cm])	2 cups	210 g
Roasted red pepper, puréed	1	
Green beans, 1-in [2.5-cm] pieces	2 cups	210 g
Salt and ground black pepper to taste		

1. Preheat the oven to 350°F [180°C].

2. Heat the canola oil in a large pot over medium-high heat. When it is hot, add the diced lamb. Season with half of the sea salt. Allow the meat to brown on one side for a few minutes before turning. When the lamb has been browned on all sides, remove it from the pan and set aside in a small bowl. Add the lard to the pot. When it is hot, add the chopped onion and cook until translucent. Add the caraway, marjoram, and paprika to the onions and cook for 1 minute. Return the browned lamb to the pot.

3. In a small bowl, combine the flour, remaining sea salt, and sour cream with a fork. Once it is mixed evenly, add it to the pot. Add the water, diced potato and carrot, and puréed red pepper. Bring to a boil and cover with a lid. Place in the oven for 45 minutes.

4. While the soup is in the oven, steam the green beans separately just until tender and set aside.

5. After 45 minutes, assess the thickness of the soup. Add more water if needed to reach the consistency of a creamy clam chowder. Add the steamed green beans, season to taste with salt and pepper, and enjoy! If not serving right away, cool the soup quickly. You can store it for up to 4 days in an airtight container in the refrigerator.

the flow of the year—
SEASONS AND HOLIDAYS

As we have a distinctive rhythm to our days, we also have a rhythm to our year. Each season brings different foods, some unique tasks, and its own energy. Our financial year begins in August, which makes sense because it coincides with the beginning of our busiest season, the fall.

FALL IN ANN ARBOR

Being in a town with a large university and having a strong connection to the Jewish community, our year starts off with a bang with the return of college students, football season, and the Jewish New Year. After what is usually a steady and peaceful summer, the increased energy of September feels like the beginning to an altogether different reality.

Michigan football is a big event in Ann Arbor—the stadium record is over 115,000 in attendance (it's the biggest stadium in the United States). Football Saturdays start on  Friday nights in the restaurants around town and continue with hours of tailgating on Saturday; the game, of course; maybe dinner out; and often Sunday brunch for out-of-towners. College football has a big impact on our community. Go Blue!

Zingerman's Delicatessen and Roadhouse are busy all weekend, and at the Bakehouse we're baking mounds of the full spectrum of breads and pastries and cakes for them. Rye bread, brownies, American cookies, and sugar cookies in the shape of an M covered in blue fondant and garnished with a football are the biggest sellers. The first big game is often a shock to our system. It takes a little mental adjustment and slight grieving for the summer, and then we embrace our busiest months of the year.

The Jewish High Holidays are our next big event—Challah Daze! All year round, we make a tasty yet simple challah in a braid and a loaf. For the Jewish holidays, we add two more challahs to the repertoire—turban-shaped challahs studded with rum-soaked golden and Flame raisins and a Moroccan challah flavored with anise and brushed with a honey glaze. We bake the challah at the start of our day, in a lower-temperature oven, and then the oven is turned up for the rest of the baking. To make it all happen, our bread team starts two hours earlier. The mixers start at midnight rather than at 2 a.m., and the first bench folks are in at 3 a.m. The sight and taste of the first turbans and Moroccans is exciting. We sample the challah ourselves in those first days, so happy to enjoy the flavors of this holiday. Fiona, our accountant, particularly loves the raisin challah. She stocks up on them and has a freezer full by the end of the season, so that she can enjoy them all year long.

During Rosh Hashanah and Yom Kippur, our pastry bakers make thousands of pieces of rugelach and mandelbrot and plenty of honey cakes. Honey is an important symbolic food for Rosh Hashanah, suggestive of the sweetness of the beginning of a new year full of hope. Regardless of our religious affiliation, many of us are also experiencing the hopefulness of our new year. We have new goals to achieve and new recipes we plan to make. It's a fresh start.

Beyond football and the Jewish holidays, our fall is busy with customers who are ready to eat. It's time for grainy breads, warm cinnamon rolls, apple desserts, and heartier soups. We also plan our first bake of Cornish Beef Pasties. This is a much-anticipated event. Customers start asking for them in August and they don't arrive until October. Our pie selection changes, pumpkin muffins and cupcakes return, and so does apple caramel cake. Our classes fill up with students happy to be inside baking after the long summer.

THE HOLIDAYS

Besides all the planning and tasks associated with changing our menus in the fall, we spend much of our mental energy from August on preparing for "THE HOLIDAYS." This phrase at the bakery refers to the baking we do in November and December for Thanksgiving and Christmas. Why in all caps? It's an intense period of work that determines a large part of our success for the year, and it has an appropriately large impact on everyone's morale. November and December for us are like the playoffs in sports. It's game time, all hands on and everyone in their best position.

During this period, we double the number of bakers in our pastry kitchen and increase the staff in other areas. The bakery is full of people and ingredients and packaging supplies. The mood is a mix of positive energy and focused attention. In the pastry kitchen, we rate the level of busyness for each day and display it in large red numbers on our production board, which shows what we are going to bake during the day. The shop is hustling, taking orders and helping guests taste our offerings as they consider how to celebrate. All of our shelves are overflowing with baked goods.

The cake crew is on a slightly different rhythm than the rest of us. They are just finishing up wedding cake season, which is their busiest time. October is the last month of the season and is often a fairly busy one. They can take a little breather in November, since customers are focused on bread and pies, so they regroup and prepare to make *Bûches de Noël* (Yule logs) in December.

The admin staff check in with the bakers daily to see if they need help. We all bake at Zingerman's Bakehouse. Randy, the sales guy (his official title), works in pastry and bread and delivery and maintenance when necessary. Ally, the sales gal, frequents pastry and cake and the shop. Fiona, our accountant, is great at making rugelach and crimping pies. There are lots of cookies to make—Alex and Jason from purchasing are there to help. Sara, our marketing manager, a former pastry baker and shop manager, frequents her old haunts to contribute wherever she can. Delivery needs help slicing and bagging—we all move over. The shop has lines and more food to merchandise; we're there. It's a team effort.

We (Frankenamy) spend most of our time in November and December in the bakery doing hands-on work—actual baking. It's a time that we particularly love. We get to do the baking that inspired us from the beginning. It's a couple of months when we connect more with everyone on the staff, spending hours standing side by side, often doing repetitive work that allows us to listen, chat, counsel, and joke around. We get to know people better and they get to know us better.

For Thanksgiving, we make thousands of pies, loaves of bread of all kinds, and rolls. An annual favorite from the bread bakery is Cranberry Pecan Bread. It is the same as our Pecan Raisin, but using cranberries instead of raisins. Guests adore it and buy it as gifts and for their own enjoyment.

The bakery is like a mini-United Nations at Christmas, with holiday traditions from all over the world being made. *Beigli*, a Hungarian yeasted walnut or poppy roll, is our newest hit. A longtime favorite is Stollen, the German Christmas bread. There's also the French *Bûche de Noël* from the Cake Studio. Our pastry kitchen could be called the House of Coffee Cakes, sour cream being the biggest seller. Hours are spent each day measuring ingredients, mixing batters, filling pans, baking, and depanning. The smell of cinnamon and toasted walnuts is inescapable (and delicious).

Our biggest single day of baking is the Tuesday before Thanksgiving. Christmas is celebrated by people over a period of days, but Thanksgiving is celebrated by almost all of us on the same day, and most of us shop for the most perishable parts of our meals on the Wednesday before Thanksgiving Day. We bake most of our Thanksgiving food on Tuesday and deliver to our customers on Wednesday, so they're stocked and ready to sell. We are baking around the clock in the bread bakery and the pastry kitchen on this day.

Although we all work harder, longer, and on more varied things during "THE HOLIDAYS," this is many staff members' favorite time of year. I believe that people actually prefer being challenged, stretched a little. We like the feeling of learning and growing. This season of the year requires our mental and physical concentration. I also think it's a beloved time because of the camaraderie and cooperation that it requires. We are all in it together. We

are a team that has made a commitment to our customers and to each other to make sure that we're successful. Many of us come in early, stay late, work six days and sometimes seven, and help on projects we're less familiar with.

It's not easy, but we do things to support one another. Although we express our appreciation for each other with written and verbal thanks throughout the year, it happens even more readily during this intense time. We end all of our meetings with appreciations, and at this time of year the appreciating goes on for a long time. Just when we think it's done, there's a long silence and then someone comes up with a new one, and another round begins. We bring in treats to brighten days. We buy coffee for one another. We make playlists for people to enjoy. Lots of caretaking goes on.

During Thanksgiving week and again during Christmas week we have a special day of catered meals so that we can celebrate a holiday meal together. Zingerman's Mail Order sends us pizza one day in December every year as a thank-you (since so much of what we bake gets sent out by them). It's a period of challenge, achievement, cooperation, appreciation, and plain old tons of baking. We love it! Knowing that people are excited about what we do and that we're going to contribute in a delicious way to our guests' holidays makes it worthwhile.

And then December 25th comes. The bakery that had been full of laughter and music and the energy of hustling bakers and drivers and sales staff and smells of chocolate and toasting nuts is silent and empty. It's amazing and eerie and a little hard to get used to. The change in pace is jarringly sudden. It's as if there's a big red holiday Stop button somewhere that was just hit. It's done. All over. Go home. Our holiday bakers stop coming. Our warehouse and walk-in refrigerators are almost empty. The customers' orders are so small that we laugh and then cry a little bit in relief. It was a job well done.

WINTER DOLDRUMS

Next are the slow months of January, February, and March. Time to recover. It's the slowest period of the year and it's cold outside, with gray skies day after day. Retail customers stop coming for a few weeks as they try to maintain their New Year's resolution about eating less or maybe start anticipating a tropical vacation in February. It's easy for many of us to get low during this time. We struggle to adjust to the lack of intensity. Sometimes we bicker. We get nothing done for two or three weeks, and then we try to get into a different kind of work mode—work on new food, start selling to new customers, engage in some training, try to get better at what we do.

During this period there are little holidays. We're busy for a week around Valentine's Day, and then there's the Jewish holiday of Purim, when we make Hamantaschen. There's Fat Tuesday when we makes thousands of *Pączki* (a Polish doughnut, see page 166). Our energy starts to return. We hold cake consults with newly engaged couples planning their summer weddings. We make new display cakes for our consult room. These are bright spots in the winter gloom.

SPRING AND SUMMER

Then it comes—our busy spring with Passover, Easter, and University of Michigan graduation. Each holiday has its unique set of foods that we enjoy making and eating. The pastry kitchen and cake studio make special Passover treats, like coconut macaroons. For Easter, pastry tends to make lots of our fancier desserts with fruit and lemon curd. Bread makes hot cross buns and what is now our biggest seller for Easter, the Hungarian *Somodi Kalács*, an indulgent, buttery sweet bread that none of us can seem to get enough of. Easter is also a big cake holiday, with decorations that include spring flowers, chicks, and eggs. It usually feels springlike out, and people feel celebratory. We might even have some real blooming flowers. Hope is in the air. The snow and cold have receded. The sun is out.

Before we know it, the school year is coming to an end and we're helping the community celebrate graduations, with lots of cakes. Then we move to Mother's Day, which, strangely, is a big scone holiday for us. (Father's Day isn't ever a big deal. Frank claims it's because no one cares about fathers. Amy thinks fathers want things other than bread and pastries.)

Then it's on to summer food. Special cold soups in the shop. Fruit tarts. Hamburger buns for grilling. We have big fruit pie weekends around Memorial Day, July 4, and Labor Day. As most of the bakery settles into a more predictable, calm summer routine, our Cake Studio is going full force with wedding season. Every Friday and Saturday we see gorgeous, unique creations on their way to wedding venues all over southeastern Michigan.

And then we look at the calendar and it's August again. Time to start planning for "THE HOLIDAYS." The recipes included in this chapter make us think of these seasons.

staff favorite breads and pastries

We want the staff to be able to enjoy our food and to know it well enough from their own experiences of eating it that they can actively participate in improving it. For those two reasons, we can each have a free loaf of bread for each day that we work, and we get a big discount on any sweet things we order. Here are the staff favorites, across all seasons.

Breads

- *Parmesan Pepper*
- *Pecan Raisin*
- *Cranberry Pecan*
- *Somodi Kalács*
- *Cinnamon Raisin*

Pastries

- *Mini pastries for parties—little éclairs, little lemon tarts, tiny cream puffs*
- *Decorated cupcakes*
- *Sour Cream Coffee Cake*
- *Pecan Pie*
- *Brownies*

Challah is a braided soft bread enriched with eggs, oil, and honey, first made in this form by Ashkenazi Jews in 15th-century Europe. The braiding was an adaptation from a local Teutonic bread. Challah started as a plain bread that, over the course of the 15th century, became more enriched. It was not sweetened until the early 19th century, when sugar became more available and more affordable all over Europe. Then, as now, challah was used to celebrate the Jewish Sabbath and other religious occasions.

We love our challah as it is, but we also bake two fancier versions. For the Jewish High Holidays we bake a challah studded with rum-soaked raisins and shaped like a turban. The spiral of the turban represents the circularity of life. We also make a Moroccan version of challah, flavored with sesame, poppy, and aromatic anise and brushed with a honey syrup to give it a touch of extra sweetness. We refer to the Jewish High Holidays at the bakery as "Challah Daze" because we're making so many challahs. Having the first taste of the season is something we look forward to.

Challah is wonderful as a daily bread too. The Bakehouse staff chose it as the number 1 bread for French toast.

CHALLAH

makes 1 Loaf

Rum-Soaked Raisins (for Raisin Turban Challah)

Flame raisins	½ cup (packed)	95 g
Golden raisins	½ cup (packed)	95 g
Dark rum	2 Tbsp	25 g

Seed Mix (for Moroccan Challah)

Sesame seeds	2 Tbsp	18 g
Poppy seeds	2 Tbsp	18 g
Anise seeds	2 Tbsp	18 g

Honey Wash (for Moroccan Challah)

Honey	¼ cup	55 g
Water, warm	¼ cup	55 g

Dough

Water, room temperature	¾ cup	165 g
Egg yolks	5	75 g
Corn oil	2 Tbsp plus 1 tsp	30 g
Honey	2½ Tbsp	55 g
Instant yeast	1½ tsp	5 g
All-purpose flour	3 cups plus 3 Tbsp	455 g
Sea salt	1½ tsp	9 g
Medium rye flour for dusting		
Cornmeal for dusting		
Sesame or poppy seeds for sprinkling tops (optional)		

Egg Wash

Large egg	1	
Egg yolk	1	
Water	1 Tbsp	

1. If making the Raisin Turban Challah, soak the Flame and golden raisins in the rum the night before baking.

   If making the Moroccan Challah, make the seed mix and divide in two. You'll knead one set into the dough and use the rest to coat the top of the braid. For the honey wash, evenly mix the honey and warm water together, and let cool.

continued

Mix the Dough

1. In a large bowl, combine the water, egg yolks, corn oil, honey, yeast, and half of the all-purpose flour. Mix with a wooden spoon until the mixture becomes a thick batter. Add the remaining flour and the sea salt and mix until the dough becomes a shaggy mass. Scrape the dough out of the mixing bowl onto a clean, unfloured work surface.

2. Knead the dough for 6 to 8 minutes (page 34). It will become smooth and firm during the kneading process.

3. Basic Challah: Place the dough in a lightly oiled container, cover with plastic, and ferment for 1 hour.

   Raisin Turban Challah: Knead the rum-soaked raisins into the dough until they are evenly distributed. Place the dough in a lightly oiled container, cover with plastic, and ferment for 1 hour.

   Moroccan Challah: Add one set of the seed mixture to the dough. Knead until the seeds are evenly distributed. Cut the dough into small pieces with a dough knife or bench scraper and knead them back together repeatedly until there are no pockets of seeds or streaks of plain dough. Place the dough in a lightly oiled container, cover with plastic, and ferment for 1 hour.

Shape the Basic Challah

1. After 1 hour of fermentation, turn the plain dough out of the container onto a lightly floured work surface and divide into six equal pieces. Shape each piece of dough into a round, cover, and let rest for 5 minutes.

2. Now we start braiding the challah. Form each piece into a 10-in [25-cm] long cylinder with tapered ends. Toss the strands with medium rye flour and shake off the excess. Attach three of the strands together at one end, pressing together firmly. Repeat with the three remaining strands. Then attach the two groups of strands together so that three stick out to the left and three stick out to the right.

3. Finally, shape the loaf into a six-strand braid, as shown in the illustration. Place the braid onto a cornmeal-covered work surface. Make the egg wash by beating together the egg, egg yolk, and water, and brush the braid with some of it.

Shape the Raisin Turban Challah

1. After 1 hour of fermentation, turn the raisin dough out onto a lightly floured work surface and gently shape into a loose round. Cover and let rest for 15 minutes. Then flip it over and shape into a cylinder about 2½ feet [76 cm] long. As you roll it out, one end should remain blunt while the other is tapered to a point.

2. Roll the whole cylinder in medium rye flour. The rye flour won't get absorbed into the dough, so you'll be able to see the definition of the shape. Roll the cylinder into a turban shape, beginning with the blunt end in the center and rolling the tapered tail around it gently. Be careful not to roll the turban too tightly, or it may pop out as it proofs or bakes.

3. Tuck the last bit of the tapered end under the bottom of the turban and pinch it there. Place the turban on a cornmeal-covered work surface. Make the egg wash by beating together the egg, egg yolk, and water, and brush the turban with some of it.

Shape the Moroccan Challah

1. After 1 hour of fermentation, turn the Moroccan dough out onto a lightly floured surface and divide it into five pieces. Shape each piece into a round, cover, and let rest for 5 minutes.

2. Make a five-strand braid as follows: Shape each piece into a 10-inch [25-cm] long cylinder with tapered ends. Toss the strands in medium rye flour and attach the strands together at one end, pressing firmly. Braid as shown in the illustration ending by attaching the strands together. Brush the braid with the honey wash and roll it in the remaining seed mixture. Place it onto a cornmeal-covered surface, right side up. The Moroccan Challah does not get an egg wash.

Proof and Bake the Challah

1. Let the loaves ferment for 1½ hours, until they are at least 1½ times their original size.

2. Preheat a baking stone in your oven to 325°F [165°C] for 45 minutes.

3. When fully fermented, brush the Basic Challah and Raisin Turban with egg wash a second time (and sprinkle with sesame or poppy seeds, if desired). Transfer to a lightly floured peel. Load onto the baking stone to bake for approximately 25 minutes, or until golden brown and the internal temperature is at least 190°F [88°C].

4. Remove the challah from the oven, place on a wire rack, and cool completely.

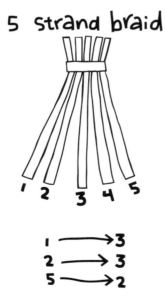

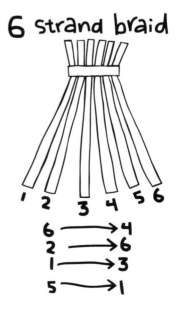

PECAN RAISIN BREAD (OR CRANBERRY PECAN)

makes 2 loaves

Water, room temperature	1¼ cups	275 g
"Put Away Farm" (page 41)	1½ cups minus 1 Tbsp	235 g
Bread flour	2½ cups	365 g
Sea salt	1½ tsp	9 g
Flame raisins (or dried cranberries)	1½ cups	235 g
Pecans	2 cups	235 g
Cornmeal for dusting		

1. Put the water in a large mixing bowl. Tear the "Put Away Farm" into small pieces and add to the water. Add half of the bread flour and beat with a wooden spoon until the dough is a smooth batter. Add the remaining bread flour and salt. Mix until the dough is rough and shaggy.

2. Turn the dough out of the bowl onto a clean, unfloured work surface, scraping any bits of dough from the bowl. Knead the dough for 6 minutes (page 34). It will be sticky at this point.

3. Spread the dough out and gently form it into a rectangle. Spread the raisins and pecans onto the rectangle. Carefully gather up the edges of the dough, keeping the raisins and pecans inside. Knead for another 2 to 3 minutes, or until the raisins and pecans are uniformly distributed in the dough.

4. Return to a lightly oiled bowl and cover with plastic. Ferment the dough for 1 hour. Uncover and place the dough on a lightly floured work surface. Fold the dough (page 34). Place it back into the bowl, cover, and ferment for 1 hour. Uncover, place on a lightly floured work surface, and fold the dough again. Place it back in the bowl, cover, and ferment for 1 hour and 45 minutes. Uncover and place the dough on a lightly floured work surface and fold the dough for a third time. Return to the bowl and cover. Ferment the dough for 1 hour. Uncover and place the dough on a lightly floured work surface. Divide into two pieces.

5. Lightly flour the work surface again and place the dough pieces down onto the flour. Flatten each into a disk 6 in [15 cm] in diameter and about 2½ in [6 cm] thick.

6. By pulling the top surface toward you and pressing back into the dough, shape each piece into a football shape. Place the loaves seam side down on a board dusted with cornmeal and cover with plastic. Proof for 2½ to 3 hours. Use the touch test (page 38) to see if the loaves are ready for the oven.

7. Forty-five minutes before baking, preheat the oven with a baking stone and a cast iron skillet (for creating steam) to 450°F [230°C].

8. Uncover and place the loaves side by side on a lightly floured peel. Using a razor blade or sharp knife, make three parallel diagonal cuts, each 2½ in [6 cm] long, that overlap each other by ½ in [1.5 cm]. Start the first cut 1½ in [4 cm] from the top point of the loaf and end the third cut 1½ in [4 cm] from the bottom point of the loaf.

9. Slide the loaves onto the baking stone and add steam to the oven (page 38). Keep covered for about 8 minutes. Uncover and continue baking for 25 to 35 minutes, until they are nicely browned and sound hollow when tapped on the bottom. Remove from the oven and cool completely on a wire rack.

Dios Beigli (di-OSH BAY-glee) *is a beloved treat in Hungary, found in bakeries all year round but especially at Christmas. It's a yeasted roll, long and narrow, with a sweet filling, usually walnut (dios) or poppy. It's a little like a yeasted rétes (strudel). The exterior has a distinctive crackled, mahogany-colored crust.*

Since pork is the primary meat in Hungary, they still use lard in their baking. You'll see that this recipe calls for a mixture of lard and butter. If you'd prefer not to use lard, just increase the amount of butter accordingly. More butter is never a bad choice! If you want to make the poppy seed version, use the poppy filling from our Hamantaschen recipe (page 151).

This recipe was taught to us by the Auguszt family, fifth-generation master Hungarian bakers residing in Budapest.

DIOS BEIGLI
HUNGARIAN WALNUT ROLL

makeS 2 rolLS, each ServinG 6

Dough

Water, room temperature	6 Tbsp	85 g
Instant yeast	1½ tsp	5 g
Cake flour	⅔ cup plus 1 Tbsp	85 g
All-purpose flour	1¾ cups	250 g
Unsalted butter, room temperature	5 Tbsp	70 g
Lard, room temperature	5 Tbsp	70 g
Powdered sugar	½ cup	65 g
Sea salt	¾ tsp	

Walnut Filling

Walnuts	2¾ cups	325 g
Dry bread crumbs	⅔ cup	85 g
Lemon zest	⅓ cup	35 g
Honey	4 Tbsp	90 g
Granulated sugar	¾ cup	160 g
Vegetable oil	⅓ cup plus 4 tsp	90 g
Water	⅓ cup	75 g
Flame raisins	¼ cup	35 g

Egg Wash

Large eggs, separated	2	

Make the Dough

1. In a mixing bowl, combine the water, instant yeast, and cake flour. Add the all-purpose flour, butter, lard, powdered sugar, and salt. Stir minimally and then use your hands to knead the mixture until it comes together into a ball and the dough feels smooth.

2. Turn the dough out of the bowl and cut it into two pieces of equal size. Flatten each piece into a 6-in [15-cm] square and wrap in plastic wrap. Refrigerate for 1 hour (or longer, but no longer than 8 hours), and take this time to prepare the filling.

continued

Make the Filling

1. Grind two-thirds of the walnuts finely in a food processor. Roughly chop the remaining walnuts.

2. In a large bowl, use a wooden spoon to mix the ground and chopped walnuts with the bread crumbs and lemon zest.

3. In a small saucepan, combine the honey, granulated sugar, oil, water, and raisins. Bring to a boil. Remove from the heat, add to the nut mixture, and stir well. Spread the filling out on a baking sheet to cool.

Assemble and Bake the Beigli

1. When the dough has chilled, remove it from the refrigerator. Place on a lightly floured work surface, and use a rolling pin to gently tap it to soften it enough to roll.

2. Roll each piece to a rectangle that is 10 by 12 in [25 by 30 cm], with the short edge closest to you. Brush the edges with water and fold over ½ in [1.5 cm] of dough on each side and on the bottom short edge closest to you.

3. Place half of the filling on each piece of dough and spread evenly all the way to the folded edges, leaving about 1 in [2.5 cm] without filling on the short side farthest from you. Starting from the short side closest to you, roll up the dough into a cylinder and place on a baking sheet lined with parchment paper, seam side down.

4. To make the egg wash, using a fork, gently beat the egg whites in one bowl and the egg yolks in another bowl. Brush the exterior of the beigli with the beaten egg yolks. Set the whites aside.

5. Cover loosely with plastic wrap, and ferment by letting sit at a warm temperature for about 40 minutes. Brush with the beaten egg whites.

6. Chill the beigli for 30 minutes and preheat the oven to 350°F [180°C]. The chilling will help create the crackled appearance of the exterior.

7. After the beigli have chilled, use a fork (or an ice pick if you have one) to make delicate holes, evenly spaced, along the body and sides of the beigli. Push the fork deeply into the rolls. Fifteen piercings will be adequate. This allows steam to escape from the rolls as they are baking and helps the beigli to maintain their cylindrical shape.

8. Bake for 20 minutes, and then lower the temperature to 325°F [165°C] and bake for another 35 to 40 minutes, or until the beigli are a beautiful mahogany color. Let cool completely, and then slice and serve.

This quintessential German Christmas bread is one of the all-time best treats from the Bakehouse and has an all-star list of ingredients. We've been making it since 1993, and we can't imagine Christmas without it. It is a bit of a project in that there are numerous steps, but none of them is actually difficult. They just take time. The dried fruit needs to be macerated the day before, and then it takes about four hours of total time before baking, only two of which are actual work time.

We first learned this recipe from Michael London, and it is a classic Michael London delight. What do we mean by that? Michael's recipes are super indulgent with ingredients. He has taught us not to be skimpy, to put that little bit more in. It makes a huge difference. In this stollen there's almost not enough dough to hold all of the dried fruit together, and it is brushed with rum butter three times and coated in cinnamon sugar and then in powdered sugar. It's all worth it!

STOLLEN

makes 2 Loaves

Filling

Flame raisins	⅓ cup	40 g
Golden raisins	⅔ cup	80 g
Currants	⅔ cup	80 g
Dried cherries	½ cup	70 g
Candied orange peel	2 Tbsp	30 g
Candied lemon peel	2 Tbsp	30 g
Chopped toasted almonds	⅓ cup	40 g
Lemon zest	1½ Tbsp	
Lemon juice	1 Tbsp	8 g
Orange zest	1½ Tbsp	
Orange juice	1 Tbsp	5 g
White rum	3 Tbsp	40 g

Sponge

Instant yeast	2 tsp	8 g
Granulated sugar	1 Tbsp	20 g
Whole milk	¼ cup plus 1 Tbsp	80 g
All-purpose flour	¾ cup plus 2 Tbsp	125 g

Final Dough

Whole milk	3 Tbsp	45 g
Large egg	1	
Vanilla extract	1 tsp	
Granulated sugar	1 Tbsp	20 g
All-purpose flour	1⅔ cups	240 g
Sea salt	1 tsp	
Unsalted butter, room temperature	½ cup plus 3 Tbsp	150 g

Rum Butter

Unsalted butter, melted	½ cup	115 g
White rum	¼ cup	55 g

Finishing

Granulated sugar	½ cup	90 g
Ground cinnamon	2 tsp	
Powdered sugar for dusting		

continued

Mix the Filling

1. Combine the Flame raisins, golden raisins, currants, cherries, orange and lemon peel, almonds, lemon zest and juice, orange zest and juice, and rum in a medium bowl. Cover and refrigerate overnight.

Make the Sponge

1. In a medium bowl, combine the yeast, sugar, and milk. Mix to combine. Add the flour and mix with a wooden spoon until the mixture is well combined. Cover and ferment for 1 hour at room temperature.

Make the Dough

1. In a large bowl, using a wooden spoon, mix the milk, egg, and vanilla extract. Add the sugar and stir well.

2. Tear the sponge into 2-in [5-cm] pieces and combine with the egg mixture. It will not be homogeneous at this point. Add half of the flour and stir with the spoon until the mixture is a thick batter. Add the remaining flour and the salt. Mix until the dough is a shaggy mass.

3. Turn the dough out onto a clean, unfloured work surface and knead for 3 minutes (page 34). It may be sticky at first, and you may be tempted to add flour, but don't!

4. Now add the soft butter bit by bit while kneading until all the butter is incorporated. This will take several minutes of kneading. The dough will be sticky; use a scraper to keep scraping the dough off the work surface. At the end of the kneading, the dough will feel buttery and will have developed some integrity.

5. Let the dough rest on the work surface for 5 minutes. Pat the dough into a flat disk. Add the fruit filling and enclose it in the dough. Knead the dough until the fruit mixture is evenly distributed throughout the dough, 1 to 2 minutes. Some of the fruit will fall out of the dough. Be patient: add it back in and keep kneading. Place the dough in a lightly oiled bowl, cover the bowl, and ferment for 1 hour.

Shape and Bake the Stollen

1. Turn the dough out onto a lightly floured work surface and divide into two equal pieces. Shape each piece into a batard or football shape about 9 in [23 cm] long (page 35). Make this shape as tight as you can roll it.

2. Now it's time to make the traditional stollen shape. Using a lightly floured dowel rod or wooden spoon handle, press down on each loaf 2 in [5 cm] from the edge, from one end to the other, and repeat on the other side. This creates a clear indentation on both sides of the football shape and a concentrated amount of dough in the center. Make the indentations very deep. They will fill in during baking. Repeat on the second loaf. This shape is supposed to be reminiscent of baby Jesus wrapped in a blanket.

3. Place the stollen on a parchment-lined baking pan. Make the rum butter by combining the butter and rum, and brush the stollen with some of it. Cover lightly with plastic wrap and proof for 1 hour.

continued

4. Preheat the oven to 325°F [165°C].

5. Brush the stollen with more of the rum butter once again before baking. Bake for 30 to 40 minutes, or until nicely browned and cooked through.

6. Remove the stollen from the oven and poke all over with a fork or skewer. While still warm, brush with the rum butter once again. Combine the granulated sugar and cinnamon and dust the stollen with this mixture. Cool completely. Dust with powdered sugar before serving.

AMY: *This scrumptious triangular filled cookie is eaten to celebrate the Jewish holiday Purim in late winter or early spring. Haman was a vizier of ancient Persia who plotted to kill all the Jews in the empire, and Purim celebrates his defeat by the Persian (and Jewish) queen Esther. It was one of my favorite holidays when I was little, because we were encouraged to make lots of noise in synagogue to drown out the name of the evil Haman as the rabbi read the story. It was probably the most joyful day of the year in synagogue from my child's perspective.*

Why are these cookies triangular, and what does the name mean, anyway? Oy. It's quite a story. The name is German and means "Haman's pocket" and may refer to the bribes Haman took as vizier. It has also come to mean "Haman's hat." Either way, it's clear that these cookies are a celebration of the delicious sweetness of life.

Hamantaschen are traditionally made either with a short cookie dough or with a yeasted dough. Both are good, and they are quite different. This recipe is for the cookie version, and we've included three fillings for you to choose from: cream cheese, poppy seed, and apricot.

Although this is a traditional Jewish cookie and made for a very specific holiday, it's eaten year round by our guests of all heritages. Cream cheese and apricot are the most popular flavors. Poppy seed and prune are favored by the traditionalists.

HAMANTASCHEN

makes 30 cookies

Filling of your choice	all	
Unsalted butter, room temperature	¾ cup plus 1 Tbsp	175 g
Granulated sugar	⅓ cup plus 1 Tbsp	80 g
Large egg, room temperature	1	
Vanilla extract	1 tsp	
Sea salt	¼ tsp	
All-purpose flour	2 cups plus 1 Tbsp	290 g

Make the Filling

1. Make the cream cheese, poppy seed, or apricot filling; see the recipes that follow. Each filling recipe makes enough for one batch of cookie dough.

Make the Dough

1. In a mixing bowl, cream the butter and sugar until light and creamy. This can be done by hand or in a stand mixer fitted with the paddle attachment on medium speed. Add the egg, vanilla, and salt to the butter mixture and mix until thoroughly combined. Add the flour gradually, and mix until the ingredients are completely combined.

2. Remove the dough from the mixer, press it into a flat square, and wrap it with plastic wrap. Refrigerate for 45 minutes before rolling out and filling. The dough can be kept in the refrigerator for up to a week in this state.

Roll, Fill, and Bake the Hamantaschen

1. Preheat the oven to 350°F [180°C].

2. Remove the dough from the refrigerator. Tap on the dough with your rolling pin to soften it. Once it is more flexible, remove the plastic wrap.

3. Lightly flour the work surface. Place the dough on the floured surface. Lightly flour the top of the dough and roll the dough out until it is ¼ in [6 mm] thick.

4. Using a round cutter 3 in [7.5 cm] in diameter, cut out pieces of the rolled dough and place on a parchment-lined baking sheet. Continue rolling and cutting out the disks. This dough can be reworked and rolled out again.

5. Place a rounded teaspoon of filling in the center of each disk. Brush the edges with water. Now fold the edges up and pinch together three corners to make a triangle shape, with the filling visible in the center. You can start with two sides, making an A shape, and then fold in the third side to finish the triangle. Repeat with all the dough circles. Make sure to pinch the edges well.

continued

6. Bake for 18 to 20 minutes, or until the edges and bottoms of the hamantaschen are golden brown. There is a tendency to underbake these cookies. Go for some color. It will give them a nice toasty flavor.

POPPY SEED FILLING

makes enough for 30 hamantaschen

Poppy seeds	1 cup	135 g
Honey	½ cup	165 g
Granulated sugar	2 tsp	
Heavy cream, room temperature	½ cup plus 2 Tbsp	135 g
Unsalted butter, room temperature	1 Tbsp	20 g
Lemon zest	½ Tbsp	
Orange zest	½ Tbsp	
Chopped Flame raisins	¼ cup	35 g

1. Grind the poppy seeds in a coffee grinder or food grinder as fine as you can make them. The closer they are to the consistency of flour, the better.

2. Put the poppy seeds, honey, sugar, and heavy cream in a saucepan and cook over medium-high heat, stirring occasionally, until the mixture comes to a full boil. Turn the heat down to medium-low and boil, stirring frequently, until the mixture thickens considerably, 6 to 8 minutes. Be careful not to let it burn. When it is properly thickened, it will look like hot boiling mud.

3. Remove from the heat and add the butter, lemon zest, orange zest, and chopped raisins. Stir well. Let cool to room temperature before using.

APRICOT FILLING

makes enough for 30 hamantaschen

Apricot preserves	1½ cups	435 g
Fresh bread crumbs	5 Tbsp	40 g

1. In a bowl, combine the apricot preserves and bread crumbs.

CREAM CHEESE FILLING

makes enough for 30 hamantaschen

Cream cheese, room temperature	1 cup	225 g
Unsalted butter, room temperature	1½ tsp	10 g
Granulated sugar	¼ cup	47 g
Vanilla bean	½ bean	
Extra-large egg yolk	½	
Vanilla extract	1 tsp	

1. In a bowl, combine the cream cheese, butter, and sugar. Beat until smooth. Split the half vanilla bean down the center and scrape out the seeds. (For ways to use the pod, see page 29.)

2. Add the half egg yolk with the vanilla extract and vanilla seeds and mix until smooth. Store in the refrigerator until ready for use.

cream cheese

One of the many perks of working in Zingerman's Community of Businesses is having ready access to the wonderful food our fellow businesses make. Fresh cream cheese made by Zingerman's Creamery has been a real ingredient upgrade for some of our cream cheese needs. What makes it different from the grocery store cream cheese we're all familiar with? It's made as fresh cream cheese was made a hundred years ago: very simply. It's milk, rennet, salt, and cream, and as with many of our breads, the cream cheese benefits from patience and time— the many hours necessary to let it drain naturally. It's free of vegetable gums and preservatives that are common components today.

We use it in our cream cheese filling for hamantaschen, and we eat it with our bagels. This cream cheese is available from Zingerman's Mail Order, www.zingermans.com. You may also be able to find similar cream cheese from artisan dairy producers near you. Using this more flavorful cheese will make a real difference.

Rugelach are the most popular and well-known Jewish cookies in the United States and are definitely the most popular Jewish cookies we make at the bakery. This version is a mix between a cookie and a pastry, with a delicate and flaky dough (two-thirds of the dough is fat—butter and cream cheese) encasing special fillings, sprinkled with sugar, and baked until golden brown.

Rugelach evolved from the Eastern European Jewish cookie called kipfel. In the early 1950s, the name "rugelach" appeared, and now it has taken over. The word seems to come from rug (Slavic for "horn") and lakh (a diminutive plural), thus "little horns."

The original cookie was made with a yeasted dough. The now very common unleavened form was first introduced in the United States in the 20th century because it was easier to make and stayed fresh longer than the yeasted version. The use of cream cheese in the dough started in the early 1950s.

The popularity of rugelach is surprising to us because they're plain looking, without a lot of eye appeal. People who have never tried them are shocked at how good they are. Rugelach can be made in many different flavors—apricot, raspberry, and chocolate, to name a few. This is our most popular flavor—walnuts and currants.

WALNUT AND CURRANT RUGELACH

makes 16 rugelach

Dough

Unsalted butter, room temperature	¾ cup	170 g
Philadelphia cream cheese, room temperature	¾ cup	170 g
Sea salt	½ tsp	
Pastry flour	1 cup plus 3 Tbsp	170 g

Filling

Walnuts	½ cup	55 g
Currants	⅓ cup plus 1 Tbsp	55 g
Granulated sugar	⅓ cup	65 g
Ground cinnamon	1 tsp	

Assembly

Unsalted butter, melted	¼ cup	55 g
Ground cinnamon	1 Tbsp	
Granulated sugar	½ cup plus 2 Tbsp	140 g

Make the Dough

1. Using a stand mixer fitted with the paddle attachment, cream the butter, cream cheese, and salt. Mix until well combined but not airy. Add the flour and mix until fully incorporated.

2. Remove the dough from the mixing bowl and flatten out into an even disk about 8 in [20 cm] in diameter. Wrap in plastic wrap. Refrigerate for at least 30 minutes. The dough needs to chill completely before it is rolled out.

Make the Filling

1. Toast the walnuts on a sheet tray in a 325°F [165°C] oven for 10 to 15 minutes, or until they're a deep golden brown. Let cool, then chop them in a food processor or with a knife until they are the same size as the currants.

2. In a medium bowl, mix the walnuts, currants, sugar, and cinnamon together. Set aside.

continued

Assemble and Bake the Rugelach

1. Preheat the oven to 350°F [180°C].

2. Remove the dough from the refrigerator and unwrap it. Lightly flour a work surface and place the disk of dough on it. Lightly flour the top of the dough and roll the dough into a 14-in [35-cm] circle about ⅛ in [4 mm] thick. Keep moving the dough as you're rolling it to make sure it doesn't stick.

3. Brush the surface of the dough with melted butter and spread the filling mixture on it evenly. With a pastry wheel cutter, cut the dough circle into 16 even, triangular wedges. Starting at the outer edge, roll each piece to the center. The resulting cookie will look like a crescent or a little horn.

4. Mix the cinnamon and sugar. Place the rolled rugelach on a parchment-lined baking sheet, brush the tops with melted butter, and sprinkle with cinnamon sugar. Bake for 28 to 30 minutes. The rugelach should be golden brown and flaky.

Chocolate Chess Pie brings chocolate to the Thanksgiving table, and no one is unhappy with that!

The filling in this pie is smooth and supremely chocolaty. It's like a flourless chocolate cake in a pie crust. To make sure that the filling doesn't separate while baking, it is critical that the eggs be at room temperature. The pie looks unassuming when it's done and could do with a little pie makeup. It's good with whipped cream and chocolate shavings on top, or if you're a fan of meringue, that would work too. Want to keep it simple? Serve it with some citrus or red berries.

Since this pie is all about chocolate, we want a very special chocolate to be the primary ingredient. Fortunately, we have some passionate local chocolatiers to help us out. We use an unsweetened chocolate from a local Michigan company called Mindo. Mindo has a great story. After retiring from the car repair shop they had owned for many years, Jose Meza and Barbara Wilson returned to Meza's home of Ecuador (after 41 years!) and ended up starting a chocolate-making company, with its production kitchen near Ann Arbor. Their chocolate is fantastic (all of the beans they use to make it come from Ecuador), and it's great working with such passionate, innovative, and community-minded people. If you can't find Mindo chocolate, choose another unsweetened chocolate of premier quality when making this pie.

CHOCOLATE CHESS PIE

makes one 9-in [23-cm] pie

Chopped unsweetened chocolate	¼ cup plus 1 Tbsp	55 g
Unsalted butter	¾ cup	170 g
Granulated sugar	1½ cups	315 g
Large eggs	4	
Egg yolk	1	
Sea salt	½ tsp	
Vanilla extract	1½ tsp	
9-in [23-cm] single pie crust, partially blind baked (page 61)		

1. Preheat the oven to 350°F [180°C].

2. In a double boiler, melt the unsweetened chocolate and butter. Set aside to cool slightly. Combine the sugar, whole eggs, egg yolk, sea salt, and vanilla extract in a mixing bowl. Whisk by hand or with an electric mixer until the mixture is smooth and homogeneous. Add the melted chocolate and butter mixture to the egg mixture. Whisk until fully combined.

3. Pour into the cooled, partially baked pie crust. Bake for 45 to 50 minutes, or until the center is set. Test with a toothpick if you're uncertain. Remove from the oven and cool to room temperature before serving.

Coconut Cream Pie marks the beginning of spring at the bakery. We start to make it in April, often just in time for Easter. By April we're all ready to start to eat some nonwinter foods, but it's too early in Michigan for any local fruit. So we decided that creamy and tropical pies—coconut cream and key lime—could mark the beginning of spring for us. Random maybe, but life isn't always rational.

This pie is super indulgent. It has about 3 pounds of thick, rich, creamy filling, and whipped cream on top. Use the most flavorful, full-fat coconut milk you can find, both for texture and for flavor. Notice the toasted coconut that's stirred in. It gives a nice contrasting color in the filling and helps to intensify the coconut flavor.

We have one more tip for a great eating experience. When you prebake the crust, let it get really toasty brown. The toasted butter flavor will make the pie more interesting, and the browning will help the crust hold up better if the pie isn't eaten right away. Bake the crust until it's darker than you're comfortable with. Really! It will taste better.

Although cream pies need to be stored in the fridge, I personally think they have more flavor when they are eaten at room temperature. We highly recommend letting this pie come to room temperature for an hour or two before eating. The texture will be lighter too. Don't worry about the whipped cream. If you use a high-quality cream it will keep its shape at room temperature for a couple of hours.

COCONUT CREAM PIE

makes one 9-in [23-cm] pie

Pie

9-in [23-cm] single pie crust, fully blind baked (page 61)		
Unsweetened flaked coconut	1¼ cups	100 g
Granulated sugar	¾ cup plus 2 Tbsp	180 g
Cornstarch	¼ cup plus 1 ½ tsp	41 g
Sea salt	½ tsp	
Whole milk	1½ cups	340 g
Coconut milk	1½ cups	340 g
Egg yolks	3	45 g
Vanilla extract	1½ tsp	
Unsalted butter	1 Tbsp	15 g

Sweetened Whipped Cream

Vanilla bean	½ bean	
Heavy cream	1½ cups	315 g
Vanilla extract	2 tsp	
Granulated sugar	2 Tbsp	25 g

1. Blind-bake the crust (page 64) and set aside to cool.

Make the Filling and Fill the Pie

1. Lower the oven temperature to 300°F [150°C].

2. Spread the coconut onto a sheet tray. Toast in the oven for 8 minutes. Stir and toast for 2 more minutes, or until golden. Set aside to cool.

3. In a medium saucepan, stir together the sugar, cornstarch, and salt. Add the milk, coconut milk, and egg yolks to the pan and whisk to combine.

4. Cook the filling over medium heat, stirring constantly, until the mixture thickens and comes to a light boil. Continue to cook and stir for 1 minute. Remove from the heat and stir in the toasted coconut (reserving ¼ cup [20 g] for garnish) and the vanilla and butter. Stir until well blended. The mixture will be smooth.

5. Pour the filling into a clean bowl and cover with plastic wrap, making sure the plastic is pressed directly onto the surface of the filling to prevent a skin from forming. Let the cooked filling cool for 30 minutes at room temperature.

continued

6. Stir the mixture again, and pour into the baked pie shell. Press the plastic wrap onto the top of the filling. Refrigerate until completely chilled, at least 2 hours.

Make the Whipped Cream and Top the Pie

1. Prepare the whipped cream while the filling is cooling. Start by splitting the half vanilla bean down the center and scraping out the flavorful seeds. (For ways to use the pod, see page 29.)

2. Put the cream, vanilla extract, vanilla seeds, and sugar in the bowl of a stand mixer fitted with the whisk attachment, and beat until soft peaks form. This can also be whipped by hand in a cold metal bowl, using a balloon whisk. Cover and refrigerate until it is time to cover the pie.

3. Once the pie is chilled, cover it with the sweetened whipped cream. Use a spatula to make decorative peaks in the cream. Garnish with the reserved toasted coconut.

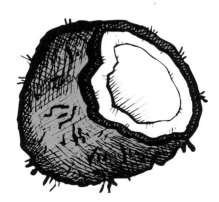

Making Bûche de Noël *at the bakery during December is a joyful sign of the holidays. We start to anticipate and plan in October, start making the decorative mushrooms in November, and then have log-rolling parties in December. It wouldn't be Christmas at the bakery without* Bûche de Noël!

The cake is composed of a rolled sponge or genoiselike cake filled most commonly with chocolate butter-cream and decorated to look like a fallen log. Our version has chocolate buttercream on the exterior and wal-nut rum buttercream on the interior. You could use other combinations if you prefer. Use your imagination!

Creating this holiday centerpiece is a project. You can spread it over many weeks if you prefer. The mush-rooms can be made ahead and kept in an airtight container. The cake can be made, filled with buttercream, rolled, and then frozen a month prior to eating. The remaining buttercream can be frozen too. The final assembly and decorating is best done the day before or the day of serving. You'll need a 12-by-18-in [30-by-46-cm] rectangular cake board.

BÛCHE DE NOËL
makes one 12-in [30-cm] cake

Chiffon Cake

Granulated sugar	1 cup plus 2 Tbsp	230 g
Cake flour	1 cup plus 1 Tbsp	125 g
Baking powder	1½ tsp	
Sea salt	¼ tsp	
Large eggs, separated	4	
Vegetable oil	¼ cup	65 g
Water	⅓ cup	80 g
Vanilla extract	1 tsp	
Cream of tartar	½ tsp	

Buttercreams

Egg whites	6	180 g
Sea salt	½ tsp	
Granulated sugar	1½ cups	295 g
Unsalted butter, room temperature	2 cups	455 g
Vanilla extract	½ tsp	
Chopped chocolate (65% cacao)	½ cup	75 g
Walnuts	1 cup	95 g
Dark rum	½ cup	120 g

Meringue Mushrooms

Egg whites	3	90 g
Granulated sugar	¾ cup	145 g
Cream of tartar	¼ tsp	
Sea salt	¼ tsp	
Vanilla extract	½ tsp	
Chopped chocolate (65% cacao)	2 Tbsp	25 g
Unsweetened cocoa powder for dusting		

Rum Simple Syrup

Water	½ cup	115 g
Granulated sugar	¼ cup	55 g
Dark rum	2 Tbsp	25 g

continued

Make the Cake

1. Preheat the oven to 375°F [190°C]. Line a half-sheet pan (13 by 18 in [33 by 46 cm]) with parchment paper. Do not grease or spray the sides of the pan.

2. In a small bowl, combine ½ cup plus 1 Tbsp [115 g] of the sugar with the cake flour, baking powder, and salt. Stir together with a whisk to combine. Set aside.

3. In a stand mixer fitted with the whisk attachment, combine the egg yolks, oil, water, and vanilla. Mix on low speed to combine. Add the dry ingredients to the wet ingredients. Using the whisk attachment, beat on low speed until the mixture becomes smooth. Scrape the sides of the bowl and mix again to break up any lumps. Set aside. If you have only one mixing bowl, transfer this batter to another large bowl and thoroughly clean the mixing bowl for the next step.

4. In a clean mixing bowl fitted with a clean whisk attachment, add the egg whites and cream of tartar. Whip on medium-high speed until the whites start to form soft peaks. Gradually add the remaining ½ cup plus 1 Tbsp [115 g] sugar to the egg whites in a slow and steady stream. Beat on high speed until the sugar is incorporated and the egg whites are beaten to stiff peaks. Do not overbeat the egg whites or they will become dry and lumpy and will not properly leaven the cake.

5. Working by hand, fold one-fourth of the whipped egg whites into the egg yolk batter to lighten the mixture. Add another one-fourth of the egg whites and fold to combine. Add the last half of the egg whites and fold in. Don't fold too much or the mixture will deflate.

6. Pour the batter gently into the prepared half-sheet pan. Bake the cake for 13 to 15 minutes, or until golden brown and the top springs back when touched.

7. Remove the cake from the oven. While the cake is still warm, run a spatula between the cake and the edges of the pan. Invert the cake onto a new sheet of parchment, remove the existing parchment that lined the baking pan, and tightly roll the cake and clean parchment paper into a tube shape. Roll from the long side (landscape orientation). Cool to room temperature in this shape. This will help the cake "remember" the rolled shape and be less likely to crack when rolled up with the filling.

Make the Buttercream

1. In a mixing bowl, combine the egg whites, salt, and sugar and stir to combine. Place over a pan of simmering water and heat the mixture until the sugar is completely dissolved and the temperature reaches 180°F [82°C]. Stir occasionally during this process. Use a candy or meat thermometer to assess the temperature.

continued

2. Transfer the egg white mixture to the bowl of a stand mixer fitted with the whisk attachment. Whip the mixture on high speed until it doubles in volume, becomes thick and shiny, and has cooled to room temperature. Touch the bottom of the mixing bowl to assess the temperature. The next step is to add the butter. If the egg white mixture is too hot, the butter will melt and ruin the buttercream.

3. Now that the egg mixture is at room temperature, with the mixer on medium speed, add the soft butter, a bit at a time, until all is incorporated. The butter should be approximately the same temperature as the egg mixture to ensure easy incorporation and a smooth texture. Add the vanilla and beat to incorporate. Beat on high speed for 1 minute to ensure that all the butter is combined with the whipped egg white and sugar mixture.

4. Use the buttercream immediately or place in an airtight container and refrigerate for up to 1 week (or freeze for up to 3 months). If you refrigerate it, let it come to room temperature before using. This could take at least 6 hours, so we recommend removing it from the refrigerator the day before you will use it. Be sure to rewhip the buttercream before using to get the best texture.

Make the Chocolate Buttercream

1. Melt the chocolate and cool to room temperature. Divide the buttercream in half and add the chocolate to one half. Mix until thoroughly combined.

Make the Walnut Rum Buttercream

1. Toast the walnuts on a sheet tray at 325°F [165°C] for 10 to 15 minutes until they are golden brown. Let them cool, then chop into fine pieces. Add the walnuts and rum to the remaining half of the buttercream. Mix until it's completely incorporated. This will be the filling for your log.

Make the Meringue Mushrooms

1. Preheat the oven to 225°F [110°C].

2. In a mixing bowl fitted with the whisk attachment, combine the egg whites, sugar, cream of tartar, salt, and vanilla. Whip on high speed until the meringue holds stiff, shiny peaks.

3. Line a baking sheet with parchment paper. Place half of the meringue into a pastry bag fitted with a ½-in [12-mm] plain round tip. Pipe small mounds onto the parchment for the mushroom caps; pull the bag off to the side to avoid forming tips on the mushroom caps. To pipe the stems, pipe the meringue into a tall candy kiss shape. Do not worry about making all the pieces exactly the same. The mushrooms will look more natural if the pieces are different sizes.

4. Bake for 1 hour, or until the caps and stems are dried out. Cool completely.

5. To assemble the mushrooms: Melt the chocolate. Using a small knife, poke a small hole in the bottom of a mushroom cap, dip the tip of the stem into the chocolate, and insert it into the hole in the bottom of the cap. Let the chocolate set. Dust the mushroom caps lightly with cocoa powder. Store at room temperature in an airtight container for up to 3 days.

Make the Rum Simple Syrup

1. In a saucepan, combine the water and sugar. Bring to a boil to dissolve the sugar. Remove from the heat, let cool, and add the rum. Store at room temperature for up to 1 week.

Fill, Roll, and Assemble the Cake

1. Unroll the cooled cake and leave it on the parchment paper. Brush the entire surface with the rum simple syrup. Use an offset spatula to ice the surface of the cake with the walnut rum buttercream. Spread the buttercream out evenly over the cake, right up to the edges.

2. Place the cake in landscape orientation (with a long side facing you). Starting at the edge closest to you, roll up the cake tightly. Once the cake is rolled completely, try to tighten the roll even more. Refrigerate for 30 minutes to let the buttercream firm up.

3. Remove the cake from the refrigerator. Cut off a piece of cake at an angle, one-third the length of the cake.

4. Spread a tablespoon or two of buttercream on a 12-by-18-in [30-by-46-cm] rectangular cake board, and place the largest piece of cake onto the cake board. Attach the remaining shorter piece at a spot of your choosing along the main trunk. It should look like a branch coming off the tree trunk.

5. Using an offset spatula, ice the cake roughly, using the chocolate buttercream. Use a fork to draw lines from end to end on the trunk and the branch. This helps the buttercream resemble tree bark. Decorate the bûche with the meringue mushrooms.

6. Serve at room temperature. The Bûche de Noël can be refrigerated and enjoyed for up to four days. Bring to room temperature before serving.

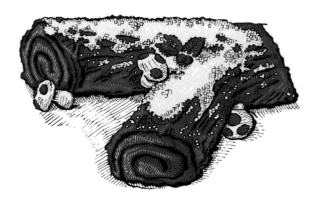

AMY: *Every year before Fat Tuesday, customers call us weeks in advance to place their* pączki *(PUN-shki) orders. Having* pączki *on Fat Tuesday is a big deal here in Michigan. The lines for* pączki *at bakeries all over southeastern Michigan are shockingly long, and the scene is always reported on the local news. We're small fry in this world and only make 3,000! It's a lot of late winter fun.*

What are pączki, *and why are they such a big deal in Michigan? They are the Polish version of filled doughnuts, and the tradition of serving* pączki *on Fat Tuesday was made popular here by the once-large Polish Catholic community in Hamtramck, a small city fully encircled by the city of Detroit. These rich, deep-fried treats are seen as a last indulgence before fasting begins for the 40 days of Lent. Polish Jews actually ate* pączki *during Hanukkah (fried foods being traditional during Hanukkah) and then took them to Israel, where* pączki *are now called* sufganiyot. *Although the* pączki *tradition in Michigan was started by Polish immigrants, it has been adopted by many as a Fat Tuesday treat.*

Pączki *have some interesting qualities. The dough includes Spirytus, a Polish grain alcohol with a scary-high proof content. It's flavorless and you won't taste it, but it keeps the dough from absorbing too much oil. If you can't find Spirytus, feel free to substitute another neutral-flavored high-proof alcohol. Pączki also have two traditional fillings:* powidla, *which is stewed plum jam, and rosehip jam.*

PĄCZKI
POLISH FILLED DOUGHNUTS
makes 10 filled doughnuts

Dough

Unsalted butter, room temperature	¼ cup plus 2 Tbsp	654 g
Granulated sugar	¼ cup plus 3 Tbsp	100 g
Whole milk	¾ cup plus 2 Tbsp	205 g
Instant yeast	4 tsp	13 g
All-purpose flour	3½ cups	510 g
Large egg	1	
Large egg yolk	1	
Spirytus vodka or other neutral, high-proof alcohol	2 Tbsp	25 g
Sea salt	1 tsp	

Ricotta Filling

Vanilla bean (optional)	½ bean	
Ricotta cheese	2 cups	455 g
Powdered sugar	½ cup	80 g
Vanilla extract	2 tsp	
Vegetable oil for deep-frying		
Powdered sugar for dusting		

Make the Dough

1. In a stand mixer fitted with the paddle attachment, cream the butter and sugar until smooth. Add the milk, yeast, half the flour, the whole egg, and the egg yolk. Stir the ingredients on low speed until a smooth batter forms. Add the vodka and mix until completely combined. Add the rest of the flour and the salt. Mix until a dough is formed.

2. Turn the dough out onto a clean, unfloured work surface and knead by hand for 6 to 8 minutes (page 34). It will be tacky but smooth. If you prefer to use your mixer, switch to the dough hook attachment and mix on medium speed for 6 minutes. You may need to scrape the dough from the sides of the bowl intermittently.

3. Place the dough in a lightly oiled bowl, cover with plastic wrap, and ferment for 1½ to 2 hours, or until doubled in size.

4. Uncover the dough and turn it out onto a lightly floured surface. Fold the dough (page 34) and place it back into the oiled bowl. Ferment for 1 more hour, or until doubled in volume.

These preserves are hard to find in the United States, but if you are able to locate them, you can substitute them for the cheese filling in this recipe.

Our favorite version of pączki, *which we now make every Sunday, has a sweetened ricotta filling. Cheese-filled doughnuts? Yes, we were skeptical, but then we tasted them. It's like eating vanilla cheesecake wrapped in fried dough. The idea came from our sales guy, Randy, who made this flavor of doughnut in Indiana during his youth.*

Make the Filling

1. If using the half vanilla bean, split it down the center and scrape out the seeds. (For ways to use the pod, see page 29.)

2. In a medium bowl, combine the ricotta cheese, powdered sugar, vanilla extract, and vanilla seeds, if using. Mix together until creamy and smooth. Keep refrigerated until ready to use.

Roll and Cut the Pączki

1. Lightly flour the work surface, and turn out the dough from the bowl. Lightly flour the top of the dough and pat it out with the flats of your hands or a rolling pin to a ½-in [1.5-cm] thickness, flouring the work surface if necessary to avoid sticking. Brush off the excess flour after the dough is the desired thickness.

2. Using a round cutter 3½ in [9 cm] in diameter, cut out rounds of dough. The pączki will not have holes, since they will be filled with the ricotta filling. Place on a lightly floured surface, cover lightly with plastic, and proof for 1 to 1½ hours, until they have risen and spring back lightly when gently touched. The scrap dough can be cut into irregular pieces or doughnut holes, proofed, and fried. Do not attempt to rework the dough.

Fry and Finish the Pączki

1. Heat 3 in [7.5 cm] of vegetable oil to 375°F [190°C] in a deep pan.

2. To fry the pączki, carefully lower proofed pieces of dough into the hot oil. The number of pączki that you fry at once depends on the size of your fryer. Do not crowd the frying pot.

3. Fry the pączki on the first side for 1 to 2 minutes, or until golden brown. With tongs, turn the pączki over and fry on the second side for 30 to 60 seconds, or until golden brown. Remove from the fryer and drain on a cooling rack placed over a sheet tray. Cool completely.

4. Fit a pastry bag with a large round tip (size 1A in the Wilton world, ½ in [1.5 cm]) and fill the bag with the ricotta filling. Make a hole in the side of each doughnut with a paring knife. Move the knife gently to make some space in the interior for the filling. Push the pastry tip into the hole and pipe in the filling. Try to put 2 to 3 Tbsp of filling into each one.

5. Sift powdered sugar on the pączki. Enjoy!

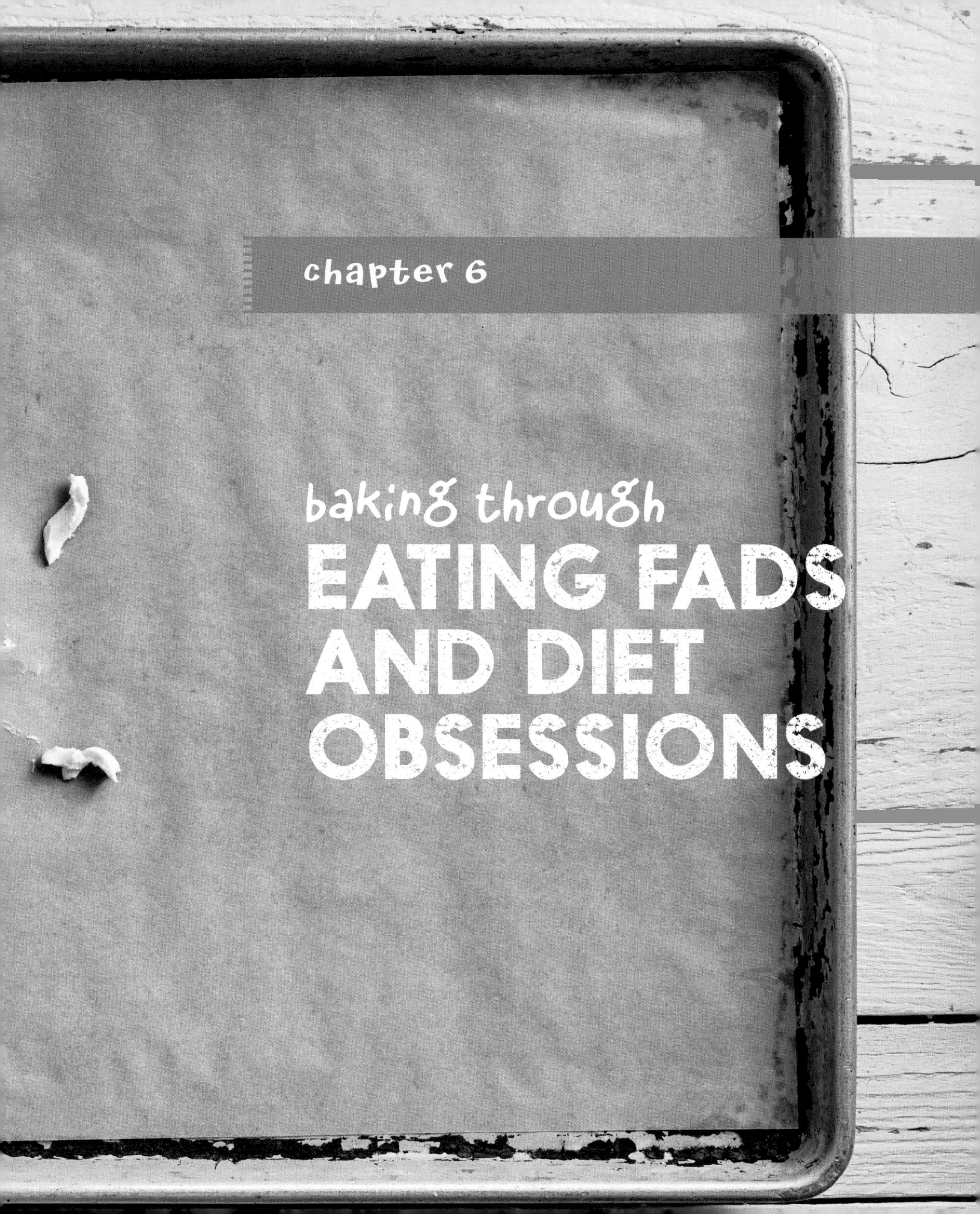

chapter 6

baking through
EATING FADS
AND DIET
OBSESSIONS

AMY: One of the more engaging and challenging parts of being a professional baker has been navigating ever-evolving eating trends and popular diets. The list is long: low salt, low fat, low carbs, no carbs, Atkins diet, paleo diet, gluten free, raw food, no corn syrup, and the rise of vegan, to name a few of the big ones. We are 100 percent behind a healthy public and for being sensitive to people's special dietary needs. We are equally committed to making traditional, full-flavored foods. Balancing these two is the source of the challenge.

In the early years, our conversations with customers focused on flavor preferences, texture, storage, and serving suggestions. We'd discuss the history of the food and how we prepared it. Today we commonly add ingredient provenance, calorie count, and a discussion about GMO to the standard conversation. We say, sort of jokingly, that we thought we had entered a benign and noncontroversial profession—being bakers—but somehow we've ended up in the thick of a contentious and important national debate about health.

During the most challenging periods (the low-fat diets and then the no-carb diets), we worried that we were slowly poisoning ourselves and our clientele with salt, sugar, fat, and wheat: our four beloved baking tools. Could it really be that the staff of life—our daily bread—or our beautiful and delicious pastry was making our community sick? Stated more dramatically, are we like drug pushers or tobacco peddlers? We don't think so.

FOOD KNOWLEDGE HAS EXPANDED

The change in our world is a result not just of health concerns but of the growing knowledge on the part of the general public about food. This is great—a more knowledgeable and interested community is a positive change.

Information about food, and access to this information, has been greatly broadened since we opened in the early 1990s. Consider the number of us who watch the Food Network and the greater appreciation we now have for the world's foods. We can all learn about unusual foods and food preparation from our living rooms. Professionals open their kitchens and bakeries on TV to the nation, sharing what was previously secret information.

Beyond television is the access many of us have to the plentiful information on the Internet. Millions of recipes, many blogs, and explanatory videos are available to us at any hour of the day from anywhere in the world. It's fantastic. Food has become popular and cool, and knowledge about it is much more democratic than in the past. Clearly, knowledge is spreading. And our conversations are now more involved than ever before because of it.

WHAT SHOULD WE EAT? WHAT SHOULD WE BAKE?

It seems that the more we know and the more elevated food has become in our culture, the more confused and uncertain we've become about what to eat and how to be healthy. In our experience, direction about what to eat comes primarily through five different perspectives: health and nutrition professionals, weight-loss diet advocates, environmental and economic sustainability concerns, popular food fads (think cronuts), and lifestyle diet advocates. The common approach of food producers to these ever-changing interests is to go with the flow and reap the profit that can be had. Reduce the flour and make low carb. Reduce the fat and make low fat.

What is our approach? We joke sometimes that we're "Zegans." By that we mean that we make full-flavored traditional foods and that our choices are dictated by that diet. Frank often jokes that he eats only gluten-rich foods. All kidding aside, our challenge has been finding a way to stay true to our mission while also providing great service to our customers—who may themselves have changing views—and staying in business.

The most proactive step we take is to send a clear message about what kind of bakery we are, so that customers can know what to expect from us. We communicate our mission clearly in many ways. We realize that we are not the bakery choice for everyone, and the more clearly we can communicate our identity, the less frustration there will be for the customer and for us as well.

This approach doesn't alleviate all of the frustration, however. There's a cultural expectation that businesses will embrace market opportunities, regardless of their mission. During the newest trends, some guests and wholesale customers are incredulous that we are not reworking our recipes to match the diet of the moment. There's also the idea that if there's a buck to be made at something, we ought to be chasing it. When you're a mission- or purpose-driven business, though, the buck is rarely, actually probably never, the primary motivator. It's the end result of having executed the mission well.

We have seen too many extreme, unsustainable diets come and go, the science refuted, to allow them to alter our basic approach to food, which is very much in line with what the food critic Michael Pollan has written in his many books (such as *The Omnivore's Dilemma*). Eat food made from real ingredients. Eat food that your ancestors would understand. Make much of your own food from basic ingredients. Eat a balanced diet in moderation. Eat with other people! Make eating a focused activity and pay attention to it. Know what you're eating. Understand the ingredients. And while we're at it, a little exercise and good emotional health go a long way, too.

Many years ago, we created our own nutritional label that included categories on it like Food with History, Food That Is Full-Flavored, Food Eaten with Others, Food That You Understand. The suggestion was that these criteria also have an impact on our health. The reductionistic approach of focusing on one element—fat or carbs, for instance—doesn't seem to have made us much healthier. Until the scientists figure it out, we're promoting the balanced middle road of eating a wide variety of real food.

On a lighter note, our partner Paul is a serial dieter. He once went on an all-pickle diet. He lost weight . . . for a while. Frank loves to say that he has personally lost the most weight of anyone at the bakery since it started, and estimates that he has lost more than 1,200 pounds since 1992. Figure that one out! Many others at the bakery are personally engaged with efforts to be healthier. We have exercise routines, try out diets. We're not immune from the challenges of our time.

In reaction to lifestyle diets like vegetarianism, veganism, and paleo, we identify the things we already make that fit them and then highlight them for people. We also do research to develop food with history and flavor that matches the eating preferences of the moment. We want customers to have choices that both meet their interests and fit with our mission. Examples? Pavlova, the Australian meringue dessert, is low fat and gluten free (and so good for Passover). The Sicilian bread *pane nero*, which we've just started making, is whole grain. Coconut macaroons are gluten-free (and also good for Passover). Most of our breads are vegan. We make vegan and vegetarian soups and sandwiches.

Sometimes people are still frustrated because they want more options in these areas, or they want us to alter their favorite item that they were eating prior to their new dietary choice to fit their new criteria. Can't we have it all? I guess that's why there are foods like Tofurky. We understand that desire. I want chocolate cake that's delicious, has zero calories, and meets all of my daily nutritional requirements. Maybe a scientist will create it one day.

In terms of health and nutritional suggestions from the medical establishment, we pay attention, look at our practices, and try to find ways to be helpful and to contain any harm we could cause. For example, allergies were a very minor topic of conversation until the last decade or so, but now they are common, and the number of things people are allergic to has dramatically increased. To help with this, we practice careful procedures to avoid cross-contact and often offer choices that are sensitive to common allergies, like not putting nuts into everything. We have actually eliminated peanuts from our bakery, since they can cause life-threatening reactions. Our mission isn't worth anyone losing their life over, and there's plenty to make without using peanuts.

Fortunately, since we use real ingredients, some of the other suggested ingredient changes have not affected us, because we are not using items like high-fructose corn syrup or trans fats.

And then there are food fads. There's always a hot new ingredient or flavor combo. Some recent ones have been bacon, *dulce de leche*, sweet and salty, pumpkin-flavored everything. Or a particular item will have a lot of buzz—artisan doughnuts, cupcakes, cronuts, French macarons. Sometimes we're making them already and we carry on. Sometimes we're equally excited and it fits with our mission, so we jump on board. And sometimes we see it as a distraction that will be short lived, so we take a pass. Most often we're coming up with our own next best thing.

Another area of focus is environmental and economic—organic, local, GMO free, fair trade. We keep all of these in mind, and whenever we can make a choice that creates the same great taste but is also organic or local, we make it.

Sometimes what we use is not available locally but could be. For instance, there is very little wheat farming in Michigan, although it is possible to grow wheat here. We are working with farmers to try to get wheat farming going again. We have paid for a season of wheat even when nothing is usable, so that people can relearn this lost skill. We are committed to reestablishing these lost foodways, even as we use grain from Kansas. Michigan has a vibrant agricultural sector, so it is easy to find local fruit (cherries and apples are widely grown) and local dairy.

We are committed to reevaluating our position on all of these topics as we learn more and as our world changes. Practically nothing is set in stone, except our desire to make full-flavored traditional foods.

This chapter includes recipes that we have developed or promote because they both meet our mission and match at least one of the trends of the last 25 years.

our approach to sugar

Recently a health focus has been on reducing sugar consumption. First it was all about avoiding high-fructose corn syrup (used in soda pop and other manufactured foods), and now it's about overall sweetener consumption. We are in support of dessert and pastries being special eating events and not necessarily consumed every day.

We have never used high-fructose corn syrup, but we do use corn syrup in a handful of recipes. Corn syrup has a structural quality to it that works differently than granulated white sugar. It doesn't crystallize and helps with viscosity and shine. Americans have been using it at least since the Civil War, long before our obesity epidemic. We use it in items that are clearly sweet, so it is not like a secret hidden ingredient, as it has become in so many processed foods. We do not believe that corn syrup is any less healthy than other sweeteners, although high-fructose corn syrup may be.

As we write, a new labeling law has been passed that requires food producers to list the percentage of added sugar in each serving. We will do this as required, of course, but we will keep using the amount of sugar we think best suits the goals of our recipes. Sweetness is one of the flavors we want in our baked sweet foods (most of our breads have no added sugar), but it is never the primary flavor we are aiming for. We regularly tweak recipes by reducing the sugar. Sugar also affects texture and color, and we carefully consider these characteristics when deciding on how much sugar to use.

We are happy to let people know what they're eating and make an informed choice, and once again we believe in moderation. Something's not special or a treat when we eat it all the time.

"know fat"

AMY: *We can have all kinds of serious responses to the latest diet issues, but sometimes it's more helpful to be playful. It's just food we're dealing with, not world peace! We count on Frank to bring in the fun. He did it masterfully in the mid-'90s when we decided to respond to the low-fat phenomenon. Low fat really didn't work for our pastry-making style. As we have mentioned once or twice, we are dedicated to using full-flavored fat to make our traditional pastries and desserts. Frank came up with a great marketing campaign. The primary visual was a winking cow saying "Know Fat." (Get it? Just know what you're eating.) People laughed, and it gave us an opportunity to explain why we weren't switching our recipes to low-fat dairy products or shortening and carried on.*

FARM BREAD WITH PEPPER AND BACON

makes 2 Loaves

Nueske's bacon	16 oz	455 g
Water, room temperature	1½ cups plus 2 Tbsp	370 g
Levain (page 42)	⅝ cup	90 g
Whole wheat flour	⅓ cup	45 g
All-purpose flour	3¾ cups plus 2 Tbsp	550 g
Sea salt	2 tsp plus a pinch	15 g
Coarsely ground black pepper	1 Tbsp	9 g
Cornmeal for dusting		
Coarsely ground black pepper for sprinkling tops		

1. Cook the bacon until it is nice and crispy (see page 186). Chop into ¼-in [6-mm] pieces.

2. Place the water into a large mixing bowl. Tear the levain into small pieces and add it to the water. Add the whole wheat flour and half of the all-purpose flour. Stir with a wooden spoon to combine and break up the levain. Add the remaining all-purpose flour and salt. Mix to combine until the dough is rough and shaggy.

3. Turn the dough out onto a clean, unfloured work surface, scraping any bits of flour or dough out of the bowl. Knead the dough for 6 minutes (page 34).

4. Spread the dough out on the work surface and gently form it into a rectangle. Sprinkle the crumbled bacon and pepper onto the rectangle. Carefully gather up the edges of the dough, keeping the bacon and pepper inside. Knead for another 2 to 3 minutes, or until the bacon and pepper are uniformly distributed in the dough.

5. Lightly oil a container, place the dough into it, and cover with plastic. Ferment for 2 hours. Uncover and place the dough on a lightly floured surface. Fold the dough (page 34). Return to the container and cover. Ferment for 1½ hours. Uncover and turn the dough out onto a lightly floured work surface.

6. Divide the dough into two equal portions. Flatten each into a disk 4½ in [11 cm] in diameter and about 1 in [2.5 cm] thick.

7. By pulling the top surface toward you and pressing it back into the dough, shape each piece into a football shape. Place the loaves seam side down on a cornmeal-coated board and cover with plastic. Allow to ferment for 1½ to 2½ hours. The loaves should approximately double in size.

8. Preheat the oven, baking stone, and a cast iron skillet (for creating steam) to 450°F [230°C] for 45 minutes before baking.

9. Remove the plastic from the loaves. Brush the top of each loaf with water and sprinkle with a bit of cracked black pepper. Score the dough with a razor blade or a very sharp knife (page 38). Slide the loaves onto a pre-heated baking stone, cover, and bake for 8 minutes with steam (page 38), then uncover and bake for an additional 25 to 30 minutes, until the loaves are golden brown. Remove the loaves from the oven and cool on a cooling rack. Let cool completely before cutting.

The name says it all. This bread has been popular since we began baking it in 1993. The organic eight-grain mix that we purchase has rye, wheat, corn, oats, barley, millet, rice, and flax in it. The honey adds a touch of sweetness to the bread, and rolling it in sunflower seeds gives it a great nutty and crunchy quality. While it's a sourdough bread, the sour flavor is mildly complementary in this popular bread. And it's arguably very healthy, since it's full of unrefined grains.

8 GRAIN 3 SEED BREAD

makes 2 loaves

Soaker

| 7-grain cereal mix | 1¾ cups | 270 g |
| Water, boiling | 1 cup plus 3 Tbsp | 270 g |

Final Dough

Water, room temperature	½ cup plus 2 Tbsp	135 g
All-purpose flour	1⅓ cups plus 1 Tbsp	190 g
Whole wheat flour	⅔ cup	90 g
Brown rice flour	2½ Tbsp	25 g
Buckwheat flour	1½ Tbsp	15 g
Honey	5 Tbsp	100 g
Levain (page 42)	1 cup	190 g
Toasted sunflower seeds	3 Tbsp	25 g
Poppy seeds	1 Tbsp plus 1 tsp	15 g
Sea salt	2½ tsp	14 g
Sunflower seeds (untoasted) for coating loaves		
Cornmeal for dusting		

Make the Soaker

1. Put the 7-grain mix into a large mixing bowl, and pour the boiling water over it. Stir to make sure the grains are moistened, then let sit until the mixture comes to room temperature, about 1 hour.

Make the Bread

1. To the cooled grains, add the water, all-purpose, whole wheat, brown rice, and buckwheat flours, and the honey, levain (torn into pieces), toasted sunflower seeds, poppy seeds, and salt. Combine thoroughly with a wooden spoon until the mixture looks stiff and dry. Press and squeeze the mixture in the bowl until it comes together into a stiff and sticky dough.

2. Scrape the dough out of the bowl and onto a clean, unfloured work surface and knead for 5 to 7 minutes (page 34), until it feels strong. The dough will be quite sticky throughout the kneading. Clean the work surface with a plastic scraper as needed.

continued

3. Put the dough into an oiled mixing bowl and cover with plastic. After 1 hour, turn the dough out onto a lightly floured work surface. Fold the dough (page 34). Turn the dough back over and return it to the oiled bowl. Cover with plastic. After 1 additional hour, place the dough on a lightly floured surface. Divide it into two pieces of equal weight.

4. Gently form each piece of dough into a round disk shape. Roll each piece into a batard (football) shape (page 35).

5. Brush the top of each loaf with water. Turn the loaf over and roll the wet surface in a tray of sunflower seeds to fully coat the top of the loaf with seeds.

6. Place on a cornmeal-covered surface with the seam side down. Let the loaves ferment for 2 to 3 hours at room temperature. Use the touch test (page 38) to see if the loaves are ready for the oven.

7. Preheat the oven, baking stone, and cast iron skillet (for creating steam) to 450°F [230°C] 45 minutes prior to baking. When ready to bake, score each loaf with a razor blade or sharp knife (page 38). Make three parallel diagonal cuts, each 2½ in [6 cm] long, that overlap each other by ½ in [1.5 cm]. Start the first cut 1½ in [4 cm] from the top point of the loaf and end the third cut 1½ in [4 cm] from the bottom point of the loaf.

8. Slide the loaves onto the preheated baking stone, cover, and bake for 8 minutes with steam (page 38), then uncover and bake for an additional 30 to 35 minutes, or until golden brown. Remove from the oven, place on a cooling rack, and cool completely before slicing.

How could focaccia be controversial or problematic? As it turns out, food safety laws have become more robust over the years, and inspectors now prohibit any focaccia with a vegetable topping from being sold commercially if it has been kept at room temperature for more than four hours, due to the possibility of contamination. Because of the timing of our bake schedule, this means that we no longer sell focaccia with vegetable toppings. It's really unfortunate. Sometimes laws put an end to delicious foods.

However, you can do whatever you like in your home, so we've included our all-time favorite focaccia recipe for you to make. The combination of caramelized onions, toasted walnuts, and Gorgonzola cheese with the tender olive-oily focaccia dough is magical. It's so good that you'll probably finish the whole thing in fewer than four hours anyway.

FOCACCIA
WITH GORGONZOLA AND CARAMELIZED ONION

makes two 10-in [25-cm] round focaccia

Poolish

All-purpose flour	¾ cup plus 1 Tbsp	115 g
Water, room temperature	½ cup	115 g
Instant yeast	⅛ tsp	

Topping

Onions	2 lb	910 g
Olive oil	¼ cup	40 g
Walnuts, coarsely chopped	⅓ cup	270 g
Crumbled Gorgonzola cheese (grape-sized chunks)	¼ cup	35 g

Final Dough

Water, room temperature	1 cup	225 g
Poolish	all	
Olive oil	¼ cup	40 g
Instant yeast	½ tsp	
All-purpose flour	3 cups	425 g
Sea salt	1½ tsp	9 g
Cornmeal for dusting		
Olive oil for brushing dough		

Make the Poolish

1. Combine the flour, water, and yeast in a medium mixing bowl and stir together until incorporated. Cover the bowl loosely with plastic wrap and allow the poolish to ferment for 8 hours. Use immediately or refrigerate and use within 24 hours for best results.

continued

Prepare the Toppings

1. Peel the onions and then cut them in half. Cut into thin half-ring slices and then toss to separate the layers. Heat the olive oil in a large skillet over medium heat. Add the onions and cook slowly, stirring often, until the onions are soft and golden brown in color. This will take 20 to 30 minutes. Depending on your pan and stovetop, you may want to put the heat on low to avoid overbrowning or burning the onions.

2. Toast the walnuts in a baking pan in a 325°F [165°C] oven for 10 to 15 minutes, or until they're a deep golden brown.

Make the Dough

1. In a large bowl, add the water, poolish, olive oil, and yeast and combine thoroughly with a wooden spoon. Add half the flour and stir to combine. The mixture will resemble thick pancake batter. Add the remaining flour and salt and stir to combine.

2. Continue mixing until the dough becomes shaggy and starts to just barely form a ball, then turn the dough out onto a clean, unfloured work surface. Knead the dough for 6 to 8 minutes (page 34).

3. Scrape the dough off the table, place it into an oiled mixing bowl, and cover with plastic. Ferment for 1 hour and 15 minutes. It will approximately double in volume.

4. Uncover the dough and turn out onto a lightly floured work surface. Divide into two equal pieces. Gently pre-shape each piece of dough into a small round (page 35). Place each focaccia on a cornmeal-covered board and cover with plastic. Let proof for 50 to 55 minutes.

Shape and Bake the Focaccia

1. Preheat the oven with a baking stone to 450°F [230°C] for 45 minutes before baking.

2. When the dough is proofed (page 38), gently press the rounds into disks approximately 10 in [25 cm] in diameter. Use your fingertips for this process. Place one disk onto a lightly floured or cornmeal-covered peel. Press your fingertips into the dough to make dimples all over the surface. Using a pastry brush, cover the focaccia with olive oil. Scatter half the onions, toasted walnuts, and Gorgonzola over the surface of the focaccia.

3. Slide the focaccia onto the baking stone in the preheated oven and bake for 15 minutes, until golden brown. Remove from the oven and place on a wire rack. Repeat for the second focaccia. Cool to room temperature before eating.

These scones, with their oats, nuts, and milk rather than cream, at least approach being "healthy." We love the way they taste, but they are also a concession to our customers who want something they can feel better about eating for breakfast. They can be even "healthier" if you switch out some of the white flour for whole wheat flour. It's possible to swap as much as half the white flour for whole wheat flour without adjusting the other ingredients. If you use more than that, you will want to increase the milk quantity, because the whole wheat absorbs more liquid than white flour.

COUNTRY SCONES

makes 12 scones

Pecans, chopped	¾ cup	90 g
All-purpose flour	2 cups plus 2 Tbsp	305 g
Granulated sugar	¾ cup	150 g
Old-fashioned rolled oats	1½ cup plus 1 Tbsp	190 g
Baking powder	1 Tbsp	14 g
Baking soda	½ tsp	
Flame raisins	⅔ cup	90 g
Sea salt	1 tsp	
Large egg	1	
Unsalted butter, melted	¾ cup plus 2 Tbsp	190 g
Whole milk	½ cup	110 g
Vanilla extract	1 tsp	

Egg Wash

Large egg	1	
Egg yolk	1	
Water	1 Tbsp	

Cinnamon Sugar

Ground cinnamon	1 Tbsp	
Granulated sugar	½ cup plus 2 Tbsp	130 g

1. Heat the oven to 325°F [165°C]. Toast the pecans on a sheet tray for 12 minutes, until toasty brown. Start checking after 8 minutes.

2. In a large bowl, combine the flour, sugar, oats, baking powder, baking soda, pecans, raisins, and salt. Stir to mix evenly.

3. In a small bowl, lightly beat the egg and then add to the dry ingredients, along with the butter, milk, and vanilla. Mix until completely homogeneous.

4. This is a very wet and sticky batter. Using a 2-oz [59-ml] portioner or a ¼-cup measure, scoop the scones onto a sheet tray with at least 2 in [5 cm] between them. Place a little flour on your hands and gently flatten the scones into disks 2 in [5 cm] thick. Chill the scones for at least 30 minutes. This will help them attain more loft as they bake.

5. Preheat the oven to 375°F [190°C]. Make the egg wash by beating together the egg, egg yolk, and water in a small bowl. In a separate small bowl, combine the cinnamon and sugar.

6. Using a pastry brush, apply egg wash to the top of each scone and then generously sprinkle with cinnamon sugar. Bake for 15 minutes, or until a nice golden color. Cool on a wire rack.

We love pizza! There's barely a pizza that exists that either of us can pass up. However, we are still surprised at how popular pizza-making classes are at BAKE!

We made pizza for our lunch customers at the bakery in the early 2000s but stopped because there was just not enough demand. Still, we thought teaching it might be worthwhile, and this time we were right. The pizza class became popular overnight and has stayed that way.

The overnight fermentation of the dough creates a chewy texture, a remarkable flavor, and a nice bubbly crust. We chose a simple topping for this version, but you can embellish it as you like. Try not to overload it, though, because that can make it difficult to transfer it to the baking stone, and it may not bake as nicely.

NEW YORK-STYLE
THIN-CRUST PIZZA

makes two 10-in [25-cm] pizzas

Pizza Dough

Water, room temperature	1 cup	225 g
Instant yeast	½ tsp	
All-purpose flour	2½ cups	345 g
Sea salt	1 tsp	

Pizza Sauce

Olive oil	¼ cup	45 g
Chopped onion	¼ cup	25 g
Finely chopped garlic	1 Tbsp	15 g
Crushed tomatoes (canned)	28-oz can	795 g
Dried oregano	1 tsp	
Dried basil	2 tsp	
Sea salt	½ tsp	
Ground black pepper	¼ tsp	

Pizza Topping

Fresh mozzarella cheese	8 oz	225 g
Fresh basil	12 leaves	

Make the Dough

1. Combine the water, instant yeast, and half of the flour in a large mixing bowl. Mix thoroughly with a spoon until the batter is smooth. Add the sea salt and remaining flour and mix with a spoon until the dough forms a shaggy mass. Scrape the dough from the bowl onto a clean, unfloured work surface and knead for 8 minutes (page 34).

2. Place the dough in a lightly oiled mixing bowl and cover with plastic. Ferment the dough for 2 hours.

3. Lightly flour the work surface and turn the dough onto the surface. With a bench scraper, divide the dough into two equal pieces. Form the pieces into tight, round balls. Place on a lightly oiled sheet tray, oil the tops of the dough balls, and cover with plastic. Refrigerate overnight or for up to 3 days before using.

Make the Sauce

1. In a saucepan, heat the olive oil and sauté the onion over medium heat until the onions become translucent. Add the garlic to the saucepan and cook for 1 minute. Add the tomatoes, oregano, basil, salt, and pepper. Bring the sauce to a simmer and cook for 10 to 15 minutes, until somewhat thickened.

2. Remove the sauce from the heat and cool slightly. Place in a food processor and blend until smooth. Adjust the seasoning to taste. You will have more sauce than you need. Cool and store in an airtight container in the refrigerator for up to 1 week.

Prepare the Pizzas for Baking

1. Preheat the oven and baking stone to 500°F [260°C], or hotter if possible, at least 1 hour before baking. The convection setting is not recommended.

2. When you are ready to make the pizzas, remove the doughs from the fridge and immediately start working with them. Shape and bake one at a time. Lightly flour a work surface and the top of the dough. Press on the dough about ½ in [1.5 cm] from the edge of the disk—this will form a rim. Press down on the center to flatten it out.

3. Place the dough on top of your knuckles with your fingertips turned down, and slowly pull your hands away from each other to stretch the dough. Make sure your knuckles are not in the center of the dough, or it will thin out the center too much.

4. Turn the dough as you stretch it until it is 10 to 12 in [25 to 30 cm] in diameter. If you are uncertain about your ability to hand-shape the pizza dough, use a rolling pin and roll the dough out on a floured work surface.

5. Once the dough is stretched to the correct diameter, place it on something that can eventually help you transfer the prepared pizza to the baking stone. There are two ways we have found that this can be done at home. The first is to use a 14-in [35-cm] cardboard cake round, and the second is to use a peel, metal or wood. We recommend purchasing a peel. It will make getting the pizza in and out of the oven much easier. For any of these scenarios, sprinkle the surface of your transfer tool with flour to help avoid sticking, and place the pizza dough on the prepared surface. Reshape the round if it has become deformed.

Top the Pizza

1. Spoon ½ cup [120 ml] of the pizza sauce onto the surface of the pizza dough, and spread it out to ½ in [1.5 cm] of the edge of the dough. Slice the mozzarella into rounds and place half of it evenly on top of the sauce. If you have additional toppings, add them now.

Bake the Pizza

1. Once you have your pizza prepared, shake the cardboard round or peel to make sure the dough is not sticking. If it is sticking, gently lift it up and sprinkle the transfer tool with flour.

2. Slide the pizza onto the baking stone. Bake for 10 to 12 minutes. Check after 5 minutes to see if the pizza is baking evenly. Turn it if necessary. Continue baking the pizza until the center is bubbly and the crust is golden brown on the bottom. Using the peel, remove the pizza from the oven and cool for 4 to 5 minutes to allow the cheese to set up.

3. Scatter half the fresh basil over the top. Repeat with the remaining dough and toppings. Cut the pizzas into 6 to 8 pieces with a pizza cutter and enjoy!

PECAN SANDIES WITH BACON

makes 2 dozen cookies

Pecans	1¼ cups	125 g
Bacon	3 slices	90 g
Unsalted butter, room temperature	1 cup plus 2 Tbsp	230 g
Granulated sugar	½ cup plus 2 Tbsp	120 g
Water	2 tsp	
Vanilla extract	2 tsp	
All-purpose flour	2 cups plus 2 Tbsp	270 g
Sea salt for sprinkling tops		
Demerara sugar for sprinkling tops		

AMY: *Bacon is beloved in America and beloved at Zingerman's. We have a three-day annual event called Camp Bacon, www.zingermanscampbacon.com, every June and a Bacon Club that you can buy through Zingerman's Mail Order. At the Bakehouse, to show our enthusiasm for bacon, we created these cookies. We make them infrequently, but when we do, not only do customers buy them, but they're a staff favorite. We sometimes think that the staff buys more of them than our customers do. My belief is, if the bakers love something, it is worth a try.*

What's so special about this cookie? It's the mix of sweet pecans, smoky bacon, and nutty browned butter. Salt, sugar, butter, and nuts are a tempting combination. Not into bacon? Leave it out. They're still super satisfying.

1. Preheat the oven to 325°F [165°C]. Toast the pecans on a sheet tray. Though this typically takes 10 to 12 minutes, start checking them after 8 minutes. The browning happens suddenly when the nuts are heated to the point that their oil comes to the surface, and they can burn quickly. Use your nose while you bake! You will notice a toasty aroma when they are nearly ready. When they are done, remove them from the oven and let them cool completely.

2. Chop the pecans with a knife or in a food processor until they're the size of peas.

3. Cook the bacon until crispy. This can be done in a frying pan or in the oven. When cool enough to touch, chop the slices into ¼-in [6-mm] pieces.

4. In a stand mixer fitted with the paddle attachment, cream the butter and sugar on medium speed. Add the water and vanilla and continue mixing. Add the flour, pecans, and bacon. Mix until evenly incorporated.

5. Scoop the dough using a 1-oz [30-ml] portioner, or shape into balls by hand, using about 2 Tbsp of dough for each. Place the cookies on a parchment-lined baking sheet and press each one down using your palm. Leave space between the cookies so that they have room to spread during baking.

6. Before placing them in the oven, lightly sprinkle each cookie with salt, and then sprinkle more generously with Demerara sugar. Bake for 16 to 18 minutes, until light brown on top and golden on the bottom. Remove from the oven and cool.

tip: *Buy tasty bacon. We use Nueske's applewood-smoked bacon because of its multidimensional flavors. Cheap bacons will add a lot of salt and just a little flavor, so don't skimp here.*

Why have macaroons landed in the chapter about eating trends? Well, luckily for us, they're wheat free. They are a fortunate combination of an item that fits our mission and one that aligns with the dietary needs of some of our guests.

Beyond all that, what's particularly appealing about these macaroons? For one, they are super chocolaty. Want the flavor to be more multidimensional? Try adding chopped candied orange peel or orange zest, chopped dried cherries, or chopped chocolate along with the coconut.

They also have a crisp exterior and a dreamily moist interior. If you want more crunch, make your macaroons smaller or bake them for a few extra minutes. Want more of the soft chew? Make them larger to increase the amount of soft center. Cooking time will need to be adjusted depending on the size.

These treats are great to serve on lots of different occasions. We made them originally to celebrate the Jewish holiday of Passover, but many of our customers buy them for Christmas.

CHOCOLATE COCONUT MACAROONS

makes 2 dozen cookies

Chopped chocolate (56% cacao or higher)	½ cup plus 1½ Tbsp	115 g
Egg whites	3	90 g
Unsweetened cocoa powder	¼ cup plus 1 Tbsp	25 g
Granulated sugar	¾ cup plus 2 tsp	160 g
Sea salt	½ tsp	
Vanilla extract	1 tsp	
Sweetened flaked coconut	2½ cups	340 g

1. Preheat the oven to 350°F [180°C].

2. Place the chocolate in a double boiler to melt. You can make your own double boiler by using a metal bowl that fits over the top of a pan. Fill the pan about one-third full of water and bring to a boil. Once boiling, reduce the heat to medium and place the metal bowl with the chocolate in it on top. Make sure the bottom of the bowl is not touching the water. Stir the chocolate until melted. Avoid overheating it. Once the chocolate is melted, set it aside to cool.

3. In a mixing bowl, by hand or with the whisk attachment on a stand mixer, stir together the egg whites, cocoa powder, sugar, salt, and vanilla. Add the melted chocolate and stir until well blended. Add the coconut and mix until evenly incorporated.

4. Using a ¾-oz [22-ml] portioner, form mounds of the mixture and place on parchment-lined pans. You can also use a spoon to roll the mixture into balls, using about 1½ Tbsp for each. They should be the size of a walnut in the shell. Leave some space between the macaroons for even baking. They will not spread.

5. Bake for 25 minutes, until the cookies are slightly crispy on the outside and still soft on the inside. If you're unsure whether they're done, squeeze one! Remove to a cooling rack and cool completely. These cookies stay very moist in a sealed container or bag for up to a week. They can also be frozen for up to 3 months.

Here is a brownie inspired by our Magic Brownies but made without wheat flour, for our friends who want gluten-free treats. It is made possible by the power of amaranth, quinoa, and eggs. Amaranth has been cultivated for centuries by other cultures, especially in Mexico and Central America. Both amaranth and quinoa are quite high in protein, making this brownie more than just a treat. It could provide a significant portion of one's protein for the day.

The name was created by our former marketing manager, Pete Garner. It's a tribute to native-born Ann Arborites (that's Ann Arbor's definition of a townie) who have been our loyal supporters and are always on top of food trends.

This version doesn't have any special mix-ins, but you can add any nut or dried fruit or chunks of chocolate to the batter.

TOWNIE BROWNIES

makes one 8-by-8 in [20-by-20-cm] pan of brownies

Chopped chocolate (56% cacao)	¾ cup plus 1 Tbsp	140 g
Unsalted butter, melted	7 Tbsp	95 g
Large eggs	3	
Granulated sugar	½ cup plus 2 tsp	110 g
Sea salt	¼ tsp	
Vanilla extract	½ tsp	
Amaranth flour	3 Tbsp	25 g
Quinoa flour	3 Tbsp	25 g

1. Preheat the oven to 350°F [180°C]. Spray an 8-by-8-in [20-by-20-cm] square baking pan with nonstick cooking spray.

2. In a double boiler, melt the chocolate and butter together. Set aside to cool.

3. In a mixing bowl, using a hand whisk, mix together the eggs, sugar, salt, and vanilla extract. Whisk rapidly for 1 minute or more, until the mixture is frothy and thick. Add the melted chocolate and butter. Stir well using a spatula or wooden spoon. Add the amaranth and quinoa flours. Using a whisk, mix to incorporate evenly.

4. Pour the batter into the prepared pan and spread evenly. Bake for 26 minutes, or until a toothpick comes out almost clean. There should be moist crumbs on the toothpick.

5. Store, covered, at room temperature for 3 to 5 days. These brownies freeze well too.

We first baked this cake during the mid-90s when low-fat eating was the primary topic of health and diet conversations. We used low-fat buttermilk and called it, unimaginatively, low-fat buttermilk cake. It was tasty and had some followers but not a huge number. In the early 2000s, after many of us had given up on low-fat diets, we decided to fatten it up and create a more evocative name. Sour cream was the key addition.

Hot Cocoa Cake is now a favorite for many, and it is definitely a Bakehouse standard. It's a versatile cake that can be eaten in the morning or as an afternoon snack, and also makes a great dessert after dinner. We enjoy it warm, served with lots of chocolate sauce and whipped cream. Fresh raspberries, whole or as a sauce, are also a nice addition. And of course it's great with an actual cup of hot cocoa.

HOT COCOA CAKE

makes one 9-in [23-cm] bundt cake

Granulated sugar	2⅓ cups plus 1½ Tbsp	485 g
Unsalted butter, room temperature	½ cup plus 2 Tbsp	140 g
Sour cream	½ cup plus 1½ Tbsp	145 g
Large eggs	2	
Egg whites	3	90 g
Vanilla extract	2 tsp	
Instant coffee powder	2 Tbsp	
Water, hot	2 Tbsp	
All-purpose flour	1½ cups	215 g
Unsweetened cocoa powder	½ cup plus 3 Tbsp	55 g
Baking powder	¼ tsp	
Baking soda	¼ tsp	
Sea salt	½ tsp	
Chocolate (56% cacao or darker), chips or chopped	¾ cup plus 2½ Tbsp	160 g

1. Preheat the oven to 350°F [180°C]. Spray a Bundt pan with nonstick cooking spray, and set aside.

2. In a stand mixer fitted with the paddle attachment, combine the sugar and butter on medium speed until the mixture resembles wet sand. Add the sour cream and mix in well. Add the eggs and then the egg whites, one at a time, beating well after each egg is added. Once all of the eggs are in, add the vanilla extract.

3. Combine the coffee powder with the hot water. Add to the mixing bowl.

4. In a separate bowl, combine the flour, cocoa powder, baking powder, baking soda, and salt. Mix until homogeneous.

5. Remove the bowl from the mixer and sift the dry ingredients into the mixture. Use a spatula to mix gently until all of the ingredients are completely combined. Add the chocolate chips and mix gently until evenly incorporated.

6. Pour the batter into the Bundt pan and bake for 50 to 55 minutes, until a toothpick comes out clean. Cool for 10 minutes in the pan, then release onto a cake circle or a plate.

AMY: *This is my favorite summer pie! Its fresh tartness is a welcome change after our winter baking, which is full of nuts, chocolate, and cinnamon. We've chosen to keep this a pure rhubarb pie—no strawberries—and with as little sugar as possible, in order to focus on the rhubarb. We understand that many people like to add strawberries to their rhubarb pie. If that's what you prefer, reduce the weight of the rhubarb and substitute some strawberries. You may also want to reduce the sugar to compensate for the sweet berries.*

We aim to use only local Michigan rhubarb, since it's widely grown here and we love baking with local ingredients in season. The funny thing is that as customers we sometimes don't want to wait for the local season. When we see rhubarb in the grocery stores, we want it. The first rhubarb that arrives in Michigan stores comes from Washington state, which has a growing season that is at least a full month earlier than ours. Holding off until Michigan rhubarb arrives is one of the tensions of being local and seasonal while living in a society in which practically everything is available regardless of the season.

Be sure to leave time for the rhubarb and sugar to meld overnight. This generous marinating time makes sure that the pie is plenty juicy and that the sugar liquefies adequately. When we created this pie we discovered that fresh rhubarb varies greatly in its moisture content, and sometimes we'd end up with a dry filling. By following this marinating process we have a consistently juicy pie.

JUST RHUBARB RHUBARB PIE

makes one 9-in [23-cm] pie

Rhubarb, cut into 1-in [2.5-cm] pieces	6½ cups	910 g
Granulated sugar	1⅓ cups	270 g
Sea salt	⅛ tsp	
Cornstarch	3½ Tbsp	34 g
9-in [23-cm] double pie crust, unbaked (page 61)		
Egg Wash		
Large egg	1	
Egg yolk	1	
Water	1 Tbsp	
Demerara sugar, for sprinkling		

1. In a mixing bowl, combine the rhubarb pieces and granulated sugar. Cover and refrigerate overnight.

2. Drain the liquid from the rhubarb into a saucepan. Put the salt and cornstarch into a small bowl. Remove one-fourth of the total liquid from the saucepan, and gradually pour it into the cornstarch, stirring to make a slurry.

3. Bring the remaining liquid in the saucepan to a boil. Stir the slurry into the liquid and simmer until the mixture is clear. Remove from the heat, and add the rhubarb pieces. Cool to room temperature.

4. Preheat the oven to 375°F [190°C] 20 minutes prior to baking.

5. Roll out the dough for the bottom crust (page 63), and fit it into a 9-in [23-cm] pie pan. Add the cooled filling to the unbaked pie shell. Make the egg wash by beating together the egg, egg yolk, and water, and brush the edge of the dough lightly.

6. Roll out the top crust, and place it on the filled pie. Follow the directions on page 64 to finish the pie crust. Brush the entire top of the pie with egg wash, cut four vents into it, and sprinkle with Demerara sugar.

7. Place the pie on a parchment-lined baking sheet and bake for 45 to 50 minutes. The pie is done when the juices are bubbling in the center and the crust is a dark golden color. Remove from the oven and let the pie cool to room temperature before serving (this will allow the juices to thicken).

chapter 7

UNEXPECTED SUCCESSES,

surprising controversies and stunning flops

At End of Night
Turn Oven Temp
Down To
160
Challah Sealer
Turn Oven Temp
Up To

FRANK: Baking and business aren't always as predictable as we'd like. Sometimes we think we're creating something that people will love, and it's a total flop. Other times, we do something on a whim and it turns into a great success. And then there are the few times when we manage to hit a nerve that we didn't know existed and we find ourselves either baking something in great demand or the recipient of scathing complaint letters. This chapter is a compilation of surprising outcomes, good and bad, and the recipes related to them.

FLOPS AND MAYBE EVEN FAILURES

I've learned that flops and failures aren't really a bad thing. From a failure can come intense concentration, motivation, and focus on never going to that spot again. Recovering from failure builds resiliency for the future. Amy says that in business and in life it's good to fail early and fail small. It allows us to learn how to fail and how to recover effectively. I'd have to agree. Failing big can help too, though.

For me an early and big failure came in 1985 when I opened another Monahan's Seafood Market, with my business partners Paul Saginaw and Michael Monahan, in Farmington Hills, Michigan, a community about 30 miles northeast of Ann Arbor. Our little shop was beautiful and located in a growing and affluent community surrounded by thousands of young professionals living in nearby apartments and condos. What could go wrong?

Well—surprise!—it didn't take off, no matter what we tried. The result of that failure was the idea in my mind that, should I have that chance again, I would do anything and everything to make certain that it succeeded. I was listening to Dan Barber, one of our country's renowned chefs, and he spoke about a similar event in his life. He said, "Every chef I know that's really successful has had a moment of really intense failure. Failure is very important. It introduces you to an idea that you don't ever want to return to." I knew exactly what he was talking about. When we started Bakehouse, the failure of the fish market was still fresh in my mind, and I was determined to do whatever I could to make the bakery successful. Relentlessness was a quality of mine that the crew saw in the early years. What they didn't know was that it was driven by my knowledge that failure was possible and that I would do anything I could to avoid it.

In the early years of the bakery we had frequent small failures—bread overproofed, batches lost when an oven went down and we weren't able to get it going in time, starters accidently thrown away. One Thanksgiving we used the wrong proportions of cinnamon and sugar in our apple pies and sent out 350 pies that just had way too much cinnamon in them. The Friday after that Thanksgiving was a challenging day as we answered all the angry phone calls from our customers letting us know that we had ruined their Thanksgiving. That was painful!

From all of these mistakes we've learned and created systems and training materials to try to avoid having them happen again. We happily share the stories with the crew so that the learning never dies. We have come to understand that talking about failures and mistakes is actually more important than discussing the successes. When we share these stories, our vulnerability creates an environment that lets everyone be open when a mistake happens. This is critical if we want to improve.

Over the years we've created foods that we thought would sell incredibly well that didn't. For instance, in the spring of 1992, Ari and I came up with the idea of putting Detroit Street toppings (the name of the street the Deli is on)—a mixture of fennel seeds, sesame seeds, and poppy seeds—on bread and rolls. We decided to garnish our large sourdough rounds with this seed mix, imagining someday baking hundreds per day. We were certain that it was going to be a signature item.

It's been more than two decades, and that day hasn't come yet. More typically, we bake about a dozen loaves with this topping a day and, on our largest baking days, about twice that number. We still think it's an interesting flavor combination, but I guess few other people do. Why do we still make them? It's easy, and honestly sometimes we fall in love with our creations and it's hard to let them go.

OUR FAVORITES THAT ARE IN PRODUCT HEAVEN

AMY: Frank and I often laugh that we don't make some of our personal all-time favorites anymore. It's an important lesson that our personal taste is not always the best indicator of what our customers want, and we need to know when to let go.

Alsatian rye: A sourdough rye that we made in the early years. Although Frank loved it and we promoted it energetically, we could never sell more than 12 to 18 a day. We finally gave up.

Marjolaine: This is a sophisticated French torte of soft hazelnut meringue layers and chocolate and coffee buttercream. It's one of my and Frank's favorites but, it seemed, hardly anyone else's. We sold it for years, regardless. We finally let it go and just bring it back from time to time or beg the cake team to make it for us when we're celebrating something special. I think we underestimated the power of the name. We wanted to keep its real name, but perhaps the lack of familiarity scared people off from even asking about it. It also looked small in size, and although it was rich and full of flavor, perhaps it didn't appear to be of great value.

2-kg rye breads and large loaves in general: Frank, Ari, and I think that the bigger loaves bake better and taste better. For years we tried to sell them to guests, either whole or in quarters. We'd waste them regularly, as they sat on the shelves looking beautiful but tempting practically no one. Perhaps it's too un-American to buy a part of something. We all want our own. These days many guests want smaller and smaller loaves. Making sandwiches from slices cut from a quarter loaf might be perplexing to some of us as well, due to the odd shape.

Flodni: This is a Jewish Hungarian sweet that is made of layers of pie crust in between apple, poppy seed, and walnut filling. It's relatively plain looking, is definitely unfamiliar, and has a foreign name, all strikes against it. A few of us and a few guests adored it. Our retail staff just couldn't get behind it, though, and I'd have to remind them daily of how we agreed to display it. They actually teased some of us when we ate it! A critical lesson in retail is that the staff has enormous influence over the success of an item. If they don't like it, good luck.

Cinn-Oh-Man: This is what we think is a fantastic cinnamon Danish that we created to replace our cinnamon roll. It has cinnamon in the dough and in the laminating butter as well as in the glaze. It is tender and tasty. The goal was to make both for a while and then to retire our more typical American cinnamon roll. We weren't pleased with the cinnamon roll and thought something different would be more interesting than working on it. Our grand plan wasn't going to be, however. Our guests divided 70 percent to 30 percent in favor of the cinnamon roll, a real frustration to me and Frank. Finally we gave in, fixed the cinnamon roll recipe, and retired the Cinn-Oh-Man to "special bake" status. I guess it's in purgatory rather than heaven. There was no value in being stubborn about this one any longer.

OUR BIGGEST FAILURE

These were all little failures, easy enough to rebound from. Probably our biggest commercial failure ever was our Christmas Cookie Club Box created in 2009. In 2008 we were told about a new novel called *The Christmas Cookie Club* being written by an Ann Arbor author and mother of a Zingerman's Roadhouse staff person. It was the story of a group of middle-aged women, friends from college, who had been getting together each year to exchange Christmas cookies while catching up with each other and exchanging life experiences.

The economy was terrible, and we were looking for ways to do new things that would help business. We collaborated with the author to do a tie-in by producing a box of Christmas cookies in a box shaped like the novel. We managed to convince Borders Books, a national chain at the time, to order 7,000 boxes and to stock some in each of their stores throughout the country and Puerto Rico. This was exciting, a hometown collaboration (Borders originated in Ann Arbor and had its corporate offices there) that would help all of us during a tough time.

We got really excited about making these delicious tiny cookies. Each box would have three different Christmas cookies from the book. We had to figure out how to make 150,000 cookies, a daunting number, at a time of the year when we were already extremely busy. So we made a plan that four days a week for three weeks several of us would come in at 4 a.m. (four hours before the pastry kitchen would begin) and try to bake 15,000 cookies. We bought a little hand-cranked cookie machine that seemed like a perfect 19th-century creation and went to work. The first couple of days were sometimes like the famous *I Love Lucy* episode, until we managed to get the production running smoothly.

We baked the cookies, boxed them, and sent them all over the country. We were wondering how we were going to make the refill orders when they came in. The book was going to be a massive success, and there was even talk of a movie the following year and more cookie sales. This was going to be fantastic, the sales boost we needed.

After four weeks we hadn't heard a word. How could this be? Each store only got 12 boxes of cookies. They had to be sold by now. If they hadn't, we thought, they'd be starting to rot in the boxes. Finally we called our contact at Borders' corporate to get the next order. Oh boy, the news was shocking. According to the sales reports, not a single box of cookies seemed to have sold! We were told that if we left them on the shelves until January 1 they'd pay for half the order.

What to do? We knew that at this point the cookies were deteriorating, and that we had thousands of reputation time bombs in many Borders stores across the country. What was more important: reputation and future sales or cash in January? We brought them all back from the stores and disposed of them ourselves. We didn't want to leave anything to chance. So all that work baking really delicious cookies in a really special package and zero sales. It was quite an audacious failure!

THE #1 CONTROVERSY OF OUR CAREERS—BAGELS!

Enough about our failures. Almost more interesting is when we create items that are controversial. We define these as ones that people have strong reactions to, both positive and negative.

Our most controversial item for the last 15 years has been our bagels. People either love 'em or hate 'em, and sometimes when they hate them they also seem to hate us!

For years we had actively chosen not to make bagels, even though the Deli used lots of them. Making bagels is a different process than making breads, and adding them would require a boiler, a different oven, a different mixer, and a shift at an entirely different time of day. We thought we'd leave bagels to those who were already making them.

Then a new opportunity came. In 2001 our organization had an opportunity to create a Zingerman's store in the newly built McNamara Terminal at Detroit Metro Airport, located about 25 miles east of the Bakehouse. The new terminal is quite nice, and as you enter it after going through security you approach a large fountain in the very center of the mile-long terminal. That fountain is located where the Zingerman's store was intended to be. During the planning for this store, our partners in the venture said that if we made bagels we would sell "a thousand a day" and that it was really important to have bagels at the airport. It seemed to make sense for us to move forward. We'd have two large customers to sell to.

We spent several months researching the history of the bagel and working on a number of different formulas. Frank had the opportunity to visit Montreal a couple of times to taste their style of bagel (which is delicious but, having no salt, was not quite what we wanted). We finally nailed down a recipe that we were happy with and, in September 2001, headed to the baking show in Las Vegas to purchase the equipment we needed for this venture. We bought a rotating deck oven, a boiler, and a large spiral mixer to complement our existing bakery equipment. Then we woke up on the morning of September 11, 2001, to the horror of what had happened in New York City.

We ended up being trapped in Las Vegas for a couple of days because all flights were canceled throughout the country and car rental companies had decided not to let people drive their cars across state lines. We were in shock, as the rest of the country was, and we didn't think for a minute about how this could affect our project at the airport. Seven days after returning to Ann Arbor, our partner in the venture pulled out of the project, and we never had our own place at the airport. But lo and behold, we now had a bagel oven, a boiler, and a mixer. The momentum was so strong at this point that we went forward. We would sell them to the Deli, in our own shop, and maybe to some of our other wholesale customers.

A couple of things about our bagels: We think of them as being very traditional. They are boiled, baked on a stone surface at a high temperature, have a hole in the center that you can stick your finger in, and have a real crust. They are what we think the bagels were like that were sold in bagel shops on the Lower East Side of Manhattan at the turn of the 20th century. They are on the small side, chewy, and very flavorful. We make them with very good ingredients—we roast 100 pounds of fresh garlic each week for our garlic and Enough Already bagels. We caramelize onions and cook them with poppy seeds and salt for our onion bagels. No dehydrated onions for us! We use great cinnamon and Flame raisins for our cinnamon raisin bagel. In all, we make 12 different varieties, all really delicious.

So what's the controversy? Many bagel lovers grew up with a bagel that they now think of as authentic, and they believe ours aren't right and that we're moronic, maybe even immoral, for making them this way. New York customers often preface their criticism by telling us that they're from New York, as if that makes them experts. (Amy's mother grew up in Brooklyn. She was born in 1936, and she says that our bagels are very evocative of the ones she grew up with. Who knows?) Customers from Milwaukee know for certain that a bagel can't be crusty or baked like ours are. The challenge is that it's very difficult to compete with someone's memory of a food, especially if it's attached to positive emotions. Bagels are one of those foods that many people have strong associations with.

The bagel craze of the '90s convinced consumers that bagels should be heavily yeasted, plump pieces of dough with a dimple in the center but definitely no hole. They should be soft and squishy and filled with blueberries. We have never worked harder to make an authentic baked good that aroused so much animosity. But we know in our hearts that what our bakers are now baking are consistently the best bagels that we've ever made.

UNEXPECTED AND SURPRISING SUCCESSES

It's really joyful when something goes well that we didn't expect. It's like getting a Community Chest card in Monopoly. Here are a few of the more surprising traditions that have started at the bakery.

Thursday Is Tipsy Turkey Day

We make some simple and delicious savory food that we sell in our bakeshop. We had been making sandwiches for several years, as a way to introduce our customers to our different breads, and we had the idea that soup would be a nice addition to our repertoire. Lots of us like to eat bread with our soup, so we give out a free roll or slice of bread with every bowl of soup we sell.

Our soup making started in 2003. Mary Kalinowski, one of our first bread bakers, had left to open her own soup shop and then returned to the Bakehouse to make soups and prepare savory foods to sell in our retail shop. One of her soups was a turkey chili. Even after Mary left, the turkey chili had such a strong following that only a fool would stop making it. So it became one of our two hot soups each Thursday. One winter Thursday, our two hot soups were turkey chili and Cheddar ale soup. They seemed like two dissimilar items that would give people a choice of flavors. We never imagined that someone would ask for us to mix a half bowl of chili with a half bowl of Cheddar ale. The shop manager at the time, Jake Blachowicz, named the combo Tipsy Turkey. That launched one of the most puzzling and eclectic concoctions that we've ever experienced in our four decades in the food business. It caught on and now is a standard on Thursdays.

Grilled Cheese Wednesday

Nearly every week someone asks us to add a menu item as a restaurant might, not really considering what a bakery can do in an 800-square-foot retail shop. Some years ago, in a weak moment, we agreed to buy a press grill and make grilled cheese sandwiches to sell each Wednesday at lunchtime. We felt we were staffed to do it and that the shop could pull it off.

Well, from the start the sandwiches were a success, and we were consistently selling all that we had prepared by 1 p.m. every Wednesday afternoon. Our sales went from 20 a day to 30 to 40 and on and on. After a couple of years, the demand outgrew our ability to grill the sandwiches on two press grills in the Bakehouse, so we developed a plan to grill them on the 12-burner stove that we have in our front BAKE! classroom. Our customers order the sandwiches in our shop and then walk across the courtyard to the classroom to pick them up. Made with sourdough bread, New York Cheddar cheese, and, if you'd like, mustard and tomatoes ("The Works," also a Jake B. term), the sandwiches make many people happy each Wednesday. They are a favorite of the staff too. Also served on Grilled Cheese Wednesday is classic American creamy tomato soup. It's definitely a comforting and tasty lunch to look forward to every week.

One Wednesday recently, when Frank saw James Brown, one of our longtime employees, setting up to grill, he asked how many sandwiches he had prepped—it was more than 200!

Dinkelbrot

In January 2012 we were fortunate to have Elisabeth Kreutzkamm-Aumueller, Tino Gierig, and Frank Reiser from the Dresdner Backhaus in Dresden, Germany, come bake with us and teach a couple of baking classes at our school. While they were here, they made their version of stollen, as well as teaching us to bake *vinschgauer,* a type of rye bread, and *dinkelbrot,* a German spelt bread.

Somehow, the *dinkelbrot* (funny name and all) is what captured the imagination and palate of our customers. We sell hundreds of loaves every week, with little promotion or education. Who would have thought? We had tried baking spelt bread in the fall of 1992 and decided that we didn't have the capacity for it, given everything else we had going on. However, we stayed in contact over the years with Don Stinchcomb of Purity Foods in Okemos, Michigan, which specializes in Michigan-grown spelt. Don had helped us many times by milling small runs of wheat that we had local farmers grow for us, and we're glad to finally be able to buy spelt from him.

Part of the love affair with *dinkelbrot* comes from customers' love for anything not baked with wheat flour. We think they believe that eating a bread made with a different grain is by definition healthier for them. So the present bias really helped people embrace and love *dinkelbrot.* Ours happens to be a wonderful bread with mashed potatoes, a bit of honey, our rye sour, a touch of malt, and a spice combination of anise, coriander, and cumin.

With that introduction, we leave you to the surprisingly successful recipes and a couple of controversial ones.

This German bread made from spelt (an ancient variety of wheat) is a dense, moist, nutty-flavored loaf coated in sunflower seeds. Its full flavor comes from spelt in the form of flour and flakes, rye flour, and a bit of ground caraway, anise, and coriander. The spices add an almost unidentifiable complexity of flavor.

We have a large German population in Ann Arbor, made up of both native Germans and folks of German heritage. They have been eager purchasers of this bread. We think it also appeals to our ideas about healthy eating. It's a hearty, tasty bread. We recommend eating it with a nut butter, or cheese, or charcuterie, or just by itself.

This recipe takes some planning to prepare. A rye sour, as well as what we call a soaker, needs to be made the day before. As in many of the bread recipes we're sharing, the steps are not difficult but they do require some coordination and forethought.

DINKELBROT
GERMAN SPELT BREAD
makes 2 Loaves

Soaker

Small Yukon Gold potato, cubed	½ cup	115g
Spelt flakes	2½ cups	270 g
Toasted sunflower seeds	¾ cup	100 g
Water, hot (140°F [60°C])	1¼ cups plus 2 Tbsp	320 g

Final Dough

Water	¼ cup plus 1 Tbsp	80 g
Whole spelt flour	2¼ cups	320 g
Rye sour (page 55)	1 cup	270 g
Barley malt syrup	3 Tbsp	70 g
Honey	1 Tbsp plus 2 tsp	30 g
Sea salt	1 Tbsp	18 g
Instant yeast	2 tsp	7 g
Ground caraway	½ tsp	
Ground anise	½ tsp	
Ground coriander	½ tsp	
Sunflower seeds (untoasted) for coating loaves		

Make the Soaker

1. Place the cubed potato in a small saucepan and cover with cool water. Set the pan over medium-high heat and bring to a boil. Boil until the potato is fork-tender. Remove the pot from the heat and drain the potatoes in a strainer, then place the potatoes back into the hot pot. This will help dry them out a bit. Mash the potatoes and set aside to cool.

2. Mix together the spelt flakes, sunflower seeds, mashed potato, and hot water. Cover and allow the soaker to sit at room temperature for 8 to 12 hours.

Make the Dough

1. After 8 to 12 hours, place the soaker in a mixing bowl. Add the water, spelt flour, rye sour, barley malt syrup, honey, sea salt, instant yeast, caraway, anise, and coriander. Stir well. Knead the dough in the bowl for 4 to 5 minutes (page 34). Then let rest, covered with plastic, for 15 to 20 minutes.

continued

Shape the Loaves

1. Coat the work surface with water. Place the dough on the water-coated surface. Wet your hands. Divide the dough into two equal pieces. Flatten the pieces into disks, and then roll each up into a football-shaped loaf.

2. Brush the loaves with water. Roll the moistened loaves in untoasted sunflower seeds to cover the top and side surfaces completely.

3. Place each loaf into a 9-by-5-in [23-by-12-cm] loaf pan that has been lightly sprayed with nonstick cooking spray. Allow to rest, covered with plastic, for 1½ hours. The loaves should approximately double in volume.

4. Preheat the oven with a baking stone and cast iron skillet (for creating steam) to 450°F [230°C] at least 45 minutes before baking.

5. Bake for 3 minutes with steam (page 38). Open the oven door to release the steam, and then bake for an additional 35 to 40 minutes, until nicely browned. Spray the top surface with water after baking to give the loaves a nice shine. Cool on a wire rack before enjoying.

This has been one of our most popular breads since we opened in 1992. Its shiny, blistery crust and compact white crumb seem really accessible to a wide range of diners. It is the bread of choice in our bakeshop to serve for our Grilled Cheese Wednesdays. It's also been one of the two house breads at Zingerman's Roadhouse since they opened 13 years ago.

Why is it named *Better Than San Francisco Sourdough*? Isn't that a pretty arrogant claim? For years we called it San Francisco Sourdough in honor of the naturally leavened bread traditional in the Bay Area, dating back to the Gold Rush era. One day, however, we were contacted by the lawyer of a San Francisco company that objected to our using the name. This was our first run-in with intellectual property law. It seemed a little far-fetched to us that they could claim ownership of the name, but we weren't interested in a lawsuit. Our partner Paul, always quick witted, offered to call it "Better Than San Francisco Sourdough" instead, and much to everyone's surprise, they were fine with that.

We had to change the name of a pastry years later for a similar reason, and then we got smart by doing some research before using what we thought were fun, harmless names. Later, we were on the winning side of one of these battles, and a company paid us to use one of our names!

BETTER THAN SAN FRANCISCO SOURDOUGH BREAD

makes two loaves

Water	2 cups plus 1 Tbsp	470 g
"Put Away Farm" (page 41)	2¾ cups	410 g
Bread flour	5 cups plus 1 Tbsp	695 g
Sea salt	2½ tsp	14 g
Cornmeal for dusting		

1. Pour the water into a large mixing bowl. Tear the "Put Away Farm" into small pieces and add to the water. Add half the flour and beat with a wooden spoon until the dough is a smooth batter. Add the remaining flour and salt. Mix until the dough is rough and shaggy.

2. Turn the dough out of the bowl onto a clean, unfloured work surface. Scrape any bits of dough from the bowl. Knead the dough for 6 to 8 minutes (page 34). The dough will be slightly sticky during the kneading. Place in a lightly oiled bowl and cover with plastic. Ferment the dough for 1 hour.

3. Uncover and place the dough on a lightly floured work surface. Fold the dough (page 34). Place back into the bowl and cover. Ferment for 1 more hour. Uncover and place the dough on a lightly floured work surface. Fold the dough a second time. Place back into the bowl and cover. Ferment for 1 more hour. Uncover and place the dough on a lightly floured work surface. Fold the dough a third time. Place back into the bowl and cover. Ferment for 1 more hour. Uncover and place the dough on a lightly floured surface and divide into two equal pieces.

4. Pre-shape the pieces into rounds (page 35). Cover and let rest for 30 minutes.

5. Uncover and shape into round loaves (page 35). Place the loaves seam side down on a cornmeal-covered surface. Cover with plastic. Proof for 2½ to 3½ hours. Use the touch test (page 38) to see if the loaves are ready for the oven.

6. Preheat the oven with a baking stone and cast iron skillet (for creating steam) to 450°F [230°C] at least 45 minutes before baking.

7. Uncover your loaves and place them on a lightly floured peel. With a razor or sharp knife, cut a tic-tac-toe pattern onto the tops of the rounds that covers a 5-by-5 in [12-by-12-cm] area.

8. When ready, slide the loaves onto the baking stone and bake with lots of steam (page 38) for 10 minutes, uncover, then bake for an additional 25 to 30 minutes, or until they sound hollow when tapped on the bottom. Remove from the oven and cool completely on a wire rack.

AMY: *We were teaching one of our week-long BAKE!-cations—four days of baking classes—and it was bagel-making afternoon. Unexpectedly, my relationship to bagels changed forever. I have to admit that until that afternoon, bagels didn't do much for me.*

What happened? Well, we made our bagels. They were still warm and had a nice contrast between the crispy exterior and the interior chewiness, a contrast that gets lost after being out of the oven for several hours. As we always do in class, we were going to taste what we made. I decided to make the tasting a little more indulgent—I ran over to Zingerman's Creamery, just next door, to get some smoked salmon and fresh cream cheese. I was lucky and it was a Tuesday, their cream-cheese-making day, and they had just made a batch. The cream cheese was still slightly warm. Back in class, we cut our super-fresh bagels, covered them with this just-made cream cheese, and then topped them with pieces of smoked salmon. The combination was unbelievable. Really out of this world, which is an expression I almost never think and have probably never actually spoken. I had one of those moments of confirmation, thinking that all of the trouble we go to when we use traditional methods is worth it—you really can taste the difference.

BAKEHOUSE BAGELS

makes 16 bagels

Onion Mix

Medium onion	1	270 g
Vegetable oil	4 tsp	30 g
Sea salt	2 tsp	12 g
Poppy seeds	3 Tbsp	30 g

Dough

Water, room temperature	2¾ cups	615 g
Barley malt syrup	3 Tbsp	70 g
Demerara sugar	1 Tbsp	20 g
Instant yeast	1 tsp	
Bread flour	8¾ cups	1,226 g
Sea salt	1 Tbsp plus 1 tsp	25 g
Sesame seeds, poppy seeds, or sea salt for sprinkling tops (optional)		

Prepare the Onion Mix

1. You'll prepare the onion mix first so that it has time to cool before it's added to the dough. Preheat the oven to 400°F [200°C].

2. Cut the onion into ¼-in [6-mm] dice. Mix the onion, oil, salt, and poppy seeds in a small bowl. Spread the mixture on a baking tray. Bake for 30 minutes, or until the onions pass through the translucent stage and are just starting to brown. Let the mixture cool completely before adding it to the dough. You'll need ¼ cup [105 g].

Mix the Dough

1. In a bowl, add the water, barley malt syrup, Demerara sugar, and yeast. Stir together with a wooden spoon. Add half of the flour and mix to incorporate the ingredients. It will look like a thick batter. Add the remaining flour and salt and mix until the dough is a shaggy mass.

2. Turn the dough out onto a clean, unfloured work surface. Don't worry if there is still loose flour and partially mixed dry bits of flour and liquid. These will work in as you knead the dough. Knead the dough for 3 minutes (page 34), then cut off one-fourth of the dough and set it aside, covered with plastic. You'll use this dough to make four onion bagels, using the onion mix.

3. Continue kneading the plain bagel dough for an additional 5 minutes, then put it into an oiled bowl. Cover with plastic wrap. Take the dough you set aside earlier and knead in ¼ cup [105 g] of the onion mix, giving it about 5 minutes of additional kneading. Place the onion bagel dough in a separate oiled bowl and cover with plastic. Ferment both doughs for 1 hour.

continued

Form and Bake the Bagels

1. Divide the plain bagel dough into 12 pieces and cover with plastic. Divide the onion bagel dough into 4 pieces and cover with plastic.

2. Starting with the plain bagels, roll each piece of dough into a strand 8 to 10 in [20 to 25 cm] long with bulges on both ends. Form each into a circle around your hand and wrap the ends together, overlapping them by about 1 in [2.5 cm]. Roll the seam together, using the palm of your hand to lock the ends together.

3. Place the finished bagels on a lightly floured board and lightly cover with plastic wrap. Ferment for 1 hour.

4. Preheat the oven to 450°F [230°C] for 45 minutes prior to baking.

5. Bring a stockpot filled with water to a simmer. Add the bagels to the simmering water and boil for 1 minute. Do this with only a few at a time. Remove the bagels from the water with a slotted spoon and place on a cooling rack over a sheet tray so that excess water can drip off.

6. If you'd like to put seeds or salt on your bagels, do it now, then transfer the bagels to a parchment-lined sheet tray and bake immediately. The total baking time will be 22 to 25 minutes.

7. Once the bagels are in the oven, watch for the surface to appear dry and to have a hint of color. This will take about 10 to 12 minutes. At this point, remove the tray from the oven and flip the bagels over, using a spatula. Return to the oven and bake until golden brown.

a more traditional way to bake bagels

If you want to get even more serious about bagel baking, try doing it in the traditional way. This means creating your own bagel baking boards. Here's how:

- *Cut 2-by-4 boards into lengths that match the depth or width of your baking stone. Either orientation will work.*
- *Cut pieces of jute webbing (available in fabric stores) the length of the boards, plus enough extra to wrap around to the other side for fastening.*
- *Use a staple gun to attach the jute to the board by wrapping it over the ends and stapling it to the other side.*

Now you're ready to bake your bagels. Here's how:

- *Heat a baking stone in the oven for 1 hour at 475°F [240°C].*
- *Moisten the jute-covered boards by placing them in the kitchen sink and liberally spraying them with water.*
- *After boiling the bagels, line them up on the jute-covered boards and put them in the oven, on top of the baking stone.*
- *Bake for 3 minutes on the boards and then flip the bagels onto the surface of the baking stone, remove the boards from the oven, and continue baking for 18 to 22 minutes, or until golden brown.*
- *Remove from the oven and cool completely on a cooling rack.*

For years we made pecan sticky buns that we called 'Bama Buns—'Bama referring to the state of Alabama, where pecans are common and where our head pastry baker at the time, Mitch Stamm, harkened from. Then, in 2008, Barack Obama was elected president. We couldn't help but notice the similarity between his last name and our sweet little apolitical sticky bun. We thought it would be fun to change the name, at least during his presidency, to Obama Buns. Although President Obama has eaten at Zingerman's Deli several times, we don't think he's had the chance to test out his namesake.

Some of our customers thought it was funny, especially those who knew the original name of the treat. Some didn't really care or didn't engage with it. And some, much to our surprise, were very offended. Literally every few months we fielded a furious response to the name. Generally, the ones complaining were not supporters of President Obama and were ticked off to see something named after him. Only once did someone comment that they thought it was disrespectful and beneath the office of the president to name a sticky bun after him. We think this person didn't have enough respect for our sticky buns!

But let's discuss the buns themselves. They are delicious, rich sticky buns. The dough is full of tasty butter, and the topping is made special with a mixture of honey, muscovado sugar, and an abundance of pecans.

These buns reheat really well from room temperature, even after being frozen, so there's no need to make them the day you wish to serve them. They are best made over two days. The dough is very soft when you make it, so don't be surprised. It's not incorrect.

Oh, and call them whatever you want.

OBAMA BUNS
PECAN STICKY BUNS

makes 12 buns

Poolish

Whole milk, room temperature	½ cup	115 g
Instant yeast	1 tsp	
All-purpose flour	1 cup plus 3 Tbsp	170 g

Final Dough

Unsalted butter, room temperature	½ cup	115 g
Granulated sugar	¼ cup plus 1 tsp	55 g
Sea salt	1½ tsp	9 g
Large egg	1	
Egg yolk	1	
Poolish	all	
All-purpose flour	1 cup plus 3 Tbsp	170 g

Cinnamon Sugar Filling

Muscovado brown sugar	¼ cup (packed)	55 g
Ground cinnamon	1 Tbsp	
Sea salt	pinch	

Topping

Unsalted butter, room temperature	1 cup	220 g
Granulated sugar	½ cup	55 g
Muscovado brown sugar	⅓ cup (packed)	60 g
Honey	¾ cup	255 g
Sea salt	1 tsp	
Pecan pieces	2 cups	240 g
Melted butter for brushing dough		

continued

Make the Poolish

1. Make the poolish by combining the milk, yeast, and flour in the bowl of a stand mixer. Mix with the dough hook attachment until the mixture forms a dough. This is a firm poolish. Place the poolish in a separate oiled bowl and ferment, covered, for 1 hour.

Make the Dough

1. After an hour, on low speed, with the paddle attachment, cream the butter, sugar, and salt until combined. Increase the speed to medium and beat until creamy. Add the whole egg and egg yolk. Scrape down the bowl as necessary.

2. Break the poolish up into small pieces and add to the creamed mixture. Once all the poolish is added, increase to medium speed and beat until the mixture is light and creamy, and there are few pieces of poolish left.

3. On low speed, add the flour and mix for 3 minutes, scraping down the bowl if necessary. The dough will still be sticky to the touch. Remove the dough from the bowl, wrap in plastic wrap, and refrigerate overnight or for at least 6 hours.

Make the Filling and Topping

1. To prepare the cinnamon filling, combine the muscovado brown sugar, cinnamon, and salt in a bowl and mix well. Set aside until needed to fill the rolls.

2. To make the topping, cream the butter, granulated sugar, and muscovado sugar together in a mixing bowl. Add the honey and salt and combine until well blended.

3. Toast the pecans on a sheet tray at 325°F [160°C] for 12 minutes until they are toasty brown. Start checking after 8 minutes.

4. Spread the topping on the bottom of a 9-by-13-in [23-by-33-cm] baking pan and spread the pecans evenly over the topping.

Assemble and Bake the Buns

1. Remove the sweet dough from the refrigerator. Unwrap the dough and place it on a floured surface. Flour the top of the dough.

2. Using a rolling pin, lightly tap the sweet dough into a rectangle. Check to see that the dough is not sticking to the work surface (flour lightly again if necessary). With the rolling pin, roll the dough into a 9-by-12-in [23-by-30-cm] rectangle that is ¼ in [6 mm] thick.

3. Brush any excess flour from the surface of the dough, making sure to flip the dough over to get the flour off the bottom. Arrange the dough in a landscape orientation, with a long edge facing you (12 in [30 cm] from left to right). Brush melted butter over the surface of the dough. The dough is very soft and may easily extend beyond the initial dimensions. Do your best to keep to the suggested size, but if you don't the rolls will still be tasty. What's most important is that the rolls end up being the same size.

4. Sprinkle the cinnamon sugar mixture evenly over the butter, except for 1 in [2.5 cm] along the top edge farthest from you.

5. Starting with the edge closest to you, begin rolling up the dough. Keep the roll as snug as possible. Continue rolling the dough up, then pinch the far edge to the log, making a seam.

6. Roll the log of dough onto the seam and cut it into 12 equal slices. (If you prefer smaller buns, roll the log longer and cut it into more pieces. Twelve pieces can fit nicely into the pan.)

7. Place the rolls on the sticky bun topping in a 4-by-3 pattern. With the palm of your hand press the rolls down until they are ¾ in [2 cm] thick. When the rolls proof and bake, they will grow together.

8. Cover the rolls with plastic and let proof for 1½ to 2 hours or until they are 50 percent bigger.

9. Thirty minutes prior to baking, preheat the oven to 375°F [190°C].

10. Bake for 30 to 35 minutes, until the rolls are golden brown on top and the filling is bubbling. To be certain that they are ready, take their internal temperature with a thermometer. Bake until they are 190°F [88°C]. They could get quite dark. Do not be alarmed; the interior will be moist. It's best to bake the pan on a sheet tray lined with parchment paper, to catch any of the filling that might spill over.

11. Cool the buns for 5 minutes, then place a sheet tray or serving platter on top of the pan. Using hot pads, turn the sticky buns over onto the tray or platter, removing the pan. Let cool for a few more minutes, then enjoy while still warm.

On our third research trip to learn about Hungarian baking, we went to a part of Romania called Transylvania to explore Hungarian foods still being made by the small Hungarian communities that live there. The prize of the trip was this rich cinnamon swirl celebration bread, Somodi Kalács (sho-MO-di ka-LAHTCH). Originally it was baked in a clay pot, greased with lard, in a wood-fired oven. Nowadays it is more frequently made in a loaf pan, still greased with lard but baked in a gas oven.

We already have many Christmas baking traditions at the bakery, so we decided to make it for Easter. It instantaneously became an annual Easter favorite with our customers and staff—a totally unexpected overnight success. We make it every weekend for the month around Easter. When the first month ended, the disappointment was palpable, so we decided to bake it on several weekends throughout the year. Many people have freezers full of these loaves so they can make it to its next appearance in our store.

SOMODI KALÁCS
TRANSYLVANIAN CINNAMON SWIRL BREAD

makes 1 loaf

Water, room temperature	½ cup plus 1 Tbsp	125 g
Egg yolks	4	60 g
Corn oil	2 Tbsp	25 g
Honey	2 Tbsp	40 g
Instant yeast	1¾ tsp	5 g
All-purpose flour	2⅓ cups	325 g
Sea salt	¾ tsp	
Ground cinnamon	2 tsp	
Granulated sugar	⅔ cup	165 g
Melted butter or lard for brushing dough		
Egg Wash		
Large egg	1	
Egg yolk	1	
Water	1 Tbsp	

1. In a large bowl, combine the water, egg yolks, corn oil, honey, yeast, and half of the flour. Mix with a wooden spoon until the mixture becomes a thick batter. Add the remaining flour and sea salt and mix until the dough becomes a shaggy mass. Scrape the dough out of the mixing bowl onto a clean, unfloured work surface.

2. Knead the dough for 6 to 8 minutes (page 34). Scrape down the work surface as necessary; the dough will become smooth and elastic during the kneading process.

3. Put the dough into a lightly oiled bowl and cover with plastic. Ferment the dough for 1 hour at room temperature. Combine the cinnamon and sugar in a small bowl.

4. After an hour, turn the dough out of the bowl onto a well-floured surface and use a rolling pin to roll it out to a 13-by-15-in [33-by-38-cm] rectangle. Position the dough in a landscape orientation (with the long side facing you), and brush the entire surface with melted butter. Place half the total cinnamon sugar on the buttered surface and spread it across the dough.

5. Fold the long edges at the top and bottom of the dough so that they meet along the middle of the length of the rectangle. Brush the newly exposed surface with more melted butter and about half of the remaining cinnamon sugar.

continued

6. Grab the left side of the dough and fold it two-thirds of the way over to the right. Brush butter onto the newly exposed surface and rub half of the remaining cinnamon sugar on it. Fold the right side of the dough over to the left. Turn the dough 90 degrees counter-clockwise. Brush the surface with melted butter and spread the remaining cinnamon sugar on this surface.

7. Beginning at the side closest to you, roll the dough into a cylinder. Place the loaf with the seam side down in a 4-by-8-in [10-by-20-cm] metal loaf pan that has been brushed on the inside with melted butter.

8. Make the egg wash by beating together the egg, egg yolk, and water. Brush the loaf with some of the egg wash and allow it to proof in a draft-free area for 1½ to 2 hours, or until it has risen significantly in the loaf pan and responds properly to the touch test (page 38).

9. Preheat the oven to 335°F [168°C].

10. When the loaf is fully proofed, brush it with egg wash a second time and lightly score the surface with a paring knife in three spots to prevent air gaps. Bake for 15 minutes, then reduce the oven temperature to 320°F [160°C] and bake for another 25 minutes. Using a meat thermometer, take the temperature of the loaf. Remove it from the oven at 195° to 200°F [90° to 93°C]. Let cool for at least 20 minutes before removing from the pan. Remove carefully, placing it onto parchment paper or aluminum foil.

discovering somodi kalács

Why visit Romania to learn about Hungarian traditions? Transylvania was an important part of Hungary until the Treaty of Trianon after World War I, when it was given to Romania. After the treaty, many Hungarians left the region, but plenty stayed. To this day there are villages in Transylvania in which everyone considers themselves Hungarian.

We traveled to a village named Torockó, which is the home of somodi kalács. *This village was originally very prosperous. About 400 years ago it was an iron mining town known for its wrought iron pieces, which were exported to Italy. Some village families also owned gold mines. The lucrative trade in metals enabled many of the villagers to afford sugar and cinnamon, a real luxury in 1600, which they used to make this "cake." It was served for Christmas, Easter, and Pentecost (and still is), and until the 20th century it was the customary wedding cake.*

To learn to make somodi kalács, *we visited the bed-and-breakfast of Melinda Király, who grew up in Torockó and learned to cook and bake in her parents' restaurant. Most interesting to us was the special folding technique Melinda used to achieve the unique distribution of the cinnamon sugar inside the bread. Although not all traditions are kept in their pure form, Melinda still greases her pans with lard. The result is a sticky, sweet, cinnamony crust that tastes slightly of bacon. This is one of those breads you may devour by the loaf and then lick your fingers at the end to get every last little sticky bit! We encourage you to try making it with melted lard, but if that doesn't fit your lifestyle, use butter instead.*

BOSTON CREAM PIE

makes one 9-in [23-cm] two-layer cake

AMY: *This cake has been a huge customer favorite from the moment we started selling it. We love to make classic foods—the ones that have passed the test of time. It says something, to us at least, if a food continues to be loved from one generation to the next. Boston cream pie lands in that category. We also like to make things at the bakery that we crave. Boston cream pie lands in that category too.*

We're not sure why it took us more than a decade to consider making Boston cream pie. Perhaps it was the challenge of making it suitable for display in a refrigerated pastry case. A traditional Boston cream pie is not iced on the sides, leaving exposed, bare cake. When a bare cake sits in a display case, it can dry out. Although it's not traditional, we decided to put a relatively thin layer of white buttercream all over the cake to protect it. Then we glaze the top with chocolate ganache. Although we're usually sticklers for tradition, we love this version as much as the original.

There are five component recipes in this cake, so it takes a little while to make. Give it a try! You won't be disappointed, and you'll develop several important baking techniques in the process.

Chiffon Cake

Granulated sugar	1 cup plus 2 Tbsp	230 g
Cake flour	1 cup plus 1 Tbsp	125 g
Baking powder	1½ tsp	
Fine sea salt	¼ tsp	
Extra-large eggs, separated	4	
Vegetable oil	¼ cup	65 g
Water	⅓ cup	80 g
Vanilla extract	1 tsp	
Cream of tartar	½ tsp	

Pastry Cream

Vanilla bean	½ bean	
Whole milk	¾ cup plus 1 Tbsp	190 g
Heavy cream	¾ cup plus 1 Tbsp	190 g
Granulated sugar	7 Tbsp plus 2 tsp	90 g
Sea salt	⅛ tsp	
Egg yolks	5	75 g
Cornstarch	2½ Tbsp	25 g
Vanilla extract	2 tsp	
Unsalted butter	3 Tbsp	45 g

Swiss Buttercream

Egg whites	3	90 g
Sea salt	¼ tsp	
Granulated sugar	¾ cup	150 g
Unsalted butter, room temperature	1 cup	225 g
Vanilla extract	¼ tsp	

Chocolate Glaze

Chopped chocolate (60% to 65% cacao)	1 cup	225 g
Light corn syrup	¼ cup	85 g
Unsalted butter	¼ cup	115 g

continued

Simple Syrup

Water	½ cup	115 g
Granulated sugar	⅓ cup	75 g
Light corn syrup	2 Tbsp	40 g
Vanilla extract	¼ tsp	

Make the Cake

1. Place 9-in [23-cm] parchment rounds in the bottom of two cake pans, 9 in [23 cm] in diameter and 2 in [5 cm] deep. Set aside. (No greasing or buttering of the pans is necessary.) Preheat the oven to 375°F [190°C].

2. Combine in a mixing bowl ½ cup plus 1 Tbsp [115 g] of the sugar with the cake flour, baking powder, and salt. Stir together with a whisk to combine. Set aside.

3. In a separate mixing bowl, combine the egg yolks, oil, water, and vanilla. Beat to combine.

4. Add the wet ingredients to the dry ingredients and whisk until the mixture becomes smooth. If using a stand mixer, use the paddle attachment and scrape the sides and bottom of the bowl. Lumps sometimes form when making this batter. It's important to break them up and mix thoroughly.

5. In a clean bowl of a stand mixer fitted with a whisk attachment, add the egg whites and cream of tartar. Whip on medium-high speed until the whites start to form soft peaks. Gradually add the remaining ½ cup plus 1 Tbsp [115 g] sugar to the egg whites in a slow and steady stream. Beat on high speed until the sugar is incorporated and the egg whites form stiff peaks. Be careful not to overmix at this point. If the whites start to break apart into clumps, you have gone too far.

6. Fold the egg whites into the batter, one-third at a time. Don't fold too much! You don't want to deflate the whites. A little bit of unmixed egg white is better than overfolding and deflating the batter too much. Divide the mixture between the prepared cake pans. Bake the cakes for 16 to 18 minutes, or until golden brown and the top springs back when touched.

7. Remove the cake pans from the oven, immediately turn them upside down on a sheet tray, and cool to room temperature. When cool, turn the cakes out onto cooling racks, remove the parchment paper, and set aside. If you have trouble releasing the cakes from the pans, use a plastic knife to help. Run it along the edges and try again.

tip: *Why don't we grease the pans prior to baking? The dry sides of the pan allow the batter to grip and rise in the oven. If they were greased, our painstakingly made batter would keep sliding down the sides, and we'd end up with a low and dense cake.*

Make the Pastry Cream

1. Split the half vanilla bean down the center and scrape out the seeds. In a medium saucepan, combine the milk, heavy cream, sugar, sea salt, and the vanilla bean seeds and scraped pod. Bring to a simmer and then turn off the heat. Let stand for 30 minutes for the vanilla to infuse the liquid.

2. In a medium bowl, whisk together the egg yolks and cornstarch.

3. Reheat the milk mixture and temper the eggs with it. To do this, ladle small amounts of the hot milk into the egg yolk and cornstarch mixture while stirring. This prepares the yolks to be added to the hot mixture and reduces the possibility that they will curdle.

4. Pour the egg yolk mixture into the saucepan. Over medium heat, cook the mixture while stirring constantly with a wooden spoon or a whisk, and bring to a light boil. Cook for 1 minute while stirring vigorously. Remove the pastry cream from the heat and pour it into a clean bowl. Beat it with a clean whisk for a couple of minutes, until it cools slightly and becomes smooth and shiny. It is not possible to overbeat the cream. Add the vanilla extract and butter, and whisk until smooth.

5. Place plastic wrap directly onto the surface of the pastry cream to prevent a skin from forming. Refrigerate until completely cold before using. When ready to use, beat with a wire whisk or an electric mixer to make it spreadable.

Make the Buttercream

1. In a metal mixing bowl, combine the egg whites, salt, and sugar and stir to combine. Place over a double boiler with gently simmering water and heat the egg white mixture until the sugar is completely dissolved and the temperature reaches 180°F [82°C]. Stir every couple of minutes during this process.

2. Transfer the egg white mixture to the bowl of a stand mixer. Using the whisk attachment, whip the egg white mixture on high until it doubles in volume, becomes thick and shiny, and has cooled to room temperature.

3. With the mixer on medium speed, add the soft butter, a piece at a time, until all is incorporated. The butter should be the same temperature as the egg mixture to aid successful incorporation. Add the vanilla and beat to incorporate. Beat on high speed for 1 minute to ensure that all the butter is combined with the meringue. Scrape down the sides of the bowl as necessary.

4. Use immediately or place in an airtight container and refrigerate for up to 1 week or freeze for up to 3 months. Let stand at room temperature to soften before using. It can take several hours for this to happen.

Make the Chocolate Glaze

1. In a double boiler, combine the chocolate, corn syrup, and butter. Heat and stir until the mixture is melted and smooth. If using right away, remove the glaze from the double boiler and let stand at room temperature until barely warm. When you are ready to use it, warm it just enough to be able to glaze the cake but not melt the buttercream. The glaze can be refrigerated for a week.

Make the Simple Syrup

1. In a small saucepan, combine the water, sugar, and corn syrup. Bring to a boil over medium heat. Remove from the heat and add the vanilla extract. Cool to room temperature.

continued

Assemble the Cake

1. Place one cake layer on a 10-in [25-cm] cardboard cake round or serving platter, bottom side up. Brush the top of the cake with half of the simple syrup. Spread all of the pastry cream over the cake layer to within ½ in [1.5 cm] of the edge of the cake.

2. Place the second cake layer on top of the pastry cream, bottom side up, and press to secure it. Brush the top of the second cake layer with the remaining simple syrup. Neatly ice the top and sides of the cake with the buttercream. Make the top of the cake as smooth as possible.

3. Place the cake in the refrigerator for 1 hour to let the buttercream firm up.

4. Once the buttercream is firm, place the cake on a cake turntable or serving platter. Use slightly warm, not hot, chocolate glaze. It should be fluid enough that it will drip down the sides of the cake slightly. If your glaze has cooled too much, rewarm it in the double boiler or microwave it for a few seconds. Pour all of the chocolate glaze on the center of the top of the cake. Use an offset spatula to smooth the chocolate glaze to the edge of the cake. Let some of the glaze fall over the side of the cake, but do not smooth the sides. The glaze should drip unevenly over the edges of the cake. Place the cake in the refrigerator to let the chocolate glaze firm up.

5. Keep the cake refrigerated until 1 hour prior to eating. To serve the cake, use a hot knife to cut cleanly through the chocolate glaze. Take a chef's knife and either let hot water run on it or fill a pitcher with hot water and let the knife warm up in it. Dry the knife with a towel and then cut the cake. You may need to reheat the knife after cutting several pieces.

Let them eat cake, but they need to know how

AMY: *Somehow we've lost the knowledge of how to store and serve most American cakes. We know this at the Bakehouse because for some period of time we kept getting complaints about our cakes being dry. We were initially puzzled, and then we realized after we started asking questions that our customers were eating them cold. You bet! Cold butter-based cakes and icing are dry and crumbly.*

Cakes iced with buttercream and made with butter are best eaten at room temperature, 72°F [22°C]. They can be left out for many hours, really a full day, before eating. The only time I refrigerate a cake is if I know I am not going to serve it for a day or two. I always let my cakes come to room temperature prior to serving, which can take four to five hours to ensure that they're smooth, creamy, and moist and that the flavors are most fully available. Most cakes are not perishable, and there are no health risks to leaving them unrefrigerated. The only cakes we regularly recommend refrigerating are those with cream fillings or cream cheese frosting.

We created a sticker to put on each cake box explaining how best to enjoy it, and since then we mainly hear compliments about our cakes.

This turkey chili is made particularly flavorful with dried pepper flakes from the region of Urfa in Turkey and green chile powder. It's a testament to how the choice of ingredients can make a noticeable difference in a simple recipe.

Red-black Urfa pepper flakes have a sweet, earthy, and smoky flavor profile. They are made from a special deep-purple pepper that is picked, cut, and then dried in the sun during the day and wrapped and sweated at night for a week. As the days pass, the color changes from purple to burgundy to almost black. They have a moderate level of heat.

If you like, do as some of our customers do and make both this chili and the Cheddar ale soup, and suggest that your dining mates mix them together. People swear by the combination; the actual proportions are a personal choice. Personally, we like this chili with a chunk of sourdough or Paesano bread.

TURKEY URFA CHILI

makes 4 to 6 servings

Canola oil	2 Tbsp	25 g
Diced onion (¼ in [6 mm])	1½ cups	170 g
Ground turkey	16 oz	454 g
Minced garlic (3 cloves)	1 Tbsp	25 g
Ground cumin	2½ tsp	7 g
Green chile powder	2½ tsp	7 g
Urfa pepper flakes	1½ Tbsp	13 g
Sea salt	1 Tbsp	12 g
Ground black pepper	1 tsp	
Kidney beans, drained	three 15-oz cans	1,275 g
Diced tomatoes (canned)	28-oz can	795 g
Crushed tomatoes (canned)	28-oz can	795 g
Sour cream for topping		
Chopped green onions for topping		

1. In a large stockpot, heat the oil and sauté the onions over medium to low heat until they are translucent. Add the ground turkey and minced garlic. Stir frequently and actively break up the turkey to avoid clumping. Cook the turkey completely. Add the cumin, green chile powder, Urfa pepper, salt, and pepper. Stir to incorporate the spices and cook over low heat for 2 minutes.

2. Add the beans and both kinds of tomatoes. Mix well. Bring to a simmer and cook for 30 minutes. Stir frequently to avoid scorching. Serve hot in bowls with sour cream and chopped green onions as tasty garnishes.

This soup has been a Thursday standard in our shop for at least a decade. It's been so long that none of us can remember exactly when we started to make it. Whether summer or winter, it seems to satisfy. Its distinctive flavor comes from well-chosen beer, Cheddar cheese, and sherry vinegar. A less familiar ingredient to home cooks is Marash pepper. Marash peppers hail from Turkey and can be used fresh or dried and ground. The dried version is fruity and earthy in flavor and has a medium heat. It adds a wonderful complexity to this soup. It's also great sprinkled on other dishes, like salad and fish, and mixed with oil for dipping bread. It's readily available online through Zingerman's Mail Order and other purveyors.

CHEDDAR ALE SOUP

makes 6 to 8 servings

Vegetable Stock

Medium carrots	2	185 g
Small onion	1	165 g
Large celery stalks	2	140 g
Bay leaf	1	
Parsley stems	2	
Thyme sprig	1	
Black peppercorns	2	
Water	6 cups [1.4 l]	1,416 g

Soup

Unsalted butter	½ cup	112 g
Diced onion (½ in [1.5 cm])	1¼ cups	150 g
Diced carrot (½ in [1.5 cm])	1¼ cups	150 g
Diced celery (½ in [1.5 cm])	1¼ cups	150 g
Minced garlic	2 Tbsp	25 g
Kosher salt	1 Tbsp	20 g
Amber ale	1¾ cups [420 ml]	410 g
Vegetable stock	4 cups [960 ml]	910 g
All-purpose flour	1 cup	140 g
Whole milk	4¾ cups [1.1 l]	1,211 g
Grated sharp Cheddar	8 cups	600 g
Sherry vinegar	2 tsp	10 g
Marash pepper flakes	2½ tsp	6 g
Ground white pepper	¾ tsp	

Make the Vegetable Stock

1. Cut all of the vegetables for the stock into large pieces. Place them and the bay leaf, parsley, thyme, and peppercorns in a pot. Add the water. Bring to a boil and simmer gently for 45 minutes.

2. Pour the stock into a large bowl through a strainer to remove the vegetables. Any extra stock can be refrigerated or frozen for a later use.

Make the Soup

1. In a large stockpot, melt the butter. Turn the heat to medium and cook the onions, carrots, celery, and garlic until tender. Add the salt after the vegetables begin to soften. Be careful not to brown them. Add the beer and simmer for 5 minutes.

2. In a separate pot, bring the vegetable stock to a simmer. Add the flour to the beer and vegetable mixture. Stir and cook until the mixture thickens and starts to stick to the pan. Gradually pour in the milk, stirring as you do, and then bring the soup back to a simmer.

3. Add 4 cups [945 ml] of the hot vegetable stock to the soup. Remove the pot from the heat and purée with an immersion blender. Put the puréed soup back onto the stove on medium to low heat. Slowly add the grated cheese, stirring constantly to avoid scorching.

4. Turn off the burner and season the soup with sherry vinegar, Marash pepper, and white pepper. The soup is now ready to serve.

chapter 8

our
NEXT
VISION

FRANK: It's funny that Amy and I decided that I would write the introduction to this chapter, because I'm actually the historian of the two of us and she's the one who dreams about the future. Although we opened in 1992, I didn't begin to consider the future of the Bakehouse until 2000. Prior to this I was fully focused on the present, fearful of failure. After eight years of dedicated attention to the daily details, I felt as if the Bakehouse was established and stable, and I could begin to dream. The future finally felt hopeful, full of positive choices, exciting even.

As Zingerman's Community of Businesses has grown, we have learned and then taught approaches that can be helpful in life and in business. One of the most powerful tools we now use consistently is visioning. Simply put, visioning is accomplished by allowing oneself the freedom to describe in detail a preferred vision of how one's business (or life) may look at a specific point in the future. We teach that visions have four critical qualities. The first is that they are inspiring. They describe a future that we feel excited about—so excited that we'll do whatever it takes to reach it. Second, the vision must be strategically sound. To stay motivated, it must be possible to achieve the vision. The vision also needs to be documented. This keeps it real and keeps us accountable to it. It makes it easier to share it, and it also helps us know when we've achieved it, so that we can celebrate. Finally, the vision needs to be communicated. The more people there are who know about it, the more there are who can help make it happen. In the Bakehouse we often create the visions together, so that excitement and commitment are created right from the start.

Currently we're finishing up a 10-year vision that took us to Hungary, led to many improvements in our baking, grew our baking school, increased our green initiatives, improved the quality of work life for the staff, and inspired us to write this book. It's now time to think about a new vision!

TIME FOR BRAINSTORMING

Amy and I have a few ideas. There are small things we'd like to accomplish, like having more professional bakers visit us and our school. We're remodeling the bakery to flow more efficiently, as well as beautifying our exterior. We have educational goals for the staff, hoping to support their professional development. We plan to continue our work on improving everyone's quality of work life and compensation.

We have a few larger projects on our minds as well. We want to explore another baking tradition. We're considering where to go next. It's a tough and exciting choice when the world is available—China? Brazil? Australia? North Africa? The Baltics? We're actively researching the baking traditions of these regions and gathering information that will help us make a decision. We're looking for delicious breads and pastries made by bakers who will welcome us and teach us.

Heirloom grains and locally grown grains are also interesting to us. We have always preferred local ingredients in other areas of our baking, but until the last few years we hadn't believed that the wheat and rye we use could be grown in Michigan. We're now actively participating in and supporting the reestablishment of grain farming in Michigan. We're also considering milling our own grain. Milling is a craft in its own right and would require significant learning that we're eager to engage with.

These are our next projects, but in the Bakehouse there are 150 other people with their own aspirations and interests. Their dreams are in many ways more important than our own. We expect that they may be here longer than us to carry them out, and so this needs to be a bakery they're excited about. When we write our next vision, it will be a whole Bakehouse project and the group interaction may lead to a very different vision than I'm imagining at the moment. Through this process we hope to engage everyone at a personal level, to make the bakery and the future be even more theirs. Maybe this next vision will even include a reference to our last big project—successfully handing over the bakery to an excited, engaged, and prepared group of new owners.

Whatever the content it will be written with courage—from the heart. Come and visit us and see what happens!

The recipes in this chapter are our newest ones—two new breads using Michigan grain and many of our Hungarian favorites. Enjoy!

hungry for hungary!

You'll discover a number of Hungarian recipes in this book and, after reading our bios and seeing that neither one of us is Hungarian, you might wonder why. Let us tell you!

One of the best parts of being bakers is the seemingly infinite opportunity to keep learning. The variety of breads and pastries around the world is remarkable, and the techniques to make them well often take years of practice and observation to master. The only trying aspect of this opportunity is deciding where to focus our attention! Our most recent choice has been to study Hungarian foodways.

Not all of the world's cuisines have great baking traditions. Hungary has it all. Its baked goods include incredible breads and desserts, in both professional and home versions. An added bonus for us is that soup, which we've been serving for years in our shop, is a critical element of a traditional Hungarian meal.

One of the interesting aspects of Hungarian cuisine is its combination of many different cultural influences. The three primary influences are from the Magyars (the ethnic founders of Hungary and the creators of gulyás [goulash]), the Turkish Ottoman Empire, and the Hapsburgs of Austria. Communist rule after World War II also left its mark on Hungarian foodways by destroying many local traditions and nationalizing elements of food production.

Over the centuries, the cuisine has evolved not just through invasion but also through invitation. At different times Hungarian nobility invited both French and Italian court chefs to their own kitchens, creating an interesting meld of flavors, dishes, and techniques.

The final reason we chose Hungary is its connection to Eastern European Jewish history and cooking. Hungary had a large Jewish population before World War II, which was decimated in the final months of the war and suppressed during communism. Since the early 1990s, however, there's been a renaissance of Jewish life and cooking in Budapest. The largest Jewish population in Eastern Europe lives in Budapest. This connection of our organization's roots with traditional Ashkenazi Jewish food is very compelling. Oh, and Hungarian words are fun to try to say!

To learn about Hungarian food, we visited the country many times. During our visits we trained with local bakers and cooks as well as tasted and ate widely. Our most influential baking teachers are the Auguszt family. They are the longest-standing baking family in Hungary, with the fifth generation now carrying on the tradition. They welcomed us warmly into their world, shared some of their exacting recipes and ingredient choices, and even came to Ann Arbor to teach our baking students. Through our conversations we learned that part of the family had actually lived in Ann

Arbor for six months. Mr. Auguszt had even visited the Delicatessen and remembered the long line and the satisfying rye bread. What a joyful coincidence!

For explanations and instruction in Jewish cooking, we enjoyed the mentorship of Tibor Rosenstein of Rosenstein's. Mr. Rosenstein survived World War II along with his sister and two grandmothers. When it was time to prepare him for a life of work, the grandmothers decided he should become a chef, because then he would never have to worry about eating. In the early 1990s Mr. Rosenstein opened his own restaurant for the first time, featuring both Jewish and Hungarian standards in an elegant setting. He is incredibly inspirational, knowledgeable, and charming.

Going to Hungary was one obvious way to learn about Hungarian baking, but another was to learn from our very own Hungarian neighbors here in Michigan. Hungarians came to the United States primarily in three waves: the '48ers (1848, that is), the great wave of immigration at the turn of the 19th to the 20th century, and then the '56ers (1956, that is). The '48ers and '56ers were essentially political refugees leaving after failed revolutions, and those who came during the great wave were economic immigrants looking for a better life, just as many other European immigrants were doing at that time. Many of them made homes in the industrial Midwest. A Hungarian community developed in the Detroit neighborhood of Del Ray and later spread across greater southeastern Michigan.

This community persists and continues to evolve. We connected with them and sought out ways to help each other. We were very fortunate to make the acquaintance of Elizabeth Krajz, a fantastic cook and baker of Hungarian nationality. Elizabeth has her own catering business and teaches Hungarian cooking. She taught us to make pork crackling pogácsa, which we then transformed into the dill version featured in the book (page 231). Thank you, Elizabeth! At first Elizabeth greeted us with reserve and a critical eye concerning the Hungarian specialties we were already making. After several visits together, however, the reserve melted, and we were last greeted with a hearty hug and a huge smile.

How has our Hungarian adventure been received by our customers? Overall, the reactions have been very positive. For many it is an introduction to something they've never even imagined. To some it was a wonderful surprise, actually often tear inducing, to walk into our shop and see food from their childhood or that their grandmother made for them. It made our place feel even more like their place.

Frank and I love food, but we also love people, and this project has been an incredible combination of both, enabling us to make meaningful connections with many people in new ways and across different worlds. The power of food to bring people together is remarkable.

TRUE NORTH BREAD

makes 2 loaves

FRANK: *We've been buying a small quantity of Michigan-grown wheat for the past seven years, and to highlight it to our guests we often make a particular bread out of it rather than mixing it with our other flours. True North is our most recent loaf made with Michigan flour. The flour comes from hard red wheat and is grown and milled by Grand Traverse Culinary Oils in Traverse City, Michigan. It is stone milled and contains most of the germ and some of the bran. If you're not in Michigan and you can't locate this flour, try to find one with similar qualities and support your local grain farmers and millers. They'll appreciate it! To approximate this flour at home, use 4 parts all-purpose flour and 1 part well-sifted whole wheat flour. Use a super-fine sifter to remove the larger bran particles from the whole wheat flour.*

We bake this loaf dark, and that enhances the flavor of the wheat. If you're adventurous, bake one big round loaf with this recipe and leave it in for 10 or 15 minutes longer than we recommend—don't be afraid of the dark crumb.

Water, room temperature	3 cups plus 3 Tbsp	725 g
Levain (page 42)	⅔ cup	145 g
Stone-ground hard red wheat flour	6¾ cups plus 2 Tbsp	965 g
Sea salt	1½ Tbsp	27 g

1. Place the water in a mixing bowl. Tear the levain into small pieces and add to the water. Add half the flour and stir with a wooden spoon to combine and break up the levain. Add the remaining flour and salt. Mix to combine until the dough is rough and shaggy.

2. Turn the dough out onto a clean, unfloured work surface, scraping any bits of flour or dough out of the bowl. Knead the dough for 6 to 8 minutes (page 34). It will be sticky, so keep your plastic scraper in your non-kneading hand to clean the work surface.

3. Place the dough in a lightly oiled container and cover with plastic. Let the dough ferment for 1 hour. Place the dough on a lightly floured work surface and fold (page 34). Place it back in the container and cover. Ferment for 1 hour. Place the dough on a lightly floured surface and fold it a second time. Place it back in the container and cover. Ferment for 1 hour. Place the dough on a lightly floured surface and fold for a third time. Place it back in the container and cover. Ferment for 1 hour.

4. Lightly flour the work surface and place the dough on the surface. Divide the dough into two equal portions. Pre-shape each into a round (page 35), cover, and let relax for 30 minutes.

5. Shape each round into a batard (page 35) and place side by side on a well-floured linen couche (page 33) with the seam side down. Cover with plastic. Let ferment for 1½ hours at room temperature. Use the touch test (page 38) to see if the loaves are ready for the oven.

6. Preheat the oven with a baking stone and cast iron skillet (for creating steam) to 450°F [230°C] for 45 minutes prior to baking the bread.

7. Gently place each loaf on a lightly floured peel. With a razor blade or sharp knife, make two 6-in [15-cm] long diagonal cuts on each loaf (page 38). The cuts should be separated by about 4 in [10 cm]. The first cut should start on the right side of the loaf about 2 in [5 cm] from the top. The cut should be at a 45-degree angle. The second cut should start about 2 in [5 cm] above the midpoint of the loaf and end about 2 in [5 cm] above the bottom of the loaf.

8. Slide the loaves onto the preheated baking stone and bake for 8 minutes with steam (page 38), then uncover and bake for an additional 40 to 45 minutes, until the loaves are dark brown. Remove the loaves from the oven and cool on a cooling rack. Cool completely before cutting.

FRANK: *In late 2014 we started baking our Chestnut Baguette, made with chestnut flour from western Michigan and Michigan-grown hard red spring wheat from northern Michigan. This is an example of a Bakehouse bread that was more than 10 years in the making. We first played around with chestnut flour in 2002 or 2003. At the time, we had no real local source for chestnut flour and a lot less experience with breads made with a dough as wet as the chestnut bread is. It landed in a pile of ideas that reside on the left side of my desk.*

The American chestnut tree was devastated by a fungal blight in the early 20th century. Michigan has since become one of the leading states in its revival. To help in this effort, Rodger Bowser, Zingerman's Delicatessen partner, began working with Michigan chestnut growers to promote the fruits of their labor. In the summer of 2014, we got a sample of the chestnut flour and decided to try it in a baguette with some of our other Michigan wheat flour. We fell in love with the flavor of the bread (especially the dark crust) and the beautiful color of the crumb. The addition of the chestnut flour gives the crumb a slight purple color and rich depth of flavor.

It's become my favorite bread to choose when I'm asked to bring an appetizer to a dinner. I grab a Chestnut Baguette and run next door to Zingerman's Creamery and have them pick out a really ripe Manchester cheese for me. The combination is a real crowd pleaser.

CHESTNUT BAGUETTES

makes 4 demi-baguettes

Water, room temperature	1½ cups plus 1 Tbsp	365 g
Levain (page 42)	½ cup	70 g
Chestnut flour	½ cup	70 g
Stone-ground hard red wheat flour	2¾ cups	385 g
Sea salt	1½ tsp	9 g

1. Place the water in a mixing bowl. Tear the levain into small pieces and add to the water. Add the chestnut flour and half of the wheat flour and beat with a wooden spoon until the dough is a smooth batter. Add the remaining wheat flour and the salt. Mix until the dough is rough and shaggy.

2. Turn the dough out of the bowl onto a clean, unfloured work surface, scraping any bits of dough from the bowl. Knead the dough for 6 to 7 minutes (page 34). The dough will be sticky at this point.

3. Place the dough in a lightly oiled bowl and cover with plastic. Ferment for 30 minutes.

4. Turn the dough out onto a lightly floured work surface and fold (page 34). Return the dough to the bowl and cover. Ferment for another 30 minutes. Turn the dough out onto a lightly floured work surface and fold for a second time. Return to the bowl and cover. Ferment for 1 hour. Turn the dough out onto a lightly floured work surface and fold it a third time. Return to the bowl and cover. Ferment for 1 hour.

5. With a bench scraper, divide the dough into four equal pieces. Gently form the pieces of dough into loose rounds. Place them on a lightly floured work surface and cover with plastic. Let rest for 30 minutes.

6. After 30 minutes, uncover the dough and lightly dust the tops with flour. Follow the instructions for Final Shaping and Final Fermentation (page 38) to roll each piece into the final baguette shape, approximately 8 in [20 cm] in length. Place the baguettes in a linen couche (page 33) dusted with wheat flour, separated by pleats. Cover with plastic. Allow to rest for 45 minutes. Use the touch test (page 38) to see if the dough is ready for the oven.

7. Forty-five minutes before baking, preheat the oven with a baking stone and cast iron skillet (for creating steam) to 450°F [230°C] (page 38).

continued

The wheat flour we use (the same as in our True North Bread) is made of hard red wheat that is stone ground and then sifted so it retains the germ and some of the bran. These small parts of the grain add to the deliciousness of the bread. To approximate this flour at home, use 4 parts all-purpose flour and 1 part well-sifted whole wheat flour. Use a superfine sifter to remove the larger bran particles from the whole wheat flour.

8. Uncover and, using a transfer peel or baguette board, place the baguettes side by side on a flour-dusted peel. Lightly dust the top surface of the baguettes with flour. With a razor blade or sharp knife, make two overlapping cuts, each 3½ in [9 cm] long, the first starting about 1 in [2.5 cm] from the top end of the baguette and the second ending about 1 in [2.5 cm] from the bottom of the baguette.

9. Place the loaves on the baking stone and add steam to the oven (page 38). Keep covered for 10 minutes.

10. Uncover and bake for an additional 15 to 20 minutes, or until the baguettes are nicely browned and sound hollow when tapped on the bottom. It is important for them to get dark brown in color. Remove from the oven and cool completely on a wire rack.

growing wheat isn't simple! in michigan anyway

FRANK: *Wheat farming isn't common in Michigan these days, and it seems to be a skill that requires some support to be revived. It's definitely possible, and we're trying to play a positive role in making it happen.*

Michigan State University has an important place in agriculture in Michigan, and a man by the name of Phil Tocco from the Michigan State University Extension has supplied much of the energy for reviving the growing of wheat in the state. Over the years, he has found a number of different farmers who have grown hard red wheat for us to bake with. Our first year we got 150 pounds of flour that allowed us to experiment with the performance of Michigan-grown wheat. In our most successful year, we received 12,000 pounds, and we used it to bake our Farm Bread for a month.

In the summer of 2015, I was very optimistic, as we had 11 acres of wheat in Eaton Rapids (about 70 miles west of Ann Arbor) and 70 acres in Saline (exactly 8 miles from the Bakehouse). I visited both fields in early July and they looked spectacular (to me, the city boy). As it turned out, although they looked good in early July, we had had so much rain in June that both fields were entirely lost due to a toxin that made the wheat unusable. I was a bit discouraged to have lost an entire season without any of our own Michigan wheat to bake with.

In October 2015, I was visited by Bill Koucky from Grand Traverse Culinary Oils in Traverse City, Michigan. He brought me some canola oil that he produces, as well as some hard red wheat that he had grown on the Leelenau Peninsula in northern Michigan. While the summer of 2015 had been a bust for hard red wheat grown in southeastern Michigan, the microclimate of the Leelenau Peninsula just 225 miles northwest of Ann Arbor had yielded an incredible harvest of more than 300,000 pounds. Bill was nice enough to leave me a couple bags to experiment with. He stone-mills the wheat and sifts it some, so we get a delicious wheat that bakes beautifully. We now use this flour in two of our favorite new breads—True North and the Chestnut Baguette—and the inclusion of this flour adds incredible flavor as well as connecting us to the agriculture of our state.

AMY: Pogácsa (poh-GOTCHA) *are rich and delicious rolls made in Hungary. They are eaten at breakfast, for a snack, for appetizers, and to accompany dinner. I'd say that they are the Hungarian cousin to our southern American biscuit. Interestingly, the origins of this roll are Turkish. They were introduced to Hungary when the Ottoman Turks ruled the territory for about 150 years (and they are still made in Turkey).*

The most common pogácsa are made with unflavored dough garnished with poppy or sesame seeds. There are also variations that have ingredients folded into the dough. Goose and pork cracklings are common additions, and sweet versions are available featuring cinnamon and sugar.

If you want to make a true Hungarian meal, pogácsa are an essential component. They are also a great addition to our standard American meals. Try them with your morning eggs, a bowl of creamy soup, or alongside a roast chicken and mashed potatoes. For plain rolls, just leave out the dill.

POGÁCSA
THE ICONIC HUNGARIAN ROLL

makes twelve 2.5-in [6-cm] rolls

Dough

All-purpose flour	2 cups plus 1 Tbsp	305 g
Granulated sugar	1 tsp	
Sea salt	2¼ tsp	15 g
Rum (light)	2 tsp	9 g
Whole milk	⅔ cup	160 g
Sour cream	⅓ cup	85 g
Egg yolks	2	30 g
Instant yeast	2½ tsp	9 g
Unsalted butter, room temperature	1 Tbsp	15 g

Filling

All-purpose flour	1½ tsp	5 g
Unsalted butter, room temperature	½ cup plus 1 Tbsp	135 g
Lemon juice	½ tsp	5 g
Chopped fresh dill	1 cup	25 g

Egg Wash

Large egg	1
Egg yolk	1
Water	1 Tbsp

Make the Dough

1. Combine the flour, sugar, salt, rum, milk, sour cream, egg yolks, yeast, and butter in the bowl of a stand mixer fitted with the paddle attachment. Mix until the ingredients are well incorporated. When the dough is homogeneous, mix for 3 minutes to develop the gluten. The dough will be wet and sticky.

2. Remove the dough from the bowl and wrap it in plastic wrap, forming it into a square. Chill it in the refrigerator for at least 30 minutes.

Make the Filling

1. Combine the flour, butter, lemon juice, and dill in a medium bowl and mix with a wooden spoon until combined. Set aside.

continued

Assemble and Bake the Pogácsa

1. Place the chilled dough on a well-floured work surface. Expect it to be very sticky. You may have to scrape it off the plastic wrap. Flour the top of the dough and roll it into a 12-by-10-in [30-by-25-cm] rectangle. Have a short edge facing you. Brush away any excess flour.

2. Visually divide the dough into thirds horizontally. Spread one-third of the filling evenly over the middle third of the dough. Fold the bottom third of the dough up and over the filling. Spread another one-third of the filling evenly over it. Fold the remaining top third of the dough down and over the filling.

3. Turn the dough 90 degrees. You'll repeat the process in step 2. If your dough seems too compact to fold easily, gently roll it to make it slightly wider. Visually divide the dough into thirds horizontally. Spread half of the remaining filling evenly over the middle portion of the dough. Fold the top third of the dough over the filling. Spread the remaining filling over the recently folded dough. Fold the bottom third of the dough over the filling.

4. Wrap the dough in plastic and refrigerate it for 30 minutes before you begin the laminating process, which will make the pogácsa multilayered.

5. Place the chilled dough on a floured work surface. Flour the top and roll the dough to approximately 8 by 12 in [20 by 30 cm]. Have a long edge facing you. Brush away the excess flour. Visually divide the dough into thirds vertically. Fold the right third on top of the middle third. Fold the left third on top of the middle third.

6. Cover and let the dough rest in the refrigerator for 30 minutes. Repeat step 5, then cover and let rest in the refrigerator for another 30 minutes.

7. Preheat the oven to 400°F [200°C].

8. Place the dough on your floured work surface, with the open edges toward you. Flour the top and roll the dough to approximately 1 in [2.5 cm] thick. Brush away the excess flour. Using a 2½-in [6-cm] round cookie cutter, cut out the pogácsa. Line them up on a cookie sheet, leaving at least 1 in [2.5 cm] of space between them.

9. Gather the scraps of dough and gently form them back into a dough ball, working as minimally as possible. Flour the work surface and dough and roll it again to 1 in [2.5 cm] thick. Repeat step 9. This time, discard the remaining scraps.

10. Using a paring knife, gently draw light vertical lines and then light horizontal lines across the tops of your pogácsa. The result should be a cross-hatch marking on top. Make egg wash by beating together the egg, egg yolk, and water, and brush the tops of the pogácsa generously with it.

11. Bake for 18 to 20 minutes. The tops of the pogácsa should be a rich, golden color. Serve warm or at room temperature.

Langós (LON-gowsh) *is a deep-fried flatbread eaten with a variety of garnishes like sour cream and dill, or cheese and ham, and it's Hungary's most popular street food. Who doesn't love fried dough? Hungarians certainly do. There are* langós *stands in many food markets, and they are regular features at street fairs and public events. It's common to see people standing at counters eating hot fried dough mounded with amazing combinations of meat, cheese, and vegetables. Some* langós *dough is very simple: water, flour, salt, and yeast. A slightly more flavorful version includes mashed potatoes or even chopped cabbage. Ours is made with potatoes.*

Langós *didn't start as a fried treat made in a public setting. It was originally a snack made at breakfast time on bread-making day in Hungarian homes. The bread dough was mixed, a fire was started in the wood-fired oven, and then small pieces of the proofing dough were baked near the flames. It was a morning treat that sustained the bakers and their children while bread making continued. It's been a long time since most Hungarians baked their own bread, but as that tradition faded,* langós *evolved into a fried street food.*

Expect to eat langós *soon after it's fried. At most* langós *stands, you'll have a choice of many toppings, plus the opportunity to brush your warm dough with garlic water.*

LANGÓS
HUNGARIAN SAVORY FRIED DOUGH

makes two 7-in [17-cm] Langós

Small potato	1	30 g
Whole milk	⅓ cup	80 g
Powdered sugar	1 Tbsp	
Vegetable oil	2 tsp	
Instant yeast	½ tsp	
All-purpose flour	¾ cup	105 g
Sea salt	½ tsp	

Frying		
Vegetable oil	3 cups	TK g

Topping		
Garlic, minced	2 cloves	10 g
Water	½ cup	115 g
Sour cream	3 Tbsp	45 g
Shredded gouda cheese	½ cup	55 g
Julienned ham	½ cup	55 g
Fresh dill	1 tsp	
Paprika	⅛ tsp	

Prepare the Potato

1. Cut the potato into 1- to 2-in [2.5- to 5-cm] cubes. Place the potato in a small saucepan and cover with cool water. Bring to a boil over medium-high heat. Boil until the potato is fork-tender.

2. Remove from the heat and pour the potato pieces into a strainer. Drain all the water and then place the potato pieces back into the hot pot. This will help dry the potato.

3. Mash the potato and set aside to cool. Once it has cooled, measure 1 Tbsp (30 g) and place it in a mixing bowl. Reserve the rest of the mashed potato for another use.

Make the Dough

1. In the mixing bowl combine the mashed potato, milk, powdered sugar, vegetable oil, instant yeast, and half the flour. Mix together with a wooden spoon until a batter is formed. Add the remaining flour and the salt. Mix until the dough has taken up most of the dry bits.

2. Scrape the dough out of the bowl onto a clean, unfloured work surface and knead for 8 minutes (page 34), or until smooth and elastic. Place into an oiled bowl and cover with plastic. Leave to ferment at room temperature for 30 minutes.

3. Uncover the dough and turn it out onto a lightly floured work surface. Fold the dough (page 34). Brush any excess flour from each fold. Turn the dough over, return it to the oiled bowl, and ferment for 30 more minutes.

4. Turn the dough out onto the lightly floured surface. Fold the dough again as in step 3. Turn the dough over, return it to the oiled bowl and ferment for 30 more minutes.

Shape the Dough

1. Remove the dough from the container onto a lightly floured surface. Divide the dough into two pieces of equal size.

2. Shape each piece into a small ball. Put it seam side down on your work surface and allow it to rest, covered in plastic, for 1½ hours. After 1½ hours, press each round out to a thin disk 7 in [17 cm] in diameter.

Fry and Serve the Langós

1. Preheat 2 to 3 in [5 to 7.5 cm] of vegetable oil in a pan with high sides. Heat it to 375°F [190°C].

2. Prepare the garlic water. Finely mince the garlic and add it to the ½ cup [115 g] of water.

3. Place one of the langós in the hot oil gently to avoid splashing the oil. Fry until golden brown on the first side, and then flip the dough over with tongs. Fry until the second side is golden brown. Each side will take about 1½ minutes.

4. With the tongs, carefully remove the langós from the oil and place it on a sheet tray lined with paper towels. Allow the oil to drain off for 15 seconds and then flip to the other side and drain for 15 seconds more. Repeat with the second langós.

5. Brush each langós with garlic water. Spread half of the sour cream on each langós before sprinkling with the gouda, ham, dill, and paprika. Serve immediately.

RÉTES
SWEET AND SAVORY STRUDEL

makes 2 rétes, each 15 in [38 cm] long and 3½ in [9 cm] wide

AMY: *One of our favorite Hungarian treats is* rétes *(RAY-tesh), better known to most of us by the German name strudel. Why do we like it so much? The dough is one of those wonders of the baking world that is rewarding to make. It's like doing a magic trick! There are an unlimited variety of fillings, making* rétes *super versatile. And it tastes great.*

To make rétes, *we carefully hand-stretch dough over an 8-foot table until it's thin enough to see through. Then we brush it with melted butter and a sprinkle of cake or bread crumbs, wrap it around fresh fillings, and bake until golden brown.*

Although the sweet versions are the most familiar to Americans, we think the savory ones are perhaps even more interesting. We've included recipes for many options for you to choose from. Once you become comfortable with the process, you can easily create your own fillings. Frank is always threatening to make a chicken noodle rétes! *It makes us laugh every time because it's so ridiculous.*

All of these can be eaten warm or at room temperature. They can all be made and frozen raw and baked straight from the freezer. Convenience food!

Dough		
All-purpose flour	3 cups	425 g
Sea salt	½ tsp	
Large eggs	2	
Unsalted butter, melted	1 Tbsp	

Assembly		
Unsalted butter, melted	½ cup	115 g
Dry bread or cake crumbs	⅓ cup	45 g

Make the Dough

1. Combine the flour and salt in a mixing bowl. Create a well in the center of the flour mixture.

2. In a measuring cup, lightly beat the eggs, and then add enough warm water to make a total of 1¼ cups [300 ml]. Add the melted butter and stir the liquid until well mixed.

3. Pour the egg mixture into the center of the flour well. With a fork, slowly combine the flour and liquid, working from the center out. Continue to mix until the dough comes together and forms a ball. The dough should be fairly soft and sticky.

4. Turn the dough out onto a clean, unfloured work surface. Knead for a minute or two.

5. Now comes the fun! In order to develop the gluten, the dough must be forcefully kneaded. In one continuous motion, pick up the dough with your hand, lift, and turn your hand over so that your wrist is facing up, then slap the dough down hard. (It's a motion similar to playing with a yo-yo.) This is a common traditional way of hand-kneading a very wet dough. If done well, it can make a nice slapping sound, so we nicknamed it the "beaver slap"! Fold the dough back on itself, and detach it from the surface with a plastic bench scraper. Repeat this 100 times. Really count. As you work the dough, it will become less sticky and more elastic. After the first 20 strokes, gently knead the dough a few times and then return to slapping. When the dough is ready, it will be satin smooth, with small bubbles just under the surface. Don't become discouraged if at first the dough sticks to your hand. As you develop the dough it will pick up any dough stuck to your hand. (You can always scrape the dough pieces off with a plastic bench scraper.)

continued

6. Oil a small mixing bowl. Place the dough in the container, turning it over so that the dough is lightly coated with oil. Press plastic wrap against the dough's surface, and let rest at room temperature for 2 hours. It can be left for even longer if need be. We leave it for 4 to 5 hours at room temperature in our pastry kitchen.

7. While the dough is resting, prepare your fillings.

Pull the Dough

1. (A 30-by-48-in [75-by-120-cm] work surface is ideal for this.) To stretch the dough, cover a rectangular counter or table with a tablecloth or a sheet. Generously sift flour over it, then rub the flour into the material. Place the dough in the center of the sheet, making sure not to fold the dough. It will be quite smooth and elastic at this point.

2. Stretch the dough from the center toward each end of the work area, making a long, thin rectangle. Pull as far as the dough easily stretches.

3. Close your dominant hand into a loose fist. Put this hand under the dough and place your other hand on the dough on top of your dominant wrist. Pull the dough from the center out toward the edges of the table. Do not try to pull the dough all the way from the center to the edge in the first try. Just stretch it a few inches and then move to the next section of dough. Repeat this motion while moving around the table. Do not hurry the process by stretching the dough with your fingers. The dough will tear.

4. Once the dough is large enough, anchor one end over the edge of the table and pull from the other direction. The goal is to stretch the dough over the entire work area and then to continue to stretch it until it is possible to read a piece of paper through it. You may circle the table twice before pulling the dough all the way to the edges. Excess dough may be hanging over the edge of the work area. That's to be expected.

5. When the dough is transparent, paper-thin, and covers the entire table, trim the excess dough around the edge of the surface. To get to the correct thinness, the dough will extend over the edge. Leave at least 1 inch [2 cm] of extra dough on all sides. If the dough has torn, patch it with the excess dough from the edges.

6. To patch the dough, cut out a section from the excess, using scissors or a paring knife, and lay the patch on the hole, securing its edges to the edges of the area it is patching. Holes are not a big problem as long as you patch them. The dough is rolled and will have multiple layers, so the imperfections will not be visible and will have zero impact on the eating experience. What's most important is that the dough is stretched thin enough. Dough that is too thick will be tough.

7. Brush the entire surface of the dough with melted butter. Let it dry for 5 to 8 minutes.

8. Preheat the oven to 380°F [193°C].

Fill and Bake the Rétes

1. Lightly sprinkle the surface of the dough with dried bread or cake crumbs, being a bit more generous on the end where the filling will be, the short edge. On one of the short edges, place the fillings. This dough makes two rétes at a time. Each filling should be about 2 in [5 cm] thick and 12 in [30 cm] wide. Leave 3 in [7.5 cm] between the two logs of filling.

2. Use the cloth to lift the slight excess dough and fold it over the filling. Continue to gather the cloth in your hands and to use it as a tool to roll the rétes up into a cylinder. Do not roll them too tightly.

3. Cut the rétes apart and fold each end under the bottom of the rétes to seal in the filling. Place the rétes on a parchment-lined baking sheet. Brush the entire surface with melted butter. Cut five vents into the rétes at 45-degree angles every 2 in [5 cm].

4. Bake for 25 to 30 minutes, or until the crust is crisp and a deep golden color. Let cool at least 10 minutes before cutting to serve.

ASPARAGUS FILLING

makes enough for 1 rétes

Asparagus	20 spears	340 g
Shredded Parmesan cheese	½ cup	65 g
Unsalted butter, melted	2 Tbsp	
Sea salt	¼ tsp	
Ground black pepper	¼ tsp	

1. Remove the woody ends from the asparagus.

2. Place the asparagus on the bread crumbs. Sprinkle with the Parmesan cheese, butter, sea salt, and pepper.

CABBAGE FILLING

makes enough for 1 rétes

Cabbage, coarsely chopped	½ small	455 g
Melted goose fat	3 Tbsp	
Sea salt	¾ tsp	
Ground black pepper	½ tsp	
Granulated sugar	½ tsp	

1. Core the cabbage and dice into ¼- to ½-in [6- to 12-mm] pieces. Toss the cabbage with the goose fat, salt, pepper, and sugar. If you do not have goose fat, use any other melted fat: butter, lard, olive oil, or chicken schmaltz.

POTATO BACON FILLING

makes enough for 1 rétes

Medium potatoes	2	230 g
Bacon	4 slices	115 g
Small onion	1	230 g
Chopped parsley	¼ cup	
Sea salt	1 tsp	6 g
Ground black pepper	¼ tsp	

1. Cut the potatoes into 1-in [2.5-cm] cubes. Boil until tender but still well intact. You can leave the skins on if you wish.

2. Dice the bacon into ¼-in [6-mm] pieces and sauté in a skillet over medium heat until crisp.

3. Slice the onion into thin half-rings and add to the sautéing bacon. Turn the heat down to medium-low. Cook until the onion starts to caramelize, 5 to 8 minutes.

4. Combine the potatoes, bacon, caramelized onion, parsley, salt, and pepper.

SWEET APPLE FILLING

makes enough for 1 rétes

Medium apples	3	650 g
Lemon juice	1 Tbsp	
Granulated sugar	¼ cup	50 g
Ground nutmeg	¼ tsp	
Ground cinnamon	¼ tsp	
Flame raisins (optional)	¼ cup	40 g
Dry bread crumbs	¼ cup	20 g

1. Peel, halve, core, and thinly slice the apples. In a bowl, toss the apple slices with the lemon juice.

2. In a separate bowl combine the sugar, nutmeg, cinnamon, raisins (if using), and bread crumbs. Add the sugar mixture to the sliced apples and toss to combine.

APRICOT AND SWEET CHEESE FILLING

makes enough for 1 rétes

Sweet Cheese Filling

Cream cheese, room temperature	8oz	225 g
Unsalted butter, room temperature	½ Tbsp	9 g
Granulated sugar	¼ cup	45 g
Cornstarch	1 Tbsp	9 g
Egg yolk	1	
Vanilla extract	1 tsp	

Apricot Filling

Apricot preserves	1 cup	290 g
Dry bread crumbs	½ cup	70 g

Make the Sweet Cheese Filling

1. In a medium bowl, combine the cream cheese and butter. Beat until smooth. Add the sugar, cornstarch, egg yolk, and vanilla and mix until smooth. Store in the refrigerator until ready for use.

Make the Apricot Filling and Fill the Rétes

1. Stir the preserves and crumbs together. Fill one pastry bag with the apricot filling and a second pastry bag with the cheese filling. Use a very large round tip. Pipe one row of apricot filling, then a row of cheese filling, and then a row of apricot filling onto the rétes dough.

This cake was a famous coffeehouse dessert of the Austro-Hungarian Empire in the 19th century. It was named after the Austrian prince and diplomat Paul III Anton Esterházy (the name of the baker has been forgotten). The cake has thin, soft walnut cake layers, walnut cream filling, and a distinctive decoration on top resembling the traditional French Napoleon pastry.

This classic Hungarian torta is pure elegance—petite and beautiful to look at, refined and balanced in flavor, with a perfect level of sweetness—and it's satisfying in delicate-sized pieces. Esterházy could end up being your hallmark dessert, the perfect finish to an inspired meal. We have served it cut into small squares reminiscent of petits fours alongside a platter of handmade chocolates.

Note that you will need a quarter-sheet cake board (9 by 13 in [23 by 33 cm]) to assemble the torta.

ESTERHÁZY TORTA
HUNGARIAN WALNUT CREAM CAKE

makes one 9-by-13-in [23-by-33-cm] cake

Cake

Walnuts	⅔ cup	80 g
All-purpose flour	⅓ cup plus 1 Tbsp	55 g
Baking powder	½ tsp	
Sea salt	½ tsp	
Large eggs, separated	5	
Vanilla extract	1 tsp	
Granulated sugar	½ cup plus 1 Tbsp	115 g

Pastry Cream

Whole milk	½ cup	115 g
Heavy cream	½ cup	115 g
Granulated sugar	¼ cup	55 g
Sea salt	pinch	
Cornstarch	2 Tbsp	20 g
Egg yolks	3	45 g
Vanilla extract	1 tsp	
Unsalted butter, room temperature	2 Tbsp	25 g

Walnut Cream Filling

Heavy cream, cold	1 cup	250 g
Granulated sugar	2 Tbsp	25 g
Pastry cream	1⅓ cups	320 g
Walnuts	1 cup	115 g

White Chocolate Ganache

Chopped white chocolate	1 cup	165 g
Heavy cream	¼ cup	55 g

Assembly

Melted chocolate (56% cacao or higher), slightly warm	¼ cup	40 g
Walnuts	1 cup	115 g

continued

Make the Cake

1. Line a half-sheet baking pan (13 by 18 in [33 by 46 cm]) with parchment paper (do not grease the pan). Set aside.

2. You will need a total of about 2⅔ cups [310 g] toasted, ground walnuts for the cake layers and the filling, and for coating the sides of the cake. On a sheet tray in a 325°F [165°C] oven, toast all of the walnuts for 10 to 15 minutes, or until they're a deep golden brown. Allow the nuts to cool completely before grinding. Grind them in a food processor until they are as fine as coarse cornmeal. If ground too much, it will turn into nut butter. After the walnuts are toasted, turn the oven up to 350°F [180°C].

3. In a large mixing bowl, combine the flour, ⅔ cup [80 g] of the ground walnuts, baking powder, and salt. Set aside.

4. Make sure the egg whites are clean, meaning that they contain no fat (yolk). Use a stand mixer with a whisk attachment to beat them on high speed until they come to stiff but moist (not dry) peaks. Place the whipped whites in a separate bowl; set aside.

5. In the mixer bowl, combine the egg yolks, vanilla extract, and sugar. Using the whisk attachment, whip the mixture on high for 3 to 4 minutes. The egg yolk mixture will become very light in color and will thicken and triple in volume.

6. Add half of the whipped yolk mixture to the bowl with the dry ingredients. Fold it in well, using a rubber spatula. Once it is completely incorporated, add the rest of the whipped yolk mixture and fold again.

7. Once all of the yolk mixture is folded into the dry ingredients, fold in half of the beaten egg whites. Then fold in the other half.

8. Transfer the batter to the prepared half-sheet pan. Use an offset spatula to spread the batter evenly across the pan. Bake for 10 minutes, or until the top springs back when touched. Remove from the oven and cool to room temperature.

Make the Pastry Cream

1. In a small saucepan, combine the milk, heavy cream, half the sugar, and the salt. Cook over medium heat until the mixture comes to a boil. Remove from the heat.

2. In a mixing bowl, whisk together the cornstarch and remaining sugar until blended. Add the egg yolks and whisk until smooth. Slowly pour 1 cup of the hot cream mixture into the egg mixture while whisking constantly. This step tempers the egg yolks so they won't curdle. Pour the tempered egg yolk mixture back into the saucepan with the hot cream mixture and return to medium heat.

3. Continue to cook the pastry cream while constantly stirring with a heatproof rubber spatula or a wooden spoon, and bring to a light boil. The pastry cream will thicken as it cooks. Remove the pastry cream from the heat, and pour it into a clean medium bowl. Whisk until it cools slightly, and then beat in the vanilla extract and butter.

4. Continue beating until the pastry cream is just warm, not hot. Cover with plastic wrap, making sure it is pressed directly onto the surface of the pastry cream to prevent a skin from forming.

Make the Walnut Cream Filling

1. In a metal mixing bowl, combine the heavy cream and sugar. Whip until the cream comes to stiff peaks.

2. Whisk the pastry cream to soften it. Fold half of the whipped cream into the pastry cream. Once it is incorporated, fold in the other half of the whipped cream. Fold in 1 cup [115 g] of the finely ground walnuts. Keep refrigerated until ready for use.

Make the White Chocolate Ganache

1. Place the white chocolate into a heatproof mixing bowl. In a small saucepan, bring the heavy cream to a light boil over medium heat. Remove the pan from the heat and pour the hot cream over the white chocolate.

2. Let stand for 1 to 2 minutes to melt the chocolate. Use a whisk to combine the chocolate and hot cream until smooth. If the chocolate is not melted, heat it for 10 seconds or less in a microwave.

3. Cool the ganache until just slightly warm. If it is too warm, it will melt the walnut cream filling on top of the cake.

Assemble the Cake

1. You will want to assemble the cake on a quarter-sheet cardboard cake board (9 by 13 in [23 by 33 cm]) and then transfer it to a serving tray when it is complete.

2. To remove the cake from the pan, run a metal spatula around the sides of the pan to loosen it. Keep the parchment paper attached for easy transfer while assembling.

3. Divide the cake into four equal pieces, each 6 by 8 in [15 by 20 cm].

4. Place a teaspoon of walnut cream filling on the cake board, and then place one layer of cake on the board. The filling will stop your cake from moving around as you assemble it.

5. Using an offset spatula, spread one-quarter of the walnut cream filling evenly over the cake layer. Place a second piece of cake on top of the filling, pressing gently to adhere the layers together. Repeat this two more times to build the cake. Do not top the fourth layer with filling. It will be iced.

6. With the remaining fourth of the walnut cream filling, cover the sides of the cake. Clean off any extra filling and square up the sides of the cake with the offset spatula.

7. Pour the slightly warm white chocolate ganache over the center of the cake, spreading it to the edge of the cake with an offset spatula. If the chocolate is too cool, it will not be as smooth as we would like.

continued

8. Now create the distinctive Esterházy decorated top. Place the slightly warm melted dark chocolate into a small piping bag or a plastic condiment squeeze bottle and pipe four stripes, equidistant from one another, on the white chocolate ganache, the length of the cake. Use a toothpick to draw through the chocolate ganache, making stripes across the short length of the cake.

9. Using an offset spatula, clean off any ganache that has flowed down the sides of the cake. Using your hand, coat the sides of the cake with the remaining 1 cup [115 g] ground walnuts.

10. Refrigerate the cake for at least 2 hours so that it can firm up and will cut nicely when served. If the cake has been refrigerated for many hours, bring it to room temperature before serving.

Rigó Jancsi (ree-GO YAN-chee) *is one of the classic late 19th-century Austria-Hungarian coffeehouse cakes, in the same historical category as Esterházy torta, Gerbeaud slice, and Dobos torta. Rigó, as we refer to it in the bakery, is a regal torte made with two light layers of chocolate sponge cake, filled with rum-flavored chocolate whipped cream, iced with a thin layer of apricot glaze, and finished with a dark chocolate ganache. It is a rich chocolate delight with a colorful creation story.*

The dessert is named after a famous Hungarian gypsy violinist, Rigó Jancsi (1858 to 1927). The most common version of the story is that Rigó sang and played for Clara Ward, an American woman who traveled in the upper echelons of European society of the time, and her royal husband, the Belgian Prince Joseph. As the story goes, Ward was smitten with Rigó and secretly slipped him her diamond ring as he serenaded the room. They soon ran away together and married. Supposedly, a Hungarian baker created and named the cake to celebrate this event.

An interesting detail to us Michiganders is that Clara Ward was a native of Detroit. She was the daughter of Eber Brock Ward, who is thought to be the first Michigan millionaire. Clara led a very international life, living in many countries and marrying four times. Let's celebrate her independence and joie de vivre by making a Rigó Jancsi!

Note that you'll need a quarter-sheet cake board (9 by 13 in [23 by 33 cm]) for assembling the cake.

RIGÓ JANCSI
HUNGARIAN CHOCOLATE CREAM CAKE

makes one 9-by-13-in [23-by-33-cm] cake

Cake

All-purpose flour	¾ cup	110 g
Unsweetened cocoa powder	7 Tbsp	35 g
Sea salt	½ tsp	
Whole milk	5 Tbsp	75 g
Vegetable oil	4½ Tbsp	55 g
Vanilla extract	1 tsp	
Large eggs	5	
Granulated sugar	1⅓ cups	265 g

Chocolate Glaze

Chopped chocolate (65% cacao)	¾ cup plus 3 Tbsp	175 g
Unsalted butter, room temperature	1 Tbsp	15 g
Water, boiling	½ cup	115 g

Chocolate Cream Filling

Heavy cream, cold	3 cups	680 g
Dark rum	3 Tbsp	35 g
Vanilla extract	2 tsp	
Powdered sugar	¾ cup plus 3 Tbsp	115 g
Unsweetened cocoa powder	⅔ cup	55 g

Apricot Glaze

Apricot preserves	½ cup	145 g
Water	¼ cup	55 g

Make the Cake

1. Preheat the oven to 350°F [180°C]. Line a half-sheet baking pan (13 by 18 in [33 by 46 cm]) with parchment paper (do not grease the pan). Set aside.

2. Sift the all-purpose flour, cocoa powder, and salt three times to aerate the ingredients and to eliminate any clumps of cocoa. Put the flour mixture back into the sifter at the end. You will be sifting this mixture into the mixing bowl.

continued

3. In a small bowl, combine the milk, oil, and vanilla extract and set aside.

4. Combine the eggs and sugar in the bowl of a stand mixer. Place the bowl over a saucepan with simmering water and mix together with a hand-held whisk. Heat and mix intermittently until the egg mixture is warm but not hot.

5. Place the bowl on the stand mixer fitted with a whisk attachment. Whip the mixture on high for 12 minutes. The egg mixture will become very light in color, thicken, and triple in volume.

6. Sift half of the flour mixture over the whipped eggs and gently fold together using the whisk attachment, or whisk by hand. Follow with half of the liquid ingredients, folding to incorporate completely. Repeat one more time with the remaining dry and wet ingredients, making sure that all of the liquids have been mixed in and are not sitting at the bottom of the bowl.

7. Using a rubber spatula, fold the batter in the bowl to incorporate completely. Transfer the batter to the prepared half-sheet pan. Spread evenly. Bake for 12 minutes, or until the top springs back when touched. Remove from the oven and cool to room temperature.

Make the Chocolate Glaze

1. In a medium bowl, combine the chocolate, butter, and boiling water. Let sit for 30 seconds and then blend with a whisk until completely smooth. Set the glaze aside and cool to room temperature.

Make the Chocolate Cream Filling

1. Place the bowl of the stand mixer and the whisk attachment in the refrigerator or freezer for 20 minutes.

2. In the mixer bowl, put the heavy cream, dark rum, and vanilla extract. Mix with the whisk attachment for a few seconds just to combine. Sift the powdered sugar and cocoa powder on top of the cream mixture in the bowl and mix on low speed with the whisk attachment to completely moisten the dry ingredients.

3. Start the mixer on medium speed and whip the mixture until it begins to thicken. Slowly increase the speed of the mixer to medium-high speed. Scrape the sides of the bowl as necessary to incorporate all the dry ingredients. Whip until firm peaks form. Set aside.

Make the Apricot Glaze and Assemble the Cake

1. Heat the apricot preserves and water in a small saucepan until the mixture thickens and coats a room-temperature spoon. This will take about 5 minutes. Strain out any apricot pieces. Use while warm.

2. Loosen the cake along the edges of the pan with a metal spatula. With a knife, divide the chocolate sponge into two equal pieces, 8 by 12 in [20 by 30 cm], cutting the cake on the sheet tray through the parchment paper.

3. Spread 1 Tbsp of the chocolate cream filling on a quarter-sheet cake board (9 by 13 in [23 by 33 cm]). This will help to secure the cake layer. Lift a layer, including the parchment paper, and place it upside down on the quarter-sheet cake board. Remove the parchment.

4. Use an offset spatula to spread all of the chocolate cream filling evenly over the chocolate sponge layer. Place the second piece of chocolate sponge on top of the chocolate cream, parchment side up. Remove the parchment paper. Press gently to adhere the layers together and to make the cake as level as possible.

5. Clean off any extra cream and square up the sides of the cake with the offset spatula. Trim the cake if necessary so that you have a completely even rectangle and smooth, even sides.

6. Brush the top sponge layer with an even coat of the warm apricot glaze. Place the cake in the refrigerator to chill for 15 minutes. Remove the cake from the refrigerator and use an offset spatula to spread the chocolate glaze evenly over the top.

7. Refrigerate for at least 30 minutes before serving. In general, keep this cake refrigerated and bring to room temperature for 1 to 2 hours before serving for the best flavor and texture.

In the spring of 2011 a number of us from the bakery visited Budapest to continue our studies of Hungarian foodways. We were excited to learn more about sólet (SHOW-let), a traditional Hungarian bean and barley stew usually cooked with some sort of protein—eggs, sausages, brisket, and goose are all common.

Sólet is also a traditional Jewish dish, known by the similar name cholent. Traditionally, it was cooked overnight in the oven of the community baker (as the oven cooled down) and was eaten for lunch on the Sabbath to conform with the prohibition of cooking on the Sabbath. In Hungary, though, it is often served with pork and on any day. Hungarian and Jewish foods overlap in some surprising ways.

It's a simple but also very satisfying dish—filling and full of complex flavors, with some spicy heat.

At the bakery, we now cook sólet once a week during the cool months. We started by making it available for Saturday lunch to honor the Jewish tradition and, we hoped, to appeal to our local Jewish community. Now we make it on Fridays so it can be purchased before the weekend. Modern convenience! It's also enjoyed by our non-Jewish guests no matter what day we make it.

Our version is made with Montreal smoked meat. Feel free to use another protein of your choice. Smoked turkey, smoked pork chop, and cured sausage all make for a great dish. Substitute an equal weight of any of these. If you'd like to keep it vegetarian, it's also tasty without the meat.

SÓLET
HUNGARIAN BEAN AND BARLEY STEW
makes 6 servings

Dried cranberry beans	1¾ cups	340 g
Barley	1 cup	165 g
Goose fat, lard, or vegetable oil	½ cup	115 g
Diced onion (¼ in [6 mm])	2 cups	255 g
Minced garlic (3 cloves)	4 tsp	15 g
All-purpose flour	2 Tbsp	20 g
Hot paprika	1 Tbsp	9 g
Sweet paprika	2 tsp	6 g
Water	7 cups	1,589 g
Cubed smoked meat (1 in [2.5 cm])	16 oz	454 g
Sea salt	1 Tbsp	18 g
Ground black pepper	½ tsp	

1. Soak the beans and barley in water overnight. The following day, begin your cooking process by preheating the oven to 375°F [190°C].

2. In an oven-safe pot with a lid, heat the fat of your choice and sauté the onions over medium heat until translucent. Add the garlic and cook gently for 1 minute. Do not let it brown. Add the flour and both paprikas and cook for 1 minute, stirring constantly to make sure the paprika does not burn. The paprika is added in this step because it releases its flavor best when combined directly with fat.

3. Drain the beans and barley from their soaking liquid. Add the water, smoked meat, salt, pepper, beans, and barley to the cooking pot. Stir to mix well and bring to a boil. Cover and transfer to the oven. Cook for 2 hours or until the beans are done, stirring every 30 minutes. The sólet can be eaten right away or cooled and reheated when you are ready to serve it. If you reheat it, you will want to add a little liquid, because the beans and barley will continue to absorb the water while it sits.

RECIPE INDEX

INDEX